The

PASSION OF BELLE RIO

a novel

2nd Edition

BO MAY

Honeyville Creative

The Passion of Belle Rio – 2nd Edition (2021)

Hardcover ISBN: 978-0-578-97885-7
Paperback ISBN: 978-0-578-97886-4
eBook ISBN: 978-0-578-99116-0

BELLE RIO, FLORIDA

"The wretched poor cracker disdains work and tries to live by his rifle and fishing rod... How can he become a capitalist if he will not become a laborer? This is the true meaning of 'white trash' — idleness, rowdyism, the use of deadly weapons, and the want of material progress. This lazy, good-for-nothing way of life is very common among the poor whites of the seaboard states, but it seems to have reached its climax in Florida, which is no land of promise for the Anglo-Saxon pioneer. For generations to come, Florida will be a wilderness, the dangerous haunt of alligators, in-bred crackers, renegade Seminoles, and runaway slaves."

"Letter from The Slave States"
by James Sterling.
London, 1857. John W. Parker & Son.

"Because we are also what we have lost."

—Alejandro González Iñárritu

CHAPTER ONE

Belle Rio, 1990

MATTHEW MCCUTCHEON drove his salt-crusted Buick Century to Belle Rio instead of going home. He crossed the high arching Five Mile Bridge and the narrow causeway, where the yawning mouth of the river spread out through the marshes and mingled with the brackish water before it emptied into the bay. A cloud of seagulls trailed a fishing boat as it returned to the Belle Rio harbor, and a moist pungent breeze promised rain, relief from the hell of late September heat.

When he arrived in Belle Rio he was lost. He wasn't alone. Many people were lost in Belle Rio, where the Gulf Coast Highway threaded its way along the shoreline, separating the ever-changing sky and water from the impenetrable swamp, dark meandering rivers, marsh wetlands, and the endless, deep green pine plantation of the Gulf Royale Paper Company. The Gulf of Mexico was beyond the islands.

A squadron of pelicans cruised leisurely over the placid late afternoon water. The surf pounded the roadbed at high tide, then slipped out, leaving behind the exposed brown sand flats and the stranded cypress stumps. The highway crossed Whiskey Creek, where the tannin liquor from Tate's Hells Swamp spilled into the marsh of Yent's Bayou, then curved inland past Lighthouse Point and continued on to Three Rivers Bridge and Belle Rio Beach, the last stretch of white sand until below Cedar Key.

From Belle Rio, you could drive south through Dixie County to the real Yankee Florida, retired Republican Florida, Euro-tourist Florida, Mickey Mouse & ET's Florida, Puerto Rican exiles, anti-Castro Cubans, the Columbian Drug Cartel, Miami Vice & the Palace of Doom. South Florida was the Vacationland Mecca.

But for Matthew, Belle Rio was paradise. It had been his refuge for as long as he could remember.

Now everyone wanted a piece of it before they died.

In the cold night air Matthew stood at the water's edge staring into the vast, silent windswept space where the sky and water shaped the distant horizon above the islands. His sunburned face was covered with a salt and pepper stubble beard. His eyes had a watery-soft melancholy.

Unlike the Chicago years, there was no busy schedule, no racquetball or vanity aerobics to maintain the trim, disciplined, Spartan demeanor that accompanied the successful urban life, the fashionable wife, the overachieving offspring, the Board of Trade, good tickets to the Bears, the Bulls, the Cubs, the Northshore Tennis & Golf Club, and the *Two Day Sale* at Marshall Field's. In no particular order.

For the next four days, he retreated into the inner sanctum of his old wooden two-story summer house with no heat but the electric oven. It was November and the cold wind wailed through the trees, accompanied by rain and surging tides. At night, the dark moon was lost in the gathering clouds.

Hot water from the shower turned the bathroom into a dense haze of steam. Many non-stop days and nights were lost in the fog. How long is

twenty-five years of married life? Too long? Not long enough? Too soon
to know?

His hand wiped across the mirror, leaving an arc of uneven moisture
on which appeared, not his own image, but the ghost face that haunted
him, her eyes gazing at him quietly, through the mist of a thunderstorm.
Slowly her face vaporized off the mirror into the steam-filled room and
surrounded him, a presence without form.

Whatever it had been, it was bound to happen. They danced to the
bossa nova and fell in love. It was that simple. Afterwards, they lay in a
sweaty embrace, without knowing what there was to gain, or lose, over
the course of a life together. What there was to have, or have not.
Holding her hot body, it seemed as if they would be joined forever. And
yes, they had shared moments that would exist for all time: because the
dream that occurs with two entwined naked, sleeping bodies is a moment
that lasts forever. The momentary memory was bitter sweet.

She had recently said emphatically, "The past two years have been the
worst imaginable. You've done nothing but lose money and get ourselves
into this situation from which there seems to be no escape."

He sought relief from the anxiety and gnawing uncertainty of
incoherent activity, like falling head over heels backwards down a rocky
cliff: and that was Belle Rio. He had seen the open window of
opportunity, and the desperation to escape made him want to possess
her, as much as she wanted, desperately, not to be possessed.

After four days the unusual northern weather broke, and in the cool
golden twilight he escaped out the second-floor window and sat on the
roof while the sun disappeared, dancing across the water and through
the shimmering pines.

That night he called his Uncle Theo, who was several times removed somewhere on his mother's family tree.

The following morning, just before dawn, Theo Messina drove his pickup down the beach, the headlights bouncing and sweeping over the hard sand. Matthew was waiting near the cove, where Theo had anchored his boat overnight.

"It's a beaut," Theo said, meaning the cool morning weather. "I see you ain't forgot. And found the rope. ... Sometimes she gets lost on me. My memory ain't what it used to be. Don't work at 20/20 these days."

Theo had on chest waders, and he stood, almost to his waist, in the calm low tide and pulled the weathered wooden skiff closer to shore.

Matthew waded a few feet into the water then pulled himself over the low side into the boat. Theo climbed in stiffly, and they poled steadily out to about eight feet depth

Sixty yards of mullet gill net was piled in the back of the boat.

"You don't look too much for wear," Matthew said.

"The cold weather aint so good to me, but it oughtta make them mullet move," Theo said in his clipped, guttural accent, and with one swift jerk, cranked the motor.

"We goin west down past the point."

The sky turned from pale grey to white and then suddenly the sun burst across the channel between the mainland and the islands.

They were running southwest beyond the flats, then turned due west and continued down the shoreline past the point near Yent's bayou.

As they slowed, Theo said, "See'm yonder? They ain't runnin' in the cove like they used to but we got the right weather t' get 'em movin'."

Matthew let out the net behind the skiff while Theo drove from the front. He thought of Theo as old, but Theo was only fifty-five. True, he looked older. His skin was tough, weathered, neglected, and his mouth sucked on bad dentures which gave him a sly grin. Neither man was tall, but Theo was lean and sinewy. Matthew was stocky and broad-shouldered. They worked together well, in silence. Matthew tried to anticipate what was needed. Theo didn't talk unless it was almost too late. They moved slowly across the calm water until the net was out, then circled back and enclosed the space.

The weather was right, and the mullet were running with the incoming tide. Soon the net was weighted down with the struggling striped mullet, and as the net sank in the dark water, the corked topline dipped below the surface.

"Let's git these mullet up." They hauled in the gill net and tossed the silver mullet to the floor of the boat.

"They talk 'bout 'ketchin all the mullet', but almost any morning I seen a group a dolphin chasin' an' jumpin' outta the water, circlin' a school a mullet, an' one at a time, takin' turns, eatin' all they can eat. Dolphin ain't regulated by the gov'ment."

Soon the bottom of the boat was filled with roe mullet and they motored back up to the old beach cove. He moved Theo's truck down onto the hard sand and they emptied tubs of mullet into the truck.

"We kain't ketch'em all," Theo said. They were moving the motor back to the truck. "We been tryin' to ketch'em all since my daddy was ketchin' em, an' they's as many now as they ever was."

"That true, Theo?"

"Yes sir, that a fact. An' if tha Japanese wanta pay triple to eat the roe, we gonna catch the roe. We gotta eat too. But I can't eat the roe. Too rich for my taste.

"What's with this Net Ban Amendment?"

"Gov'ment jus' messin' with us agin. No good reason."

Theo went to East Bay to sell the mullet roe to the Japanese.

Matthew took three large mullet to the house and cleaned them. He examined the red roe, but threw it away. Maybe he'd try it next year.

He was skeptical by nature.

CHAPTER TWO

Sea Horse Tavern

IT WAS THE BEST year on the Gulf since before the Hurricane of '85. And when times were good, Belle Rio was a carnival. By mid afternoon the local seafood workers were done for the day, and the oystermen had bagged out and were headed for the bar, cash in hand, moving in unison from one watering hole to the next like migratory birds or the furies of a Greek tragedy. They smoked Gulf Royale dope and drank liquor chased with beer. As the night progressed, the conversations, names and events became confused, or changed without concern for truth, so that what was at any given moment would be for all time, and would grow into myth and become legend.

The *Seahorse Tavern* sign glared neon magenta, yellow and faded blue into the misty night. Inside, was a rowdy crowd.

A corpulent, sweaty-faced Valdosta crop duster was working on his third dozen raw oysters. He'd already eaten a smoked mullet and two pounds of rock shrimp.

"When I get to goin' it takes two field hands to clean up after me. It sho as hell does," drawled

The crop duster had flown his own Cessna to Belle Rio for a week of fishing on Billy Ray Hardaway's charter boat, and he was eating everything that wasn't nailed down. Billy Ray was making good money and his client was feeding everybody in town.

"Damn things are tasty," he said. "Y'all eat up." And you jus keep shucking them oysters, Elvis," he drawled with reverence.

"Everybody wants to be an Elvis *imposter*," Skinny Sherman said, being his usually charming self. Sherman had an elaborate curly-perm hairdo and a two thousand dollar set of pearly-white government teeth.

"Impersonator," Elvis corrected him, cracking open oysters as fast as he could.

Skinny Sherman was non-stop entertainment to himself, and occasionally to other patrons of the *Sea Horse Tavern – with* his constant police blotter gossip, and the card tricks he'd learned in the Big House. He never quit trying.

"Y'all hear about the Bartow brothers?" He announced in bold type, like he was a TV game show host: "Caught in Wakulla with naked teenage girls! The Bartow Brothers! Now locked up and charged with *attempted rape!*"

That got a hearty groan and a few laughs. Nobody ever heard of *attempted rape*.

"I wouldn't say I just tried it and not got it done," boasted Elvis. "Hey, Cutch, you a lawyer, would you ever admit to *attempted rape?*"

Agreeing with Elvis, Matthew McCutcheon said. "I would not advise 'attempted anything' … best to go ahead and admit that you got it done, or else deny that you were ever in Wakulla County." Matthew was feeling momentarily at peace with himself, and the anonymous camaraderie of Belle Rio.

Billy Ray Hardaway was shooting pool in the back room with Terri Cates and talking in his *Elmer Fudd* and *Bugs Bunny* cartoon voices, trying to get her interested in something besides his red Corvette.

Billy Ray knew how to fish, but when it came to Terri, Billy Ray was whipped pathetic.

In fact, "pathetic" was Billy Ray's middle name, and everybody knew it, long before he lost his first charter fishing boat in the big storm a few years back. He didn't have enough sense to haul her out of the rough water, and she slammed onto the shore and sank. The Polaroid pictures showed the sleek, expensive boat, nearly a fifty footer, laying keeled over, half submerged on the reef of the Island.

That's when Billy Ray went to Panama City and crewed on the charter fleet, making enough money to pay for the damage to his boat. And recently he'd won four thousand dollars in the *Saltwater Classic Fishing Tournament*. He was a likable dodo to be such a no count.

Terri Cates leaned over the pool table. Her teen queen butt was crammed into tight jeans and her platinum hair glowed with the colors of the juke box chaser lights. She was, hands down, the best-looking cougar in Belle Rio, the love child of her mother's teenage marriage to a Soldier of Fortune she called "Terry the Pirate" or "That Pirate Son of a Bitch," depending on how she felt that day. The pirate had gone off when Terri was born and had never been back.

Terri had the defiant, wild blood of her reckless parents. At seventeen, she was ahead of the game. She was good looking, and she had not gotten pregnant. That was an accomplishment in Belle Rio where they said "if you're old enough to go to the store, you're old enough to get bread."

At fourteen she had sex with her mother's youngest brother. It wasn't like she thought it would be, and it had taught her in one brisk, bloody event that sex just wasn't worth the trouble, unless there was something

9

more to be had. And she learned that when men want sex, they treat you one way, nice sometimes even; but when they get what you got, you got nothing. It was supply and demand. You got it; they want it. The more they want it, the more it's worth. When there's a lot of it around, yours ain't worth much, and if you're giving it away, it ain't worth nothing.

She had learned that the best way to have any control over her life was to make them do without. But there were times when doing what they wanted meant she might get what she wanted. She handled those as they came up.

Billy Ray's kept coming up, but she pretended not to notice. There was really nothing to gain. She already had what she wanted, for now: to be chauffeured in Billy Ray's red Corvette.

The patrons watched with envy and whistled in unison as Billy Ray escorted young Terri Cates from the Sea Horse Tavern.

"What does that cougar see in Billy Ray?" Elvis, lamented, shaking his head in disbelief.

Billy Ray's Corvette squealed from the parking lot.

"Terri likes to be chauffeured in his red Corvette," crooned Skinny Sherman, "but she don't never touch his joy stick."

Sherman laughed too loud at his own humor.

Toothless Madonna had found a home near the sympatico crop duster who was feeding her by hand, admiring her alabaster bosom and studying her business card: *Madonna   General Delivery Baytown Florida*, scrawled in childlike letters on the back of a Budweiser beer coaster.

Once the initial shock of her appearance wore off, she was attractive and appealing, especially to a South Georgia glutton with an unbridled appetite. The Valdostan slurped down another oyster and wiped the seafood sauce from his wide moustache, captivated by her toothless mouth.

Cairo Thorne made a grand appearance in the doorway. To general applause he took a seat at the bar. Cairo was dressed in camouflage from head to toe, his hunt cap backwards. He was heavy-set with a wild bush of thick reddish hair sticking out beneath his hat and a crazy Irish, Seminole renegade grin spread across his broad flat face that nobody disputed. He nodded to those over by the jukebox and the pool table. People didn't mess much with the Chief.

"Ya'll doing some eating," Cairo said to the bar. "Elvis, fix me a dozen them oysters! Aint you helping him eat, Cutch? Where's yur manners, son? I hate to see a man eat alone. Fix Cutch a dozen, too."

Elvis was shucking fast as he could.

With one arm draped affectionately around smiling Madonna, the curious crop duster addressed stone-faced Cairo.

"What's your line of work, fella?"

"I'm a farmer," Cairo replied.

The Valdostan knew when he was being took. "What you farm?"

"Row crops," Cairo answered.

"Don't nobody farm nothin' in Belle Rio."

"I do," Cairo stated bluntly for the record.

"Y'all just grow pine trees up in them woods and Gulf Royale owns the damn lot of' em."

"They don't own my crop, but I farm right alongside of 'em," Cairo said, downing a beer with a half-breed grin.

"Well, you ain't farming nothin' unless you farming contraband."

There was a pause you could drive a logging truck through.

Nobody smiled.

"I'm gonna pour us some beer," Cairo said.

"You keep tabs a that beer," Elvis cautioned.

Cairo was always generous with his friends. He drew four pitchers for the tables near the jukebox where Billy Ray's forgotten girlfriend, Darlene, had fallen in with Chad, Keith Moss, and Crazy Maxwell.

Darlene looked every bit of her twenty-eight years. She had been ridden hard and not put up, neither wet nor dry, just left out to fend for herself, and it had taken a toll on her once good looks. Her large soft brown eyes were glazed over with local weed and too much beer. She had short dark hair that was crudely cut and a soft complexion that had been abused and let go. She could be pretty when she tried, but she drank too much and forgot to care.

Chad and Keith had both worked for Hardaway Seafood Co. since they were kids. They hunted deer in the winter and chased cougar wherever they felt they might get lucky. Dressed in the local water-rat fashion of army surplus camouflage and white rubber boots, they were good friends, but they loved to fight. And there was always a reason to fight.

Crazy Maxwell made most people nervous. He was always surly, apprehensive as a three-legged dog. He looked mad at something or somebody, lurking in the shadows, watching and waiting, lost in the crowd.

Conway Twitty sang *Crazy in Love* on the juke box. Darlene danced with Cairo. The drunken laughter of the crowd mixed with the jumble of breaking pool balls.

A loud argument started at the pool table when Chad snookered Keith Moss. Keith insulted Chad's manhood, and said that Chad's mother was a not so good piece of ass, and then named the men in Belle Rio who would know. Everybody backed away and gave them room to go at it. Chad was strong, but Keith was mad. Keith tackled Chad and threw him to the floor, then hit him in the face and bloodied up his nose. It didn't look good.

Cairo had seen enough. He cracked a pool que over Keith's back, knocking him to the floor. Keith spat and cursed at Cairo who was standing over him. Keith dropped his head in defeat. He was not gonna mess with Cairo.

"Next time, Keith," snarled at Chad. "I'll kick yur ass."

"Y'all behave or get on outta here!" Elvis yelled from the bar. "I aint running a Red Cross First Aid Establishment. Have another beer. Behave or clear out!"

Rail thin and partly brain dead, Dr. Zeus stumbled through the tavern door. He had recently won thirty thousand dollars in the *Fantasy Lotto* and bought himself a new double wide and a year's supply of Quaaludes.

Dr. Zeus, the main party dude, quietly spread the word that there was a band setting up to play at a watering hole down the highway, near the beach, and then he disappeared, like he had never been there. That soon brought the tavern to a standstill. And with one mind or no mind at all, there was simultaneous exodus for the next round of excitement.

The Valdosta gentleman took advantage of the momentum to sweep Toothless Madonna out the door and down to his room at the marina.

When the dust settled, Matthew was left sitting at the bar with the half breed Cairo who was inspecting his new Barlow knife while he talked surreptitiously about the three nymphomaniac cougars that were supposed to be on the prowl and waiting for him at Moreno's trailer.

After a long silence, staring ominously at Matthew, Cairo took the blade and stuck the point below his own right eye and flicked open a small cut that bled in a fine line down his cheek into his beard.

"I do that because I am your friend. I could not hurt you without hurting myself."

Cairo handed the knife to Matthew and stared at him with a challenging ominous dare that riveted him cold. Cairo's Irish Seminole eyes revealed only a dark, ominous silence. With an unsteady hand, he stuck the blade point to his cheek below his right eye and flicked the knife. Blood rushed from the too deep cut and ran down his face. Their eyes locked together with a vengeance. Elvis handed Matthew a hunk of ice wrapped in a bar towel.

"You obviously ain't learned the trick to that yet. And now you got blood everywhere. What a mess. You're like me, Cutch. You don't really belong here. Don't try to be like them."

"Live free," Cairo said with a bold grin, "an' run wide open!"

In the pre-dawn hours under a canopy of stars, Matthew stood at the water's edge with Cairo, smoking potent Gulf Royale weed and drinking warm beer. The nymphomaniac cougars had migrated to another county, and Cairo was now traveling with a scrawny ex-con who had done time with Cairo at Raiford prison. The convict chump wasn't happy and wanted to hurt somebody but didn't know who. He was like an angry stingray, with his mean face, wanting a fight but unable to find a worthy opponent. Cairo and the ex-con Stingray were like cousins that mated by the dark of the moon.

Beneath the stars in the chill hour before dawn, the renegade half-breed and the stingray cracker babbled hostile, often unintelligible jailhouse jargon.

"You got plenty of money," snarled the agitated Stingray.

"It ain't the money," Cairo barely suppressed a blind rage. "I can shoot a gun further than any of my people ever been from this damn spot right here. My people always lived in the woods, an' on the water. An' they done took it away. The damn state took my kid. And then his dumb bitch mother got herself busted stealing underwear from the *Family Dollar* in Wakulla."

Matthew stared at Cairo. His brain was numb, understanding without thought, the pain and fear, hatred and danger, that surrounded Cairo. There was nothing he could do or say as the Chief chanted the war dance litany:

"All I ever wanted was to run wide open, to run wide fuckin' open. Let 'em try an' stop me. I jus' wanna run wide open. Run wide fuckin' open."

Matthew lost his equilibrium and sank into the sand. His brain was mush and his face hurt. He felt he had not been this near death since he got stuck for months on the all-night cross-town bus through the cold, deserted streets of Chicago.

His heart pounded an irregular reggae beat: "Live free run wide open," pounded "wide open" pounded "live free," pounded "run wide open," pounded "live free run wide open."

CHAPTER THREE

Memory

MATTHEW WOKE UP with the dawn, cold and alone. Then he drove two hours to an emergency clinic in Capital City where a young intern examined the cut beneath his eye and sewed four insignificant stitches.

The scar would not amount to much.

But mother would want to know what happened to his face.

Sitting on the cool marble tombstone beneath the tall murmuring pines, he arranged the artificial pink and yellow flowers from the *Family Dollar Store*. They were made out of some material that would last beyond the destruction of the planet. He added a Christmas Angel with wings and a gilded halo. When he finished decorating the marble headstone, it looked festive like a car wreck roadside memorial. Mother would have liked it. But now she didn't have much to say, resting next to Grandfather Patterson, who had never met a stranger, lived eighty-eight years, and died on his birthday. Grandma Patterson, silent and solemn as usual, lay beside him.

Driving back to Belle Rio from Capital City, the presence of his mother enveloped him like a narcotic. On the outskirts of Sopchoppy, in the late afternoon heat, he lapsed into a drowsy stupor hangover and pulled off the road into the parking lot of a used auto parts store and fell asleep. He could still feel her close to him, although she was slipping away.

Stranded, motionless in the sterile corridor, supported by a walker attached to a trailing plasma bottle, she had almost reached the doorway when he got there. She was surrounded by nurses encouraging her to complete the twice daily exercise routine, that was her only act of living, and make it back to the bed, which was her haven before the final resting place. It had come to this.

In the last photograph he had taken of her a few months before she went into the hospital, her face appeared white and vaporous, over-exposed from the flash, a rare event which occurred with the near dead, as if she had vaporized and disappeared from the negative, a photo-chemical existential statement of the departing soul, a metaphysical photographic phenomenon that was unexplainable by Fuji or Kodak.

"You've got to try," the nurse pleaded through the din and clutter of the hospital hallway, spoken with faint irritation and an edge of impatience at her reluctance to live, "Otherwise, you'll never get any better." It sounded futile, and no one believed it would ever be any different, certainly never any better. She had grown tired from years of waiting, and she wanted to die.

He stood impatiently and watched as she struggled to move first one leg then the other. She was in front of him, perched on the walker like a frail, helpless bird. Her drugged and listless eyes met his with recognition, then she knew, for an embarrassed moment, that he had come for her and she was not dressed for the dance. But it did not last long. Nothing lasted very long with her anymore.

"Hello, mother," he said, touching the sagging flesh without muscle that quivered while barely supporting her shrunken body.

"Tell them to let me lie down," she whispered. "My blood pressure is lower than the speed limit," she smiled wanly at him. "Am I blocking traffic?"

She wanted to make him laugh, let him know that she remembered. And he always laughed at her jokes. She leaned her face toward him, and he smelled the antiseptic perfume of dying. He kissed her.

"You want to dance, Mom?"

He wished he could comfort her in his arms like you would a small child.

"It'd have to be a slow dance," she smiled from where she was, thinking she must hurry and dress for he would soon be there, and they would dance the night until dawn. Then the war would take him away and she would have to find another sailor, another dancer.

Matthew went to the stairwell and cried against the cold concrete wall. She always had been able to make him laugh.

It was only a matter of time. All he would have left was memory.

And if memory were all there is, all there was, is all there is.

They drove through the old cemetery behind the campus where the road curved down along the river, past the eroding, vine-covered monuments, through the barren trees and darkened stones where they lay in college, he not with her but forgetting her, under the stars of the night sky, drinking gin, reciting Swinburne in misspoken drunkenness: *Between the sun dawn and the night undone, O sad, kissed mouth, I long for you.* Forgotten fragments of meaningless erotic foreplay on crumbling tombstones beneath the moon, beside the slow flowing river. He wanted to hold her, for the memory of her love was fading and he could not change that, and what he could not forget, but could not remember, but was, not is, was all there is.

"You don't come home anymore," the girl, now a woman, said.

"I always want something I can't have, that isn't here anymore," he said. Then he thought he said, "You could hold me in your arms and let me cry." But they sat in the car without talking, him wanting her to know that he had loved her, to feel that she had loved him, to see her face as it once was but was not now and would never be again, to know that he would love her forever. She had already forgotten. But he could never forget her twirling red-sequined innocent body sparkling beneath the bright stadium lights, his desire in a car parked in the dark secret whispering pines, taking pleasure that she gave him, that he gave her.

He wanted the memory to go away so that he would never again awaken with the melancholy that came with her face, that time had not taken away, would not take away. But still, the memory of her had been misplaced among the thousand nameless events, people, places and phantoms that, along with her, were all jumbled and confused, and summoned at random to haunt him.

Now they sat on the hill above the barren trees and forlorn swirling muddy water. He had loved her, but she had gone away, mailed a letter from somewhere in west Texas to him in Greenwich Village, where he was lost in a stranger's careless love. Not even a memory, just a body in a summer heat wave, that was too long ago to remember.

He only wanted to know that love was, not was not, that not all love was only memory, now that mother was becoming only memory and he could not keep her from going away, sending him a package from somewhere unknown, filled with knick-knacks and plastic angels, sending him a letter somewhere, but not home, because home faded to memory and then memory faded away and there was no place to come to.

"You went away?" she whispered against his cheek, slow dancing in the fading light. "Men always go away."

"I went home yesterday, Mom," he said, hoping to find her there, but she had gone away. "We were happy there, Mom. Remember?"

Holding her in his arms she was his sweetheart, his lover, his wife, his child, not only his mother when she held him in her arms and there was comfort in the night.

She smiled faintly from the distant horizon, her arms around his neck, slow dancing on a night that he would never forget. She opened her eyes and looked at him, but he was not who she remembered; he had gone away. Then she was gone, too. Succumbing, she sighed, and he stared, pleading, into her vacant eyes. Please, Mom, please love me. Remember me. Please. Remember forever.

He stayed with her at the hospital four days and nights, and she talked to him in the dark without knowing who he was. The wind moved through the trees and down the corridors and the cool shadows were like the breath of eternity where love was only memory. "Take care of Mother," said the telegram from Lt. Franklin McCutcheon, USN, the man he never knew. But he did not know how to take care of Mother. She needed something he could not give.

On a cold day in Chicago several months after she died, he was walking across the downtown Plaza where he had gone to close the real estate deal that he thought would change his life. A thunderstorm of pigeons rose nosily in one breath, reflected against the downtown monoliths of steel and glass, and suddenly he felt her close to him, and her voice whispered through the wind and thrash of wings, although he knew she was gone.

He recognized her, and her memory was a whisper of love. He felt her love then, at that moment, although he knew she was gone. And that would never change.

CHAPTER FOUR

Andrew Percy

ANDREW PERCY crossed the state line under a hot blue cloudless sky and breezed along the Gulf Coast Highway. The sunroof of the '90 Lincoln Continental was open, and a maudlin, heart-broke country song blared from the tape deck.

"I hate that country shit," whined the leggy, platinum blonde showgirl, reclining against the passenger door, "that whimpering, pathetic country shit." She mimicked the nasal country crooner and pushed the eject button with her big toe. Static, jumbled nonsense, noise, nothing. Percy knocked her foot away and shoved the tape back in. He cranked the volume and flicked his cigarette past her face out the passenger window. The glamour girl smiled at him, improvised a nasty rap lyric to the square beat county song. She had been trouble since they left Detroit. Percy knew that sooner or later she would goad him red-hot. He would indulge himself in shameless, brutal, unholy joy and beat her haughty beautiful face black and blue. It would cost him money, but damn, she was a bitch.

The rearview mirror image: honey brown mulatto painting her toenails. His serpent stirred when he looked at the shy young street urchin with large soft doe eyes, petite hands and feet, close-cropped dark hair, a gold pin pierced through her nostril. He liked Angie Bird. She would sing sweet from the cage of love.

Both girls had slept through Ohio, Kentucky, and Tennessee, the willowy platinum bitch stretched out in the back like it was a king size bed, the mulatto faun with the blameless feet curled up on the front seat like a lost kitten.

At first glance, Drew Percy appeared younger than his forty years, but stopped dead in his tracks, his hard, callous eyes were older than sin from years of corrupt, reckless living. He showed as self-confident, aggressive, even vain, rugged handsome, with coarse features and a strong jaw. Narcissism gave him an intense demanding presence, exaggerated by a sometimes crazed, abrupt, almost comic intensity. Scraggly bleached hair fell carelessly across his face. A faded, jagged scar ran down his neck from behind his right ear, curved under his chin, and stopped at the Adam's apple, a constant reminder of an attempted snuff by a crazy Bantu during his Club Fed vacation. Percy had known the Devil and was not afraid. In a haphazard world, he had learned to play it close to the vest. Long shots were useless, lost causes a waste of time.

Percy recruited young exotic dancers, debutantes, "neophytes in the ballet" he called them, from the Mustang Club in Detroit, the Solid Gold Bar in Nashville, and the Platinum Slugger in Louisville, and brought them to Panama City to work on their tans. Enjoy life in Paradise. Those that made the grade moved on to swank, classic ballet venues in West Palm or Miami or the Caribbean gambling casinos. The losers were dispatched to bush league clubs where they performed in the "Hot Stuff Revue" at Clubs like the *Toy Box Lounge* located next door to the Holiness Revival Church outside of Dothan, AL.

If the leggy Detroit bitch called him "the chauffeur pimp" one more time, he would break her nose. What the hell did she know.

Panama City: brilliant white beaches, emerald water, and scattered puffy clouds overgrown with a jungle of retail excess, the FloriBama Babylon, the redneck Sodom and Gomorra, where during the day the hot summer sun burned the fair-skinned flesh and the rolling surf pounded monotonously on the white sand; and at night, braggart fraternity brothers in a haze of beer and the heat of youth claimed the virginity of southern belle party girls and drank Pabst Blue Ribbon beer from quart bottles until they puked on the floor of their daddy's pickup truck.

Downtown was not what it used to be. Now it was waiting for block grant urban renewal. The fancy real estate had moved west to Seaside and Destiny Beach. Panama City was a jungle of *tourista* retail excess— tattoo parlors and video arcades, condominiums stacked upon condominiums, old people in luxury secured ghettos, *Salt Water Jack's Saloon*, ticky-tacky shops, *Wet Willy's* filled with bikini beach bimbos, cheese heads on a budget, *Boingo Boingo*, *Tropical Sea Breeze, the World's Largest Raw Bar, Dockter Dick's Tavern*, Beach Hog Motorcycles, *Hot Bitch Fashions*, Shells, Souvenirs, Everything *50% OFF* Vacancy. No vacancy. LOW RATES! Jungle Beach Train. Jet Skis. Banana Boats. Burgers Oysters Beer. *Bottom's Up Bar & Grill. Club Maharaja* of India. The *Seven Wonders of the World*. The Great Pyramid. Buddha. Sharks, Alligators & Tropical Birds, Monkeys & Dinosaurs. *Red-Eyed Gorilla Putt Putt*. Animal Fashions for Your Pet. Gator Restaurant. *Mikado Japanese Restaurant*. Key Largo Burlesque. *Asian Takee Outee. Wicked Willie's Bar & Grill*. Panama City Blue. *Euphoria Massage Parlor*. Gun & Pawn. $CASH$. Guys Without Shirts. Too Cool Too Good. And *Cleopatra's Temple of Love* with gaudy flashing lights: NAKED! *Adult*

Entertainment. SEE LIVE NUDE Dancers! The World's Most Beautiful Women

Cleopatra's Temple of Love on Panama City beach was a sex goddess theme park, an ornate gilded ballroom with a dance floor runway surrounded by chaser lights and gold speckled mirrors. Elaborate murals covered the walls. Jackal headed faceless gods of the underworld. Maidens with fine jewelry danced naked and performed sacred rituals. They all looked like Elizabeth Taylor. The décor of the Temple was 1950's Hollywood *femme fatal* movie fetish clip art.

Chi Chi was posed at the bar talking to a customer, her bare chocolate buttocks splashed with rhythmic colored lights from the spinning globe mirror. Men waited in line for her attention. In the flesh trade, she could suck up money like a Eureka power vac.

"We missed ya, baby," she greeted Percy in a voice flavored with salsa and mock sincerity. Her dark hair was shag cut and glitter sprayed. "Did you find what you were looking for?"

"Never," he said. "You working this evening?" He already knew the answer. She was gone.

"It's my last day. I'm going to Miami with Delgado. You'll have to get one of the new prima donnas to fill my slot."

"That'll be impossible, Chi Chi. You're irreplaceable."

Delgado tried to keep her under wraps for himself. Delgado was the jealous type. A man in the wrong business. Stupid and unfortunate, Percy thought.

"Hate to see you go. You're breaking my heart."

"Drew, you're cute when you're so sincere." She waived an expensive jeweled bauble-laden wrist. "You look tired."

She kissed him on the cheek and walked away.

He was tired. Constantly looking for new talent. The *Temple of Love* ballet was an acquired taste: like high culture, low life was no different.

He left the two debutants with Mother Teresa and drove to his other club on the east side of Panama City where the Redneck Rivera meets the River Styx.

The Doll House was a one-story building in the shape of the storybook Gingerbread house, painted pink and lavender, with cutouts of a brunette Barbie Doll on either side of the front door.

It was a rundown joint with a small stage and a dance pole that was popular with Pulp Mill workers from Port Royale who played blackjack and stud poker once a month when they got their paychecks. On the weekend local teenage boys with bad tattoos, who weren't supposed to drink beer, hung out playing pool, eating pizza and pork rinds, hoping to get a kiss from the dancing girls in the back room – a low ceiling dungeon that smelled of stale cigarettes and cheap perfume.

Percy watched the last performance of the night from his office through a two-way mirror. He was drag-ass tired and edgy. It was karaoke night, and the amateur dancers pandered their way through the last sex acts for a not too enthusiastic small crowd. The gloom of smoke hung in the humid air.

After closing he swaggered aimlessly from the office, inhaled the dank, sweaty odor, and descended on the frizzy-haired bleached-out blonde whose sister watched her kids at home, while she debauched for short-haul truckers and pulp mill boiler mechanics. Then, bent over the desk in his office, she took Percy's hard on for revenge against a life that left her frustrated and angry. His cold heart that defied gratification stabbed the writhing mother of two, coming at her from behind, both of them wet and smelly, banging her head against the wall until she whimpered and swooned and finally started crying, him still wooden, her sister at home in bed fucking her jealous husband. He left her collapsed on the sofa. He didn't need to hear another man's wife cry.

He finally came to rest on the sofa in his small house one block off the bay. His mind was fried. He hoped he would sleep, if he could turn the engine off. He dozed off and on for an hour with the smell of her sweaty acrid body and cheap perfume. Her desperation had made him feel something, more cruelty than pity, but it was something. She wanted what he wanted, escape from loneliness. Call it companionship. Call it pain. Call it what you will.

Vague non-thought and desire wandered, through his need to crash and sleep. Delgado was taking Chi Chi. She would be Betty Boop for white geezers after he had his. She deserved better. Delgado was a fool, but it was his life. What the hell. There was no way to salvage that wreck. Chi Chi was a survivor.

This reverie drifted to the soft doe-eyed mulatto dancer from Deerfield. He fantasized her bittersweet taste. He would worship her. Tan suede skin, taut butt, smart breast. Blameless, perfect feet. Damn cherry red toenails. Sweet ankles. He would crawl if he had to. Make life easy for her. Make her queen for a day. He didn't want much.

Anyway, she would never like a yahoo yokel bog trotter like him. He wasn't her type. Bet she ain't got no male type. He tried to think of her face, but she was just a body with a mood, shy and quiet. Yearn itch crave fondle nibble bite suck rut rut.

When Percy was young, he played pinball, addicted to machines with fantastic gaudy pictures, flashing colored lights, and sounds that binged and bonged and clanged and clicked and whirred, accumulating free games as he banged the side of the machine in the back room of the arcade parlor, while the dreams of the country music droned from the juke box in the bar next door, where his father drowned the afternoons. Slight of stature, until he made himself muscular in prison, he took the odds that came with other people's miscalculations and turned them to his own advantage, learned to walk away a winner, or at least to walk away. Devoted to chance, driven by the uncertain outcome of future events, the limited probability of success, the enormity of failure, he had nothing to lose but his raw animal instinct for survival. He was known as a man who threw dice and worshipped snakes.

Percy finally slept for three hours, then he threw out the cat, opened the windows and did his half hour of strenuous, non-stop calisthenics. Muscles hard. Stank skanky. The unusual fresh air from the bay felt clear and good.

He showered, then tried to talk to his parrot, Collette, while he shaved. Collette was the first pet he ever owned. Took him a long time to like the parrot. Estella got it for him when she stayed there. She left and he kept the bird. Collette sometimes talked a blue streak, but today she only repeated the punch line to one joke that Percy couldn't remember, so they squawked together in meaningless gibber.

The half bred, Cairo, came by in the early afternoon. Percy called the stoic Irish renegade pot-smuggler "Choctaw" or "Chief." Nobody messed much with Cairo. They drove to a poor section on the east side, not far from the Doll House, just outside the city limits.

In a dilapidated garage on 23rd Street, where a mechanic and torch man went to work on the Ford LTD, the acetylene flame cut the gas tank out of the big sedan. Inside the gas tank was a separate liner. Twenty kilos of Gulf Royale weed, and two pounds of blow, with a street value worth *mucho dinero*, was inside the liner.

The hard-scrabble office had only a broken desk, no telephone and a busted sofa covered by a chenille spread. Cairo had a pile of clothes thrown over in the corner.

Percy paid Cairo cash. "Don't spend it all in one place," he said.

The half-breed just smiled. He didn't say much. The cannabis Cairo grew between the pine rows on the Gulf Royal timber land was used to supplement the imported weed and nose candy that was being shipped in on Billy Ray Hardaway's charter boat. It was exchanged seventy-five miles offshore, from a shrimp trawler registered in Venezuela, that had put out from the coast of Mexico. They would unload it upriver by the Swamp River cutoff near Dead Lake.

Andrew Percy knew Dead Lake like the back of his hand.

His whole life seemed to be a warped replay of the story he heard his father, Andrew Jackson Percy, tell over and over again: "They went bust, and times was bad all over." It had shaped his life.

Later that afternoon Percy and Cairo went to the *Phantasy Club* near the Miracle Strip. Percy represented an international banker in Miami who was not happy with the manager of the Phantasy Club, a svelte South American named Ramon who owed Delgado a past due tariff for the privilege of peddling high-heeled Latin hookers to beach tourists, sailors, and Tyndall flyboys.

Cairo placed the lavender-scented Brazilian atop an expensive antique credenza, where he looked as helpless as he was scared.

"You believe in the *hereafter*, Ramon?" Percy asked.

Ramon nodded his penitent head and crossed himself.

"Well, I'm *here after* my money." Percy said.

But Ramon didn't get the joke.

"You don't stand a chance of living another night unless we either find the money you owe Delgado somewhere in this office, or your banker boyfriend delivers the money before midnight."

Ramon started begging for mercy.

Cairo said, "Shut up! Ramona, you whimpering shit."

Cairo ransacked through the office desk and threw the drawers out the window into the alley.

Then it got real quiet, except for the droning roll of the ocean waves that could be heard through the open windows.

Percy jerked Ramon's leg, and he tumbled from the credenza to the floor.

"Gawd damn, I hate to do this."

Cairo picked up Ramon and slammed the featherweight Latino against the wall where he crumpled to the floor like a rag doll. Cairo pulled him up, held him by the lapels against the wall.

Ramon pleaded for mercy in Spanish.

"Where's the damn money?" Cairo drawled. "You ain't gonna be happy 'til we get the damn money."

Ramon was slobbering, his dapper silk wardrobe ruined by his failure to deliver the overdue five grand he owed Delgado's Miami bosses.

"Call your banker boyfriend. Have the money by midnight. And clean up this place," Percy said.

They came back at midnight and collected the money from Ramon's suddenly eager to please banker.

CHAPTER FIVE

Sine Qua Non

AS THE PALE moon descended to the western horizon, Matthew returned from the water's edge to the house that stood against all odds beyond the sand dunes and scattered pines. It was the oldest house along the deserted beach west of Three Rivers, a weathered cypress ramshackle house, with a wide screen porch on three sides, two upstairs bedrooms that faced south toward the water, a vintage kitchen, a sparsely furnished living room, and Grandma's Closet, the inner sanctum of memories, cluttered with unwashed clothes, stacks of threadbare sheets and towels, and moth-eaten drab wool blankets. A formal portrait of his grandmother painted the year before she died gave the room a solemn dignity.

The top surface of an ornate dark mahogany credenza, cluttered with fading, aged photographs in tarnished frames, displayed the silent, haunting, dreamscape images: Grandfather Patterson, wearing his crumples Stetson, seated behind the wheel of his classic Packard at a political parade in downtown Capital City; the full-blossomed dark-haired woman that was his mother before the war, standing beside the

Navy Lieutenant that she had said was his father, holding the infant she had said was him, on the porch of the simple white frame house, beneath an enormous, weeping, moss-draped live oak tree.

He opened the heavy wooden shutters, and a silent gray mist crept into the empty rooms. He lay on the sofa drifting through a vague nether world along the brink of despair. He had been there so often that it had lost its thrill, and he had grown numb from the prolonged exposure to a jaded, weak-willed death wish. Time was, something mattered, but he'd be damned if it mattered now.

Forgive and forget, hell. You take those screwups as part of life and you leave them behind. Them being those you have to leave. Those you have to love. Those there are to love. What few choices there are. Stained with guilt as they are. As you are, as I am.

So, go ahead and throw stones; they won't hurt me. I'm not made of glass. And he waited apprehensively between the dark silence and the morning light.

Anne was not at home. He called twice after midnight and both times the machine had mocked him. He hung up the phone by throwing it at the wall, then he turned over the television set, which crashed to the floor facing the mirror, and the flickering images of the late-night movie and new and used Toyota commercials reflected off the glass and danced on the opposite wall. The world was properly upside down, sideways and backwards. He sat naked on the floor, amidst the silent flickering dancing images reflected in the mirror, talking incoherently to the uncomprehending sideways television, and drank warm vodka until he stammered into the maudlin silence, at last not moving. He stared blankly at the ceiling, wishing the ghost face would come again and take him home. No, home was not what he meant. He knew he could not go home. Sweet Home Chicago was not there anymore.

He stumbled outside where the wind was driving the low clouds over the face of the moon. The tall whispering pines were comforting, but the high tide waves were crashing on the beach while the aggressive outgoing tides wantonly sucked the river into the gulf. The wanton tides. Won Ton. Her favorite soup at their favorite restaurant, *The Dragon Inn*, with the ornate pagoda roof. "The Drag On In" they called it during the good years when the happy moments made memories, and the memories made a life, because the memories last when nothing else will.

But it was difficult to think of her now because there was nothing where the feeling had been, where the memories should be, and he couldn't find any memories that mattered, any reasons either, except for the unnatural reasons: the Golden Ray Sins, the Original Sins, any sins, please, except those Dancing Raisins and the Singing Choir Nuns, the *Sine Qua Non,* chanting St. Anselm's Proof for the existence of God. Meaning: that which nothing greater can be conceived, you cannot live without. Meaning: that which you cannot live without, you must live with. *Ergo:* that which you cannot live without, you must try to get at any cost. And he had failed. Therefore, he had to live without that which he could not live without.

It was dumb bad logic. But Dum Luk was better than most things on the Dragon Inn menu that night, and good, bad or indifferent, Dum Luk didn't leave you hungry for more.

The morning birds chirped and sang until the sun broke through the clouds above the island, then they fell silent as the sunlight streamed into the room and the dream slowly faded. Beethoven's *Quartet in A Minor* played on the tape deck. A ravaged soul was saved by grace, became peaceful knowing death and floated away. A solitary violin sustained the fragile breath of life. He was suddenly anxious and afraid, lost for all time, beyond time.

Only a deity could perfect a hurt so simple as not knowing who you are, knowing only that you are a thousand parts of a thousand thousand, and that you cannot know who you are because you are scattered like dust to the wind.

The ringing telephone woke him up, and he stumbled down the stairs.

"Hotel Belle Rio," he answered still half asleep.

"You Matthew McCutcheon?" the old gravel voice snapped.

"Yes sir, I believe so. Some days more so than others."

"This is the attorney Francois Taghert. I'd like for you to come in and talk to me, son, if you're interested in working. I understand you have been wasting time down here."

He responded with an appropriate impertinent silence.

"Do it before lunch. I'll be out this afternoon. I'm around the corner from the courthouse, toward the river."

"I can find it," he said, but Taghert had hung up.

CHAPTER SIX

Francois Tagert, Esq.

MATTHEW NEVER TIRED of the drive along the coast highway. The sky and water of the bay was either turbulent or serene, dramatic or pensive, beautiful or sad, everything at the same time. At least it wasn't the pot-holed Eisenhower Freeway in wintertime Chicago rush hour, captive to snow and ice and general desperation. Maybe the desperation was too much to lay at the feet of the general, but the pot-holed Eisenhower through Chicago was now a disaster, and it was one of the General's lasting contributions to the American landscape.

By late morning, the sky was layered with moody capricious clouds and the northern wind whipped and churned the water into a symphonic frenzy, punctuated first by a sonic boom, then the incoming roar of four F-15 fighter jets that streaked overhead and disappeared like noisy bothersome gnats, beyond the island in hot pursuit of phantom Iraqi target drones twenty miles out over the Gulf.

The reigning US President was obsessed with Mideast oil and the specter of Satan, the Saddam of Iraq, who was doomed by an angry cyber intelligence of random statistical immutability and a new generation of high technology weaponry. The Global Military Hardware Trade Show, broadcast worldwide to demonstrate the latest weapons available for emerging oil rich nations with plenty of cash, was the ultimate video games sales tool. It used Iraqi soldiers as computer generated munchies. Beyond the clouds, F-15 gunslingers locked in the Target Drone on the simulation monitor and the computers back at Tyndall Headquarters scored one for the USA.

The Belle Rio Five Mile Bridge rose sharply over the mouth of the river, high above the rust-stained tin roofs of the vacant and despairing stores, now mostly devoid of prosperity, a dilapidated shell of its former success. Beyond the motel and across from the harbor, the brown marsh wetlands spread inland like the plains of Serengeti to dismal Tate's Hell Swamp. He passed the Victorian Inn and the courthouse, where the two massive columns framed the flight of stairs leading to the Circuit Court.

It was the perfect façade for justice.

The town had been born a prosperous seaport when the first proud schooners left for New York City loaded with bales of Georgia cotton brought down river on sturdy paddle wheelers. It was a lawless town with only a veneer of Episcopalian respectability. At the *Bucket of Blood Saloon*, rowdy sailors shared whores with bankers and merchants from New York, London, and Amsterdam. The town prospered in the pleasant fall weather when the money flowed loose and easy. Those who stayed endured the damp rainy winter, then everyone who could, fled the summer heat when deadly fevers took their toll.

Speculators came from many cities and nations, and many of them were now buried in the dark, sandy ground: Louis Watson from New York City arrived by ship in 1828 and was dead from malaria by 1840; Anthony Messina sailed into port in 1832 from Italy, abandoned ship, and fathered eight children by two wives, none of whom lived to bury him in 1889; Evander Fontaine ran away from Quebec on a frigate that arrived on September 10, 1884 and died the next day in a knife fight; Ortega Bruni, son of Louisa and Frank Bruni from Portugal, drowned with his wife Mary during a storm in 1887; his son, Leo Bruni, became a successful sponge merchant until the bay was depleted of sponges, then he retired from the sea and opened a barbershop & saloon.

Among the most prominent stone testaments: Dr. John Faircloth, his wife and children, and his son-in-law D.W. Hardaway. The direct descendants of John Faircloth had been absorbed by time and circumstance—*sic transit Gloria mundi*—but the Hardaway descendants were still looking for a way to die.

Hanging over the vacant receptionist's desk in the foyer of Francois Gellot Taghert's office was a large vintage photograph, which featured six gangly young men wearing broad-brimmed hats, white starched shirts, and suspenders, holding their long rifles, surrounded by their dogs and a collection of trophy game taken from the woods: deer, turkey, wild boar, and a man-size black bear. They stood beneath a weathered sign over the tin-roofed cypress building that read *Taghert Bros. Mercantile & Trading Co.*

Matthew could hear Taghert coughing from his office down the hall as he called out, "Come on back, son."

Attorney Francois Taghert was a garrulous, tenacious octogenarian with an abundance of unruly white hair. His complexion was ruddy and freckled from the sun and wind. He was loose-jowled with thick wild eyebrows.

"Make yourself at home," Taghert mumbled, while he continued his telephone conversation over the snorting of his old yellow hound asleep on the floor beside his desk. "It'll never happen, darling. Don't you worry," he droned. "I'll take care of everything."

He hung up the telephone, stiffly adjusted his body towards Matthew, and kept talking without a break. Francois Taghert's demeanor was cold and haunting, reminiscent of Vlad the Impaler, as if Taghert had been alive, in the same condition, for an indeterminate period of time, trapped in a necessarily deceptive physical persona, cruel, yet courteous and gracious in the refined, self-conscious southern manner.

"The widow of my client and dear friend is younger than his two children, both obstreperous, argumentative members of the feminine persuasion. He married this young woman against all advice, good and bad. I rarely comment on a man's taste for women or the reasons a man might marry or divorce any woman. We all do things for personal reasons that defy logic and general understanding, myself included.

"The recent widow was my client's fourth wife. She delivered the man a son only seven days after his death. That amazed many people, because at the time of the conception, he was at least eighty years old. I know what many were thinking, but believe me, it was his progeny. He could state the time of ovulation and position of penetration with a vivid accuracy and enthusiasm that went beyond casual interest or idle conjecture. He had been waiting, however, until he knew the sex of the child before finalizing his last will. If it were a daughter, he was going to put everything into a generous family trust that included his daughters, but if it were a male, he was going to give him everything outright. He hadn't bothered to determine the sex prior to delivery, and unfortunately died suddenly without knowing the answer to his gender concern, and therefore, was without final will and testament. Nonetheless, it was a boy; and now his daughters, already mad as hornets because the young mother, wife, harlot though she may be, is holding all the cards according to state inheritance provisions. The estranged daughters are seeking relief from Chancery Court, claiming the young woman, fourth wife and now widow, had either another lover who fathered the child or that she held the old man captive, insinuating, without fully understanding his *vigor*, that the octogenarian curmudgeon was her sex slave. Vice versa, I would say, but I find it all rather amusing, and beyond legal recourse. She has it all."

Taghert laughed harshly, coughed, and projected a wad of mucus toward the spittoon in the corner behind his desk. Taghert himself was reputed to have at least one mistress at the courthouse who was considerably less than half his age.

"You called me," Matthew said after a silence.

"Yes, I did." Nothing was direct with Taghert, who looked squarely at Matthew for the first time and examined him coldly without commenting on the small bandage on the cheek beneath his eye.

"I knew your grandfather," Taghert said. "Hell, back then everybody in Belle Rio and Capital City knew Ol' Pat. He used to say, 'I've been a Democrat all my life, and I never met a Republican that didn't have a private life.' What he meant by that I never quite knew, but Patterson was always a politician. His election year bar-b-que turned out the voters registered or not. Dead or alive. He had all them down state boys on the string because he did them so many favors when they were in Capital City where they were either broke or lonely, or both."

Matthew remembered his grandfather Patterson as a tall imposing man with oversize ears, a loud voice, a hearty appetite, a Stetson hat, and a worn gray Packard with holes in the floorboard.

"Yep," Taghert said, "Pat was the master of the vote-getting bar-b-que. He told the young political hacks exactly what it took to get out the vote in a world that has long since outlawed as election fraud everything he lived for. He played nothing close to the vest. You always knew where you stood with Pat. He could tell you that you were full of manure, and somehow, something about the way he said it, made you think he had just paid you a compliment."

"So, what did you want to see me about, sir?" Matthew asked on the verge of insolence. He waited while Taghert spat again and composed himself in the swivel chair without disturbing the sleeping old hound.

"I need another lawyer in the office. And though I won't admit it, I'm accused of getting old. There are a lot of things I just don't care about anymore. I can't deal with all these damn water rats. They come to Belle Rio because they can't survive anywhere else. Oystering folk are lost in time. They missed the boat to the future years ago when they went against aqua culture farming, and most of them have the morals of a ..." Taghert seemed to think it better to let the subject dangle, suspended, so he concluded: "Well, they don't have any morals."

"Like lawyers," Matthew said to keep things in perspective.

Taghert looked at him across his spectacles, "In a manner of speaking, yes." And he stood from behind the desk, stretched his stiff back. The hound raised an eye. Francois wasn't as tall a man as he had seemed while he was seated. He moved slowly, going nowhere in particular.

"I thought maybe you would appreciate the opportunity to do some lawyering if you're going to be here in Belle Rio for any length of time and before you ruin whatever chance you may have of making a contribution to this community, son. And you need to make that contribution. You owe it to your grandfather ..." Taghert paused.

"Robert Strahorn told me that you could probably do what I needed done, if I could work with your peculiar nature. I understand that his son met an unfortunate end."

"Tom was my friend. He had some problems. You would have to ask Mr. Strahorn about how fortunate, or not, his son was. He died prematurely, yes."

"Irrelevant, and unrelated to the issue."

"Yes, sir."

"Robert Strahorn and his wife have a home on the island. They are a lovely couple. Robert said that you were experienced in real estate development and management."

"I did my time," Matthew stated bluntly, "and I wouldn't be interested in any lawyer work that involved real estate speculation or land development."

"Be that as it may. Here's the proposition: you work for me while you read the law to practice in Florida. At that time, if we both agree, you become a partner. Between now and then, you can do everything but stand alone before the judge in an official capacity. I have curtailed my criminal practice to a minimum. Unless the crime is amusing or unusually perverse, and the villain has several million dollars for legal fees, frankly, I am not interested. Criminal behavior in others bores me. There are also a considerable number of real estate ventures in which I have an interest and I would expect to utilize a certain amount of your expertise in that area, your moral persuasion notwithstanding. I realize that although I cannot take the money or the property with me to the grave, I can have the satisfaction of knowing that what I do in the next few years will affect this area for generations to come. In the next five years, this county will be transformed into a very exclusive 'environmentally sensitive,'" he said those words like they were distasteful, "but expensive resort community, every bit as luxurious as any other resort community on the Emerald Coast."

"And you own your share?"

"I own my share."

It was well known that Taghert had manipulated privileged information into a private fortune. Belle Rio was still dominated by independent oystermen, shrimp trawlers, and the logging of the Gulf Royale Forest, but the Key West escapees and sun belt millionaires were

41

building large houses on the island and opening foo-foo restaurants and art boutiques, which were the first symptoms of fatal, irreversible tourism.

"What exactly do you want from me, sir?"

"I trust the opinion of Robert Strahorn, and I need someone with leagal experience. You can have all of the criminal work you can stomach, because the county is once again without a Public Defender, and the court throws criminal case overload my way. I'll pay you forty thousand for the first six months. After that, we renegotiate once we determine your worth, or you do whatever you like. I certainly never intend to offend your sensibilities."

"Not that easily done, sir, I assure you."

"Be here Monday morning. You can have the office across the hall. You'll have to clean out the junk. Then go to the courthouse and introduce yourself to everybody. Tell them you are with Francois Taghert, Esquire, etc. etc. Eat lunch at the Victorian Inn, make new friends. And yes, Mr. McCutcheon, as you stated, a lawyer with excessive morals would be a waste of time. If you become totally moral and useless, I'll fire you on the spot."

"Fair enough," Matthew said. He stood abruptly, and the hound rolled over on his back as he moved to shake hands with Taghert.

Francois Taghert's cold hand conveyed the certainty of unwanted knowledge.

Later that afternoon, as the tide came in, he drank warm vodka and stared into the vast, silent, windswept twilight-space where the sky and water shaped the distant horizon above the islands. Venus appeared through the veil of the western sky, and in the descending quiet, a judicious, stoic heron gray with a gold beak, a black crown and white slash, tall and thin as Ichabod, stood vigil, then lifted in one motion and became airborne, long legs trailing behind like streamers. It circled over the water and settled again without effort, a solitary statue, aloof, disdainful of his presence.

The chill of Francois Taghert's handshake, combined with the immediate presence of Mephisto Robert Strahorn, unnerved him. His mind wandered to his young friend, Tom Strahorn, then to Lt. Franklin McCutcheon, both asleep in the sea. He wondered what peace there was, when it finally came.

As the moon appeared, he drank the last of the warm Stolichnaya. It was the best he had felt since he arrived in Belle Rio, a time when the days and nights were like one.

CHAPTER SEVEN

Roy Rogers in Jail

ATTORNEY MATTHEW MCCUTCHEON went through the courthouse and introduced himself. Everyone agreed it was about time Francois Taghert got another lawyer in his office. He had lunch at the Victorian Inn and made new friends. Nobody asked about the small bandage under his eye.

Taghert arrived at the office in the early afternoon. Taghert looked through him like he was invisible but somehow necessary to Taghert's ambitious, malevolent design for the future of Belle Rio.

"The state's going to indict that Texan over at the jail on two counts of first-degree murder. He's a talkative cuss and he's either done hung himself or Prosecuting Attorney Smith has botched the job. Either one or both are possible. The law officers in the county can be the defendant's best friend. You talk to the Texan and try to get the story straight. He may just be crazy. Either way, we'll file incompetency and put him in orbit." He paused and stared out the window.

"Criminal law is filthy work," Taghert said, "like riding a bike through the sewer."

Matthew went back across the bridge, through East Bay, past the oyster shucking and shrimp packaging wholesalers, with their refrigerator trucks crowding the highway, to the County Jail, which was located on the county road that ran sixty miles north along Tate's Hell Swamp, past the historic Negro Fort on a high bluff overlooking the river. The road continued on toward Sumatra, where the railroad spur line that hauled chemicals and timber to the Gulf Royale pulp mill, crossed the highway, then veered off at Whiskey Creek and ran straight west through the swamp to Port Royale.

Belle Rio County Jail was a tarantula pit. You wouldn't know it if you'd never been inside: the yelling, cursing, fighting, laughing, weeping. Even in the quiet of night, an angry voice cursed the dark.

This was jail, not prison. Purgatory, not Hell. People came and went, yet it remained the same.

The jail closed behind him with a loud metallic noise that reverberated in the unsettled, hostile, afternoon heat.

"My name is Matthew McCutcheon. I'll be working your case on behalf of Mr. Taghert, your court appointed attorney. I need to ask you a few questions."

The cowboy sat across the room and talked to the reflection of a crazy, tortured man in the glass.

"I don't want no court trial. I know what I done, an' I don' wanna hear 'bout it over an' over an' over. I'll jus' sit in the jail 'til it's paid for. Get me the best deal you can get me."

"There are not going to be any deals unless you can tell me something different than what I've heard already from the State's Attorney. You're charged with two counts of first-degree murder and they'll ask for the death penalty."

"That ain't good enough," he spat sarcastically.

"It's the best they got. Let's start at the top. Your name is Robert E. Rogers?"

"They call me Roy Rogers."

"Was Betty Rogers your wife?"

"She said she was."

"And what do you say?"

"She lived with Larry, then me, then she stayed with Larry again after I was gone. She was a common law good fuck. I don't know if that makes us married or not. We was all three sometimes living together."

The Texan moved slowly, hesitantly, ravaged, and confused, drawn toward the window light. He spoke in a quiet, confidential tone. "I'd known from the beginning that she was willin'. An' shit, opportunity is a willin' woman. Once was one thing, twice was a mistake. Then it got to be regular, an' I was beatin' him at poker, fuckin' his woman, lyin' all the damn time."

Roy Rogers seated himself at the table, his mind slipping gear and wandering without control.

"Larry owed me fifty dollars from last week. But when I got home, they was dead. Some damn cokehead redneck broke in an' kilt 'em both. Stole everthin' we owned. Larry an' Betty both dead. I didn't kill nobody. Betty was always sayin' he turned her daughter to a whore. She was mad at me, but there was nothin' I coulda done 'bout that. I tol' her t' tell the police. He'd made Bonnie a whore. But she wanted us to go away. I said, 'No, he was my friend.' But she wanted to go away. Like it was before. Before Bonnie came along. Larry took Bonnie to Houston after I left. I never shoulda gone an' left her ..."

The cowboy's frown turned slowly into a smile as a distant memory took over his mind, and soon he was bragging,

"They brought some fine cocks in from Mexico to entertain them Jap businessmen, all them little bastards wearing Stetsons an' takin' pictures.

Secret Service everywhere. Hell, Lyndon Byrd loved to put on a feed: all the bar-b-que you could eat, liquor by the gallon, ladies laughin', cameras flashin', Japanese gibberish, them Congressmen bettin' on the birds. The best Mexican cock they had was a big black satin bird. Proud damn bird walked with his chest all throwed out, his head back, eyes watching every move."

He sat close to Matthew and spoke directly to him in solemn confidence, "I held Alfredo and looked into his eyes. He was ready to fight. He lived to kill."

The cowboy got excited.

"The birds hit the ground an' broke free. The crowd got real still and quiet. Soon they was at each other. Two, three times, before Alfredo got to him. Ripped his eye out! The place went wild. That black satin Mexican cock was waitin' to die, scratchin' the floor, starin' at Alfredo with his one good eye. Alfredo ripped his damn head off! It was one hell of a fight."

He paused, lost in that moment.

"Proudest damn day of my life, out there on the Pedernales."

The Texan stared out the window, not talking, then returned to something not so far away, and not very pleasant.

"Men liked Bonnie. Larry said it was none of my business what she done. That he'd helped raise her, even if she was mine, like Betty said. But Larry couldn't do it. Couldn't do it normal. He took her to Johnny Raymond. He could do it. Larry took pictures of 'em. He got off on that. I seen them pictures an' I knowed he was a creep. I shoulda killed him then, an' took her an' Betty away, before he carried Bonnie down to Houston an' tried her out on some of his friends. ... Then I went to Houston. Jesus, I never shoulda done it...

"Larry laughed at me, his pants bulgin' with cheap thrills. He sucked up my swill. Ate the scraps from my lousy life!"

"Is that why you killed Larry?"

Roy Rogers did not answer. He was lost in the past.

"But I didn't recognize her then. Honest. I never woulda done it." He looked at Matthew, bewildered.

The Texan took one of the cigarettes and fired a match to it, and the smoke curled up around his head. He walked away but turned suddenly back toward Matthew.

"Alfredo was a smart old bird. Best I ever had. But Pepe he was young. Alfredo sired Pepe. Then Pepe killed Alfredo. I didn't want to match 'em. Damn people was yellin' an' beggin' for me to match 'em, an' hell, Larry was worse than any of' em with this braggin' and yahooin'. Alfredo, my friend, I watched you die."

The cowboy stood holding the bloody torn spirit of the slain gladiator cock in his hands. He stared at a faraway reflection in the corner of the bullet proof glass.

Finally, he said, "I didn't want to do it," with solemn regret.

The burnt, yellow autumn sun blazed into his face, casting his turbulent shadow on the concrete wall.

"I didn't want to do it. But Larry, he begged to die. I'd been oysterin'. An' when I came back, he was crazy, shoutin' at me, 'You was my friend since we was kids. You an' me used to fish together off Galveston.'

He came at me with a butcher knife, Betty was already layin' on the floor whimpering, bleedin' to death. Larry was my friend, but Larry was a creep. Larry deserved to die."

"In this neck of the woods, Mr. Rogers, they reserve that determination to God and the State of Florida. Not even Roy Rogers can kill anybody he wants to—even bad guys—and walk."

"Then you ain't much of a lawyer."

"That may be. I'll do the best I can, Mr. Rogers."

As Matthew drove back to the office, his mind swirled with vivid images of fighting cocks, petty greed and corruption, comic deceit, illicit passion, tragic disappointment, and violent death. It was simple enough. Roy and Larry were cousins from a small town on the Texas coast. Roy lived with Betty, and then moved to the hill country around Bandera, Texas, where he was a cowboy and raised fighting cocks. Betty came to Bandera and lived with Roy. But he felt trapped and left her and he went off prospecting in the oil fields of west Texas. Then Larry took up with Betty. Bonnie was born, possibly in Bandera. Betty and Larry came to Dallas and they lived there while Roy drove long haul trucks. And Bonnie grew up.

Then Roy and Betty got back together in Galveston. And he took up fishing. Bonnie had run away to Houston. Later Roy went to Houston, where he found out, and maybe had sexual relations with, his fourteen-year-old daughter, that Larry had made a sex kitten.

Last year Roy, Betty, and Larry came to East Bay to oyster. Larry and Betty had a fight. Larry killed Betty. Roy came home and Larry attacked him with a knife. He shot Larry in self-defense. Nothing counted for the state but the body of two victims, the weapon, and a motive. Or, Roy came home, found Larry, who had made his daughter a whore, nailing his common law wife, and killed them both. Poor son of a bitch. It was his word against the whole damn State of Florida.

Matthew drove back to Belle Rio, across the Five Mile Bridge into the setting sun. At least the trouble was not his own this time, and for that he was grateful. He felt an exhilaration that screeched to an abrupt halt when it crashed into two counts of first-degree murder and mandatory execution. Scott Fitzgerald said, "It was the mark of a great mind to simultaneously hold contradictory positions with equal conviction, and still be able to act."

But Mr. Roy Rogers had trouble because he thought too much and just got confused; he loved Bonnie, and he shouldn't have. His prized rooster, Alfredo, got too old to cut the mustard and the son, Pepe, killed Alfredo. Roy Rogers killed Larry, either because Larry made Bonnie whore, or because he fucked his own daughter, and then Larry laughed.

He said he didn't kill Betty even though she bored him to death, and after all, she was all he had, a good, but not great, common law fuck.

Attorney McCutcheon thought that he could possibly make a case for self-defense, certainly manslaughter, if he could believe that Larry had the guts to kill Betty, and he could find a way to prove it.

Meanwhile, it didn't look good for Roy Rogers.

Francois Taghert poured them both a drink. The ice tinkled in the glasses.

"We got this case because they can't keep a Public Defender in the county. Belle Rio isn't a good place to make your reputation as a defense trial lawyer. Too many guilty clients."

Matthew said, "I think we should plead not guilty and go for self-defense. Not put him on the stand. There were no witnesses. I will either make the jury believe my …"

"Or he'll fry," Taghert interjected with uncharacteristic simplicity. "What does Mr. Rogers want?"

"Maybe a plea bargain to one count manslaughter. He said he didn't kill the woman, but he did kill the man. It sounds like self-defense. But he wants to be punished."

"Welcome to the sewer, Mr. McCutcheon. He's probably brain dead. He's certainly confused. And he'll change his story tomorrow. Talk to Ronnie Smith and see what you can work out. If it looks like they won't deal, we'll file for a competency hearing."

Francois Taghert didn't like the Assistant State's Attorney Ronnie Smith. He thought the Assistant State's Attorney was punctilious, moralistic, and disgustingly self-confident.

"The longer the cowboy stays in jail before the case comes to trial, the better chance there is for a plea bargain. They'll forget about him after a while and just want to wash the docket. Something else will come along to arouse the moral indignation of the pompous Ronnie twit."

CHAPTER EIGHT

Sara "Momma" Percy

ANDREW PERCY COULD SEE the billowy breath of Gulf Royale in the distant horizon. When he got too far from the pulp mill smell, he was too far from home. Frightening, he thought, as he drove toward Port Royale; he was tethered by malodor. The putrid smell stained his memory. It was worse before government regulations. The giant exhaust towers belched evil vapors— the flatulence of industrial waste, the perfume of death—while the turbines burned ghastly green and gold against the twilight sky, creating the bizarre metallic smoking inferno of Gulf Royale by the Sea.

Before the bridge crossed over the intercoastal waterway channel into Port Royale, he turned onto a side road that ran parallel to the highway then veered off inland and dead-ended along the canal that brought the fresh water to the Gulf Royale pulp mill. Across the canal, a chemical plant manufactured turpentine, paint thinner, and heavy industrial solvents from the black liquor by-product of wood pulp. The plant was surrounded by a high steel fence, harder to get into than heaven, inaccessible without security clearance from the Pope. It was scary.

He hated Port Royale. But Momma wouldn't think of leaving. The two-story house was shabby now, but when it was painted it would look better. He paid Ted to keep up the yard once a week and do whatever needed to be done on the house and not argue with Momma about it. She watched Ted work around the place, even went out while he was working, but she never spoke to him or acknowledged what he was doing.

The white Impala he bought her ten years ago was parked askew in front of the garage. She must have been out driving. He had to talk to her about her driving. Innocent people could die.

Years ago, Sara Percy had operated a flea-market, and the house and front yard stayed covered in vintage clothes, cheap jewelry, old beauty magazines, discarded toys, used appliances, frayed doodads, weathered whatnots, and useless whatevers.

In the front room, there were three commercial hair dryers, with the green vinyl chairs sitting under them, that were left over from when she moved her downtown beauty salon to the house and continued her beauty business until her customers died off, one by one.

Momma called last week, not making any sense. The Department of Human Resources was trying to put Sister in a mental care facility. It was probably for the best, but Momma wasn't going for it. Then Sister got loose and killed a neighbor's dog with a pair of scissors. She used to love animals. She got mean when she got older. She didn't know no better. It was sad.

He carried three sacks of groceries to the kitchen. He hated to shop for groceries, but it was easier to do in Panama City, by himself, than fussing with her and taking her to the *Piggly Wiggly* for every damn thing. He replenished Momma's cupboards every month and it went unnoticed. Stuff got used up. They ate good food. But she never said a word about it. She was a proud woman. He put away the canned goods and a month's supply of paper products. As long as she got her benefits from the Gulf Royale Retirement and Disability Fund, he'd buy their damn paper goods.

She was drinking again. Not drunk, but she was committed to not dying sober. It was better to die drinking than not die at all. She looked forward to dying with a buzz on. It made her mad that he wouldn't drink with her, but she was glad to see him, even if he wouldn't drink with her. She was glad he had a vice to keep him going, meaning of course, his naked women club. She hoped his soul would go unpunished through eternity. She loved her boy.

"Your father had evil ways, but women wasn't one of them."

She grinned at him.

He hated it when she didn't wear her teeth. She was shrinking and was not much bigger than five feet, and her blonde hair had gone white and played out in an uncontrolled frenzy. Her eyes were sinking back in her head and it was hard to tell what she saw anymore. Still, what a sweetheart, he thought.

"I can't eat up all the canned beets you bring in the house. We don't eat like we used to. And I never liked beets anyway. Of course, if they all show up for dinner, I won't have enough food."

"All who shows up?"

"Aunt Jean and the girls. You know your father won't get home in time for dinner. He never did. Why start now?"

He tried to ignore the reference to his father and visits from relatives he had never met, or who didn't exist, but more and more often, they were Momma's constant companions.

"How's the car running? I see it's out front."

"I drove into town yesterday. Sister and I went to *Quick Stop* for a corn dog with cheese and potato logs."

"That sounds delicious, Momma. How's Sister?"

"What do you expect?"

"I don't know what to expect, Momma, I just asked. I don't expect it to be good, if that's what you mean. I just asked about her is all."

"She'll outlive me, and you'll put her away."

"I just asked. We need to do something."

"She needs to be here with me. Momma knows best."

"How're your eyes doing? You see alright to drive?"

"I see what's ahead of me. Not what's behind me."

"Good Momma. Make sure you don't drive backwards."

"You the one that sent me them pamphlets for the home in Panama? The nerve of naming an old people's home *The Fountain of Youth*. The damn stupidest thing I ever heard. Why you think I'll ever leave this house is beyond me."

"I'm trying to look ahead."

"What! And leave all this? You got to be kidding, son. I've lived alone for years. Except for the time I spent with A.J. I'll die alone. Long after you."

"Where's the material from DHR?"

She ignored him.

"About Sister?"

"I'll find it later." She rummaged in the refrigerator for ice, then poured herself another drink.

"I hate to be one of those women always complaining about their men."

"Then don't Momma. I can do without that too."

"A.J. used to buy me gifts and was awfully sweet most of the time. I tried to change him, and he taught me to drink instead. That's the way it goes sometimes, huh? He was right, of course. Cheers." She popped the whiskey, then slammed the glass on the countertop.

"You drink too much, Momma."

"You could bring me somethin' I could use, but there ain't much I need. Those pearls you gave me, I can't wear no place."

"I know Momma. I just want you to have something nice."

"Give 'em to Jesus."

"What would Jesus want with a strand of pearls?"

"Throw 'em to swine, I reckon. You're a damn sight better than your father when it comes to wasting money. He wasted money too, but he never had the kind of money you got."

"I earn it the old-fashioned way, Momma. I work hard for it. I earn it doing things I don't like to do. Just like everybody else."

"Hah! Like all them naked women. You a fox guarding the hen house for sure."

"I do what I have to do. That's all."

"And I done what I promised I would do—I stayed here and took care of you, and her, and you oughta be thankful to me, more than treat me like I was something disposable."

"Where you learn that kinda talk, Momma? I'm not *disposed* to stay around here much, if you're not going to give me some peace."

But once again, they had their usual argument about Jesus.

"Pearls before swine," she said. "You need them pearls for the naked women."

And she swore at him, Jesus, that is, speculating as to why Jesus spent most of his time in the company of loose women, although he was good to his mother, and why he, Drew, hadn't been to visit her in more than God only knows how many months.

No matter what, she always suspected that he was in trouble when he came home. Why else did he come home? He ran away from home the first chance he got, went to Montgomery to visit Hank Williams' grave, then joined the Navy, then sent money from Nashville, then went to prison for something or other, and then a few years later came home for two days then left again. Home and gone, home and gone, home and gone, like a duck drinking water on one of those goofy glasses from the novelty store.

After three drinks, her memory was history and she rambled on and on. Otherwise, she was in pretty good shape. She had grit. She could chew 'em up and spit 'em out. Teeth or no teeth.

"You never come see me anymore."

"You know that's not true, Momma. I was here three weeks ago."

"I forgot."

Easy as that: "I forgot." She dismissed what displeased her.

It was too hot inside, so he went outside. It was hot outside too, and the air outside smelled awful. He smoked a cigarette. There was no wind.

She came outside looking for him.

"Why don't you turn on the air conditioner?" he said.

"It broke."

"Ask Ted to fix it."

"Ted?"

"Ted, the man next door. You've known him for at least forty years. Ask him to fix it. I pay him to take care of things."

"I've seen that man around here. First, he does one favor for me, then another, then the next thing you know he wants me to return the favor." She clinked the ice in her glass.

He looked at her. She winked at him. "You know what I mean. You know how one thing leads to another."

"I know, Momma. You should be so lucky." She was damn sure gonna die trying. "What are we gonna do about Sister?"

She didn't answer, looked at him with a harsh glance, then went back in the house. She refused to deal with Sister. She could be stubborn when she wanted to.

Momma Percy gave Drew his steely determination. When he was a schoolboy, he got in fights all the time. Port Royale was a tough town, especially during the segregation trouble. Seemed like everybody was mad all the time. Sometimes he got his ass whipped behind the gym of the old school or in the alley downtown behind the *Royale Beauty Parlor*. He got his nose bloodied or his teeth knocked loose. Sometimes he bloodied the other fellow. It was because of Sister mostly, defending his crazy sister from taunts and insults by boys who should have known better, who lived in the stately brick homes on the east side of town, whose fathers ran the mill where his father was a laborer and a bootlegger. There was no real satisfaction beating up Drew Percy, if you could, because he would never quit fighting or acknowledge that he was whipped. And it was seldom that he lost a fight.

Sentiment was a short suit with Momma. The mementos, trinkets, and souvenirs he had sent Sister from all over the world when he was in the Navy were long ago lost or scattered throughout the house, or sold at the flea markets along with the other gifts that he'd sent Momma. He sent her money, too, but it was never enough. What she did with the money he didn't know. He didn't want to ask anymore.

She said, "It ain't polite. If you give somebody something, don't be asking all the time what they did with it. If you want to know everything, keep the damn money."

In the kitchen, Sister was making a buzzing sound and wouldn't stop. She couldn't focus those once pretty eyes, grown dull and vacant and listless, and she drooled and droned, "Momma Momma Momma" about something only she understood. Little Sister was crazy, and the same blood flowed in his veins. Maybe the chemicals from the plant damaged her brain.

Momma said: "God's will."

"You don't believe in God, Momma."

"Sure I do. Just because I quit the damn holy church doesn't mean I can't believe in God's Will. Who else but God could have given me such a burden?"

"What did the letter say, Momma? The letter from DHR."

"They want to take her and put her in a state place."

"It might be a good thing, Momma. It's not a bad place. I've seen it."

"It ain't gonna happen while I got a life."

"You don't have a life Momma. Look at the way you live."

"There you go insulting me again. You just wanna dispose of all of us. She's not going to the state. End of subject."

"Can I see the letter, Momma?"

"I throwed it away."

"When I get back to Panama City, I'm going to call DHR and talk to somebody."

"Where you going this time—Hell?"

"I'm doing business Momma. It's what men do."

"Hrrumpppaha," she growled. Sister groaned too.

Sister sat in a chair with her head down. She wasn't healthy like she used to be. That was a fact. Not as smart either. He had loved her even after he knew what she was. And he had fought for her. Got bloodied more than once. There was some that couldn't mind their own business. Leave well enough alone.

He stroked her head, and she made a little noise, but didn't look at him. Goddamn, he hated that.

"What'd you do with the money I sent last month?"

"There you go again. Asking about what you gave me. I kept it. Put it someplace you can't get it back."

"Why don't we put her some place, Momma. I've got some money."

"Don't never talk about that to me. As long as I am her mother, and that is forever, I will take care of her. I don't need your money."

"Get somebody to come in and help you. Don't be so hard on yourself."

"You think I like the way you talk to me. Do you think I am just some woman you can insult and not care what I think? I can take care of myself and her, and if you think I can't, you just watch me."

"Momma, you're eighty-two years old. It's OK to have help. I'm going to get you help."

"You're going to get naked women to clean my house. Some fine son you are. Smut peddler."

"Stop that Momma. Stop that."

After she went to sleep, he sat in her living room and he thought about how close he lived to the edge, about how close he had come to dying unknown somewhere. He thought about how trouble slipped up on him and he would be close to losing everything without even knowing he was in trouble. Sometimes it took a jolt to wake him. He had thought Sister would die from the kidney failure, but she lived with one kidney. It don't take but one, was what his father always said.

When Sister moaned, he almost broke in two. He hated that. He wished she could go peacefully and be with angels.

After he left home the first time, he swore he would never see Momma again, cursing the man that screwed her and brought him and his crazy sister into the world. But he never forgot Sister, even when he went to the Navy, then to Nashville, where his father had told him to look for Hank Williams. But Hank Williams was long dead, and Hank Williams had been the only man his father ever thought was worth a shit.

His father, Andrew Jackson Percy, was born in west Tennessee. He would have farmed cotton all his life, but the boll weevil ate his daddy's crop, so he left home at age sixteen and made his way to Memphis. And the way he told the story, he killed a man there for opening his mail. That was what he said, but sometimes he said it was for messing with his personal property, and one time he said a woman was the cause of it, which sounded most likely, and whatever the story was, the man was hiding from him, and when he caught up with him, he killed him in cold blood. The law chased him down to New Orleans, where he got lost in the crowd and stayed for several years in a Creole whorehouse, or so he said. He made a new reputation for himself as a dandy who had a way with women and wasn't afraid of the law or anybody else.

During the prohibition, he transported liquor to Mobile and sold the White Mule to speakeasy establishments. Wherever he went he got a bad reputation, and he didn't mind that people were afraid of him, or at least left him alone. He fell in with some bootleggers near a sawmill and that life suited him fine. When he got lit up, he could "talk his way past Saint Peter," he said. But the law caught up with him again and he went to jail for a year in Alabama, and soon he busted out, which he had to do because they was going to send him back to Memphis. He disappeared again into the deep woods of Escambia, above Pensacola near the Bagdad Lumber camp, where he sold whiskey to turpentine sappers and sawmill hands.

The Black Water River was the last of the wild, primitive, Florida panhandle forest, where men moved aimlessly from sawmill camp to sawmill camp, doing hard work for low pay and a chance to eat, sleep, drink, gamble and not be bothered by anyone who expected that life be more that it was. By the time the *Bagdad Lumber Company* closed down the sawmill, and quit the timber business, there weren't no more trees to cut.

A.J. relocated to a little town near Dead Lake, where the swamp swallowed the Chipola River as it meandered for aimless miles through the lowlands northwest of Belle Rio. He converted an old turpentine boiler onto a whiskey still, and he was back in business. The nearby small towns had a born-again, anti-liquor sentiment, and he couldn't sell much whiskey there, but Panama City was a drinking town, and the pulp mill workers at Port Royale couldn't get enough to drink. He also traveled down the river to Belle Rio, where the fishermen were glad to drink his White Mule.

He was almost forty-five years old by then and still mostly uncivilized, but he could be a charming devil when he wanted to.

In Belle Rio, he met a young beautician who was only half his age. She said that if he would give up his liquor business and get a job, she would consent to marry him. He also had to buy her a diamond ring and a big house full of new furniture and let her open a beauty parlor somewhere other than Belle Rio. She had had enough of Belle Rio.

Sarah Markham and Andrew Jackson Percy got married and moved to Port Royale. They built a two-story house out from town and she opened her beauty parlor in downtown Port Royale. A.J. went to work on the night shift at the pulp mill.

Sara Percy never told her version of the story. What she knew, she kept to herself and let A.J. talk. And talk he did, telling over and over the ever-changing stories of his wandering youth on the Mississippi, of gambling fools and fancy brothels, of whiskey drinkers and bar room brawls, of crazy turpentine days and dirt-poor cracker loggers on the Black River.

He talked and drank and smoked and died of a heart attack at fifty-nine. Sarah Percy said she didn't have any past before the day they met each other, and she never met a man who was his equal. They were as romantic as they were pathetic, the two of them.

CHAPTER NINE

Real Estate Soiree

THICK HONDURAN CIGAR smoke filled the interior of Francois Taghert's Eldorado as they drove across the Five Mile Bridge to East Bay and took the toll bridge to the Island. Within twenty minutes, they were stopped at the guard house entrance to Paradise Cove, a gated resort community.

Two Mercedes, a Lincoln Town Car, and several expensive sporty trucks with gun racks were parked in the circular driveway of the Strahorn house, which faced the gulf and was three ostentatious stories high, built with a widow's walk in the traditional island plantation style, one of eight styles available from the restrictive covenant design portfolio.

Ubiquitous Robert Strahorn had flown in from Palm Springs for the evening without his wife, and the local real estate hostess was salivating with anticipation.

A Belle Rio County Commissioner with an undisclosed interest in everything was enthralled by the presence of the famous Nashville recording artist, whose business manager had worked for the original island developers two decades ago. His company, *Island Music Management*, represented many established country music performers and songwriters. Several performers had recently built houses on the Island, and added a comforting twang to the pricey real estate chit chat.

The Nashville songwriter's ASCAP royalties and Robert Strahorn's insider trading information on the Chicago Commodities Exchange, combined with the extensive real estate holdings of Attorney Taghert and local seafood entrepreneur Bud Hardaway, generated the financial heat for this group of real estate developers. Their long-term plans included two exclusive residential communities, a hotel, a yacht club & marina, a shopping mall with haute couture clients, tennis courts, and a designer golf course, come hell or high water.

Getting the money to buy Belle Rio was no problem. The problem was exchanging the local seafood business for tourism and recreational sport fishing; and in the process, abolishing the government regulations that protected the Bay, both for and from those generations of cretins who made their living on the water. Simply put, if there were no commercial seafood industry to protect, there could be significant changes to regulations concerning development along the bay. They all agreed that overregulation had essentially ruined the fishing industry and destroyed a way of life that was the fabric of American individualism and freedom. This was simplistic and sung in unison.

Without anyone saying it directly, East Bay was the bull's eye of the development. East Bay—where dilapidated oyster packing houses were standing today could, tomorrow, be worth a fortune. East Bay had under developed beach front. It had a perfect deep water channel for a yacht marina, which had been denied for the island's Paradise Cove gated community. The best solution for the yacht marina problem was to build it in East Bay. The Island, already rich and famous, would build itself.

The Real Estate Queen got it right—as significant as the dollar amount was, no matter how you computed it, the seafood industry was just a drop in the bucket compared to the potential big-time money generated from real estate development, tourism, recreation, and pleasure. "Why, personal watercraft sales alone were up fifty-five percent. It was time for tourism. And pleasure. There was a huge pent-up demand for pleasure. Pleasure craft sales, that is … simply huge."

"Huge tracks of land," Matthew thought as he watched the heaving décolletage of the real estate czarina. He wished he could be rescued by *Monty Python's* coconut clapping knights, but no one came to his rescue, and he went outside for the ocean air.

He was standing on the balcony, watching the waves and listening to the moonlight, when a dark voice interrupted him.

"Mr. McCutcheon." He turned, drawn to the voice. "I'm Bud Hardaway. Frank Taghert said he'd like for us to get together. How about Sunday afternoon we take a ride on the water? Get a better perspective on this little corner of paradise."

"Sure. Sounds great," Matthew responded, unexpectedly agreeable. He was staring at the creature standing next to Bud Haraway. Moonlight was her light. Damn sure was. He had been staring at her ever since she arrived at the party two hours ago. Liana was serene, yet volatile like quicksilver. It was something about the way she moved without moving, something about her intense, but vacant eyes, that looked beyond the waves rolling in the moonlight, to the darkness of the horizon.

"Meet me at *Three Rivers Marina*, slip ten, around six o' clock. Billy Ray speaks highly of you. Frank, Robert, they all do. Glad to have you back in Belle Rio, son."

There was an odd comfort in Bud Hardaway's sonorous voice.

"Glad to be here, sir. Mr. Taghert, for some reasons known only to himself, has given me the opportunity to join this ambitious project."

"Great opportunity," was Bud Hardaway's solemn assessment.

Then they were gone. She disappeared without looking at him. He did not exist to her. Perhaps she really existed somewhere else, just housed temporarily in that body, which went from place to place, while she was where she was, wherever that was. Bud Hardaway he could not forget, especially the voice, a dark cello sound, weeping like the surf, peaceful but ominous, confident, with the resonance of inevitable doom. What lingered, then, was the dark voice, the soft round face, the luminous eyes, the suggestive gulf wind that moved her hair, the warm flesh of her hand, after Bud' Hardaway's rough, strong but awkward handshake, with the index finger missing from his right hand.

The party was a success. Without formal pronouncement, they had agreed that the driving force would be celebrity endorsements, a face, a name, a success story with each major phase of the development.

A County Commissioner closed the evening by recounting the rumor that was circulating through Belle Rio: a famous, gap-toothed New York cover girl, planned to buy all of the old, collapsed brick buildings that once housed the cotton and sponge exchanges on the waterfront and turn them into an art colony for Soho modernists, and followers of that cadaver Pop Artist, who wore dark glasses and painted soup cans, and whose name he couldn't remember, but it wasn't Truman Capote, the queer writer, not Harry Truman, the President either; he was dead. Anyway, nobody wanted much to do with fame and fortune that only lasted fifteen minutes. They had never heard of the *Velvet Underground*, but instinctively didn't want one in their town.

Robert Strahorn's confident arm was around his shoulder.

"When Frank told me you were in town, I knew you would be good for this team."

Suddenly, he was a starter for the home team.

"You'll even have a chance to get back to some bracing Chicago weather. You don't miss that, I'm sure."

"Not at all, sir. And you must enjoy this balmy weather."

"The view is spectacular."

Strahorn's house in Kenilworth faced out over Lake Michigan. His house in Palm Springs probably faced out over water too.

"We built one of the first houses in Paradise Cove. After we decided to participate in these projects."

"You couldn't have picked a more beautiful view."

"I understand you live over on Belle Rio Beach?" Strahorn's voice had a pariah semitone that rang out with condescension in the upper registers.

Matthew wanted to sing it back to him, but it seemed so pointless.

"Yes sir, it's an old family place not quite this comfortable."

"Well, it's all business, except when Elaine comes down, which isn't very often. She doesn't like the—what do you call them, the 'no-see-ums?'"

Robert Strahorn's eyes stole to the ripened real estate sultana who was busy supervising the party servants. This conversation won't last much longer, he thought. He'd better say it:

"I miss Tommy, sir. He was my best friend."

"Robert. Call me Robert."

"And I know it was…" he fumbled the thought. "I just wanted to express that."

"I think he's happier now," Tommy's father said. "And for that I am grateful. We're glad to have you with us, Matthew. Could you excuse me?"

The drive back over bridge seemed to take about as much time as the old ferry. Taghert drove like the eighty-year-old man he was. He didn't have the energy to conquer the world that he used to have, but he did have it all put together, nicely wrapped in his private world. And he like to talk, for memories, or reasons of his own.

"I knew your mother. She was a beautiful woman, vivacious personality, sense of humor, a kind, caring woman, educated too, before it was a popular cause for the feminist ball busters. Of course, they lived right there where the woman's college was. That was a hen house, let me tell you. Us foxes were glad to visit there."

"Now women are foxes," Matthew ventured cautiously.

"There is a considerable amount of gender confusion these days," Taghert said. "Homos belong in the ballet with the ballerinas, not in the military."

Taghert did not want to be distracted and brought up to date.

Matthew had sense enough to keep his mouth shut.

"Back in the day, when I was young, your grandfather was quite a promoter. I was impressed. He was a smooth talker. I sold him the beach house you have now. At the time, I was an attorney for the family that owned most of Belle Rio."

As an afterthought, Taghert said, "Your grandfather kept a hotel room in town for many years, after the railroad shut down."

Johnathan Patterson's life has been the Belle Rio/Tallahassee & Savannah Railroad. He started working at the terminus in Capital City when he was only fifteen and eventually became vice president of the new parent company, the *Belle Rio Land Syndicate Co.*, with offices in New York, Chicago, Savannah, Capital City, Glasgow, Scotland. The tattered, faded photos and brochures that Patterson kept in a scrapbook beneath the bed were sharp with detail: a steam engine train that brought handsome, portly gentlemen with their fancy ladies to the ornate *Landmark Hotel* with its oriental minarets, and gold-leaf wall coverings, intricate wrought iron patterns and cut glass, shaded by tall live oaks and broad magnolia trees, stately rooms for three hundred guests, a veranda for social functions beneath modern gas lights, and an elegant promenade and boardwalk, which connected the hotel with a dancing pavilion on the beach.

The Syndicate sales brochure and investment prospectus offered stock in the Land Company and called Belle Rio *"one of the most beautiful and desirable localities in Florida, the Highlands of the Gulf Coast, located near the busy commercial port of Belle Rio, where a picturesque fleet of pleasure boats is provided for the guests. Fishing cannot be surpassed on either coast. Cool breezes off the Gulf of Mexico and magnificent shade trees make the Landmark Hotel a most refreshing resort throughout the year."*

Patterson worked for the railroad and the Land & Syndicate Co. until the hotel was damaged by a hurricane and finally closed. The company promptly went bankrupt. After that, his life was never the same; he had wined and dined and smooth talked his way through many broken dreams. He wore his heart on his sleeve and never met a stranger. He made himself comfortable as a Capital City institution and settled for good ol' boy cronyism and politics as usual. He had been among the first who tried to turn the Belle Rio coast into a tourist paradise, but it couldn't compete with Florida's east coast, or the exquisite emerald water of the western panhandle. It was mostly inaccessible. Belle Rio was just swamp land the Yankees never bought.

"I believe your mother married a man she met just before or during the war. So many women did."

"Something like that," Matthew replied, staring at the darkness beyond the half-moon. Taghert had it straight so far.

"I tried to court your mother after the war, after things had time to settle. We had a few good laughs, but I just wasn't her type. Too ornery and selfish I suppose."

They rode in silent agreement.

Margaret Patterson McCutcheon lived with her parents after the war until she got a teaching job at a small college in south Alabama

As a young boy, Matthew had gathered eggs from the chicken coop behind the Patterson house in Capital City. He would chase a screeching hen, catch it, then watch as Grandma Patterson cracked its neck with one swift twisting arm motion. He was amazed that she could be so cruel and deadly, and be his grandmother at the same time.

A few years later, they returned to visit, and the house had been moved to a different location. The old white house had been repainted a mustard yellow.

The very same house, the furniture, the curtains, the radio shows old Patterson never missed—Jack Benny & Rochester, George and Gracie, Amos and Andy, the Lone Ranger and the haughty "High Ho Silver, Away!" All the musky radio memories moved to another location.

He missed the large oak tree that spread itself across the lawn. He remembered the porch of a white house, and a photo of the Navy officer she said was his father, Franklin McCutcheon, holding the child she said was him.

CHAPTER TEN

Bud Hardaway

BELLE RIO would not have been what it was, become what it became, without the descendants of grizzled, butt-headed, tenacious Don Hardaway. During the sweltering summer doldrums of 1861, after the Confederate cannons had fired on Fort Sumter, an emaciated shadow of a man straggled, half-naked and almost dead, into an isolated settlement on the Gulf, east of Belle Rio, called Three Rivers, having made his way overland through Tate's Hell Swamp.

When asked how he had arrived on the Belle Rio coast, the exhausted, wild-eyed stranger said, "I don' it tha hard way." And that was all he had to say. He ate some fatback and cornbread, drank what liquor was available, and went back to the woods. He labored in the heat and cursed the deer flies while he built a little shack for himself on the edge of the river, where he caught, then raised, wild hogs. Soon he was cutting timber and making money.

He was known as "the Man Who Done it the Hard Way," then Don Hard Way, and finally, Mister Don Hardaway. That suited him fine. He had certainly been called worse, and he had never had a name that he bothered to remember.

He didn't know his age. He had come from somewhere in the mountains of what people who knew geography assumed was North Carolina. He traveled along the low hills of the southern Appalachian plateau avoiding large towns and avoiding the war frenzy that was arousing the southern gentlemen. He remembered that much, and could tell of his long journey through Georgia plantations where he didn't meet anybody he ever wanted to see again. There were too many slaves working the large plantations and no work for an itinerant Irish convict with little sense of loyalty to the plantation society cause.

He had no intention of fighting a war for slaves. He had never owned one and didn't care if he ever saw another one. There were only a few slaves where he settled by Three Rivers, and he said he'd stay as long as there weren't any more. When they organized a local militia to defend against attacks by Union gunboats, Don Hardaway said, "I won't fight for no cause, but I'll fight just the same." And he did. Over the course of the insurrection, Union troops were often engaged by the "dogged resistance" of the ragtag militia, and he killed three of the eight dead Yankees. That was Don the Hard Way's contribution to the Civil War.

A few years after the war, Don Hardaway took all of his money and went up to a plantation near Bainbridge, Georgia and came back with a pub-wench Irish girl that he had won in a raffle. They produced a son who was duly registered and certified as "D.W. Hardaway." Before the child was a year old, the mother died from the fevers, and ornery Don Hardaway disappeared again into the woods. The boy was taken in by Belle Rio's Dr. John Faircloth Sr., who kept him full of mustache cup quinine, raised him as his own son, and eventually became his father-in-law.

Elizabeth Faircloth, the fourth child and youngest daughter of Dr. John Faircloth Sr., was an attractive, fine-boned woman with dark hair she kept tied in a bun. She wore long dresses with high collars and taught school until she was ninety years old. Elizabeth Faircloth and D.W. Hardaway were practically raised as brother and sister and were wedded in their childhood minds as lovers by fate. And wedded they were.

D.W. Hardaway was ambitious and smart. He was able to motivate men to accomplish difficult tasks. In 1890, with money he borrowed from his wife's older brothers, he opened the *Hardaway Faircloth Lumber Company & Sawmill* at the mouth of Three Rivers, not far from town.

The "Hard and Fair Co." built new wharves and docks at Three Rivers, where the steam tugs ferried virgin cypress timber to the schooners anchored offshore.

After the turn of the century a mighty hurricane struck the Belle Rio coast with a savage fury. Several large schooners—from Norway, Russia, Italy, and New York—broke loose from their anchors, floundered in the harbor where they were broken apart by the pounding waves, inundated with water, and wrecked on the beach. The Three Rivers settlement was blown away; but within five years, it was rebuilt by the same boundless and inexhaustible energy that drove the immigrant pioneers the century before, when the entire continent was attacked with a vigor and determination and a strength of will, almost unimaginable to a nation watching canned TV and eating super-sized fast-food entrees.

As time and circumstance would have it, the Faircloth family name disappeared from Belle Rio history: Elizabeth's older sister, Amanda Faircloth, quietly committed suicide in 1920 because of a stain on her honor, then the baby brother, George, was lost in a storm at sea; John

Faircloth Jr. died in 1922, a few years after his only son disappeared in Mexico while serving under General "Black Jack" Perishing during the military campaign against Pancho Villa.

Elizabeth Fairchild's childhood sweetheart and husband, D.W. Hardaway, son of Old Don the Hard Way, took over all the Faircloth business interest along the Belle Rio coast and became one of its most prominent citizens.

Then on a cold night in January 1930, the main boiler at the Three Rivers sawmill exploded. A terrible fire destroyed the *Hard & Fair Lumber Co.* and D.W. Hardaway died fighting the flames that engulfed his life's work

The timber business died out and the *Hardaway Ice & Fish Co.* dominated the waterfront. The seafood business grew and the company had an on-premises ice plant, the first of its kind, and they began operating a fleet of fishing boats in the gulf, oyster skiffs on the bay, and a sponge fleet with Greek immigrant divers. Once again, the area prospered like the pre-civil war cotton days, and the years of sawmills, timber and naval stores. There were several mercantile dry goods & variety stores, a hotel, a picture show, a pharmacy, a dress maker, a tailor, a Greek bakery and restaurant for the colony of Greek sponge merchants, the Old Gulf Bank, and the popular *Miss Duffy's* tavern, located at the ferry landing just west of Three Rivers, which was packed every night with men seeking female companionship.

Soon after Wilbur Hardaway's first son was born, he proudly changed the name of the business to *Hardaway & Sons Gulf Seafood*.

Bud Hardaway's Marlin Grady White cruised from the new Three Rivers Marina past *Hardaway & Sons Gulf Seafood*, where five off-shore shrimp trawlers were taking on supplies, then roared from the river channel into the open water. They set a course from the harbor out past through East Pass into the Gulf.

A brisk southern wind whipped the silvery emerald white-capped water, and the reckless pelicans hugged the swirling capricious currents. Matthew white-knuckled the rail, but it was nothing the Grady White couldn't handle as it cruised the eastern end of the island, then headed west along the Gulf shoreline, where the large expensive beach houses of Paradise Cove towered against the cerulean sky, a single strand of three-story residences, extending from the secure beach guardhouse checkpoint, to the western end of the island.

"Biggest damn mistake," Bud growled. He was emphatic in everything he did or said. "They could build that marina right here on the island. It's so damn obvious nobody can see it. Admit the mistake we made and move on."

When Bud Hardaway had been a County Commissioner, they had denied the island's Paradise Cove a private marina because the most productive oyster beds in the sound were along the bay shore of the island. It seemed important at the time. Now it mattered hardly at all.

"With all the regulations and water changes in the bay, there won't be enough good oysters out here to make it worth the trouble. A yacht marina couldn't hurt much now. Might even help."

"The island needs a marina if it's going to reach its economic potential," Matthew agreed, "and probably a four-star hotel with some shopping and entertainment, and maybe a casino, at least a bingo parlor."

Matthew thought he was being amusing, but Bud seemed angry as they turned toward the bridge at Belle Rio.

"St. Vincent Island over there is still wild as this island used to be. I hunted wild boar there when I was young. A doctor from New York bought the island a few years ago. Made his money in some glorified 'menstrual cure' for middle-aged women. Be damned if I've ever seen that cure work."

They headed east inside the causeway, past the brown expanse of salt marsh toward the bluffs on the eastern side of the Bay, where the Chicago lawyer Strayhorn and Francois Taghert would have their new restrictive covenant development. On the hillside there was a hammock of oaks and magnolias.

"That's where we're gonna build forty over-priced brick houses that look like an Atlanta suburb," Bud grimaced and spit the words like something tasted bad.

"Mr. Hardaway, I got the feeling something's stuck in your craw."

"I aint got nothin' to make but money from all this. Taghert and I own most of this property, and by the time we get through, we'll own most of East Bay. You'll probably own some yourself. You can vacation in Belize. It'll be nice there. Hell, son, it's gone too far now. This'll never be like Destin or Sea Side. They got the great white beaches and the emerald water. All we got here is swamp detritus and brown water and enough yellow flies and mosquitoes and carnivorous gnats to eat every damn tourist that ever comes here. Tourists won't like it here. Never have, never will. But there'll be plenty of 'em, and we'll get our share. That'll be enough to make us all filthy rich."

They went the short route back to the marina, gliding across the glassy smooth water, then speeding past the East Bay oyster houses waiting patiently to become hotels and resort condos, skimming over the oyster beds, running close to shore, parallel to the highway, where the dark woods met the ocean.

The winter sun fell into the low clouds behind them, and the horizon was a steel gray cold mist. They motored into the river channel on the

77

high tide. Here the dark water river didn't flow from the mountains of Georgia. One branch of the river came down from Telogia through Tate's Hell Swamp, and the other branch snaked around Saint James from Ochlockonee Bay twenty miles east. It was a mixture of salt water and dark tannin colored swamp water. The two rivers joined a mile from the bridge, and it was called Three Rivers.

They tied up just before dark. Only the low marsh flats broke the luminous sky reflected on the placid water. Bud cracked open a bottle of bourbon and poured them both a drink. He shot his straight.

"Take the chill off," Bud said.

Matthew asked, "Are you related to Theo Matson?"

"Theo's mother and my mother were cousins. And I got four sisters and two half-sisters. Between 'em I've had ten brother-in-laws and forty some odd nieces and nephews. There ain't hardly a kid in Belle Rio that don't call me Uncle. Ain't but one pair of jeans in Belle Rio, and at one time or another, everybody's been in 'em. Belle Rio's the shallow end of the gene pool."

Bud sat in silence with the facts that only he knew. "I had two brothers, both dead now. One had some kids. They live out west."

"And you got two boys?"

"Billy Ray you know. Donny runs the business in Belle Rio. And I got a daughter, Kate. She's at the University. I got hopes for her. I tried to get her to go to one of the Ivy League schools, but she wanted to go to the state university. She's butt-headed like me, an' she won out.

"Donny's got brains and ambition, maybe political ambition. I've always been proud of Donny. He comes off sometimes like a stuffed shirt, but that's on account of his mother and the woman he married. She's worked hard as she could to take the Hardaway out of him.

"I didn't do right by Billy Ray. He came along when I was distracted, absorbed by so many other things. He didn't learn the hard way. We gave him too many things. Too much stuff and he got the addled brain of his mother's family. Donny, now, he's all you can ask for.

"Billy Ray's a good boy. People like him."

"Billy Ray might get lucky. I ain't lost hope yet, but it'll take an act of God to get him off his ass an' make something of himself. I didn't do much of a job on Billy. And that's one of my regrets."

"He's a good boy," Matthew repeated into silence.

Bud gazed across the harbor then finally said, "In Belle Rio, like everywhere else, boys are made into men by their fathers, those who know who their fathers are. Otherwise, they have to learn to kick butt and survive from the biggest dog around, like their stepfathers, half-brothers, uncles, cousins. Their friends. Their enemies. Around here, it ain't a matter of learning enough to go somewhere else an' make somethin' of yourself; it's a matter of pride to stay at home and be tough, or tougher than the next fella. Hell, why go to New York City? This here is paradise. They go to Panama City, maybe, and show their ass on Saturday night, but they learn to be somebody here, out on the water, in the woods. I heard folks say we got limited ambition, that we're short sighted, or lack dreams. Damn. How do you call a fourteen-year-old boy 'short-sighted' when he goes out on the water for nine long hard days an' nights so he can take home the only money his family's got? He can't depend on a father he ain't don't know. He puts his ass on the line in the howlin' wind, the rain. He's seasick, insulted, beat up. He takes it and becomes a man. Takes it without a damn word. That boy was a man at fourteen. He made his own damn money. Returned to Belle Rio and gave his mother money to buy food. Found liquor to drink, dope to smoke, and got laid. He got in fights and won more than he lost.

"That's what I learned on the water: 'You want some of me? You better be ready to die.' I played football in Belle Rio. We knew how to lose. That was all we did. That was back before we had the 'skill position' players, but we played just the same, and it taught me what there was to know—kick their butt, if you get the chance, before they kick yours.

"I got a boat of my own and netted mullet, when smoked mullet was what we had to eat, until we went up in the woods in the rain, the cold, an' brought home some deer meat. I shrimped offshore. Ran the charter boat during the fifties when I was a young stud Captain. I was a tough cuss-headed hound back in them days. We caught two thousand pounds a snapper a day. I've tonged oysters from the Bay. Done construction work.

"Hell, I smuggled contraband for the government and fought the government tooth and nail. We got what we had coming. Learned to make do. To get by with that we got, and if somebody else had something we wanted, and there was a way to get it, by damn, we'd go get it. No matter what we had to do.

"The smart boys find 'em a woman, sees what's good in her, and sticks by her, and she's a wife and mother, not just a damn cougar to fuck and beat up on. You keep the good ones if you can, and when they get used up, you throw 'em overboard and the food chain takes care of 'em."

Bud sloshed another drink into his glass.

"My dad, Wilbur, died on the water. He was a local hero of sorts. One of the many casualties in the Gulf of Mexico. Chasing German subs. But I know what he died for and it never bothered me. Five years after that I lost my brother to weather off the cape. He'd been a bit older than you by now. He was my best friend. I still miss him."

He drifted into a silence where many things were left unsaid. One hand clenched in a tight fist.

He held up his whiskey glass and said, "To the American Way: You are what you get. The one with the most toys wins." They drank.

"This here is what's left of paradise. And everybody wants a piece of it before they die. They ought to have to take it the hard way."

Bud poured another.

"You didn't tell me what finally happened to *Mr. Done it the Hard Way?*"

"Well... Mr. Hard Way went off to the woods after his woman died. Left his son with Dr. Faircloth and never came back. They say he became a turpentine woods rider. Was responsible for takin' the pay an' settling up accounts with the hands. He didn't have book learning but neither did the workers at the bottom. After they totaled up their commissary bills and paid for the White Mule they'd drunk, there was nothing left. So he just kept it all... finally, Sugar Walton killed him. Sugar worked for him makin' whiskey. They got into a dispute over a woman. White or black I don't know. This stuff ain't written down. Black, I suppose. Could've been white, but I doubt it."

"You just making this up as you go along?"

"Nope. Old man Hannah has the true story from his kin. And it's certainly more likely to be accurate than the history told by any of the Faircloth/Hardaway descendants, primarily the women, who've led themselves to believe that old Mr. Hard Way was a Pentecostal teetotaler, possibly even a Confederate horse officer from Virginia. Women like to think better of men than we are. I guess it makes them feel better about themselves."

Bud emptied the glass he held in his strong hand with the index finger chopped off at the knuckle and looked, desolate and angry, into the void. After a long silence, he concluded: "We all have something to hide. We all need something to believe in."

Beneath the veneer of Bud Hardaway's good ol' boy civility was an undercurrent of remorse and violence that held the dark secret of the exuberance and uncontrolled passion that had been his life.

Some men are too large for the world they live in. This was such a man.

CHAPTER ELEVEN

Chicago Divorce

THE COUNTER GIRL at the *Quick Stop* was attractive. She had pale skin, freckles, dusty reddish hair, small, dull green eyes, and counted on her fingers. A lot of them were attractive when they were young. They ripened early in the Florida sun. She also knew where to find Old Ferry Dock Road: it was back with the rusty, shattered trailers, the gutted-hull oyster boats and junk cars.

This was transient white-trash East Bay, where sand burr yards fenced with Sears chain link held in the errant offspring and rabid dogs. East Bay extended only about two miles inland from the Coast Highway before it reached either the swamps or the Gulf Royale pine barrens. The west side of town was bordered by Bay Road. It ran north along the bluff for six miles until it reached the marsh wetlands. Just before the dead end at Tupelo Bluff, they were planning to build expensive homes for Yankee transplants, not poor transient fish heads.

There was a symmetry and a logic to it that wasn't exactly comforting, but at least you knew where you were. If you were poor enough, you could live in East Bay. If you were rich enough, you could live on the Island or on Tupelo Bluff along the Bay. If you were black, you didn't live in East Bay, no matter whether you were rich or poor. East Bay was reserved for whites only.

The winter sun was unusually warm. A solitary fisherman repaired his outboard motor in front of his aluminum siding two-bedroom house. Yards were littered with partial automobiles and broken-hulled oyster boats. *Support Your Local Police* and *Praise the Lord* were plastered on anything that moved, but mostly there were abandoned cars and junk body parts, piled and rusted in the overgrown lots that separated the desperate double-wide mobile homes. The road curved left, then back right, past a concrete block oyster schucking business next to a trailer park. It was a mile back off the water surrounded on two sides by a fifteen-foot-high mound of oyster shells.

Matthew made the wrong turn onto a sandy road and followed it a half mile before driving through a gate where the road stopped at the Waste Water Treatment Plant. It had the ominous desolate roar of the dragon's mouth. Dark water poured out of the filthy smudgy condenser unit beside the large concrete building. Behind the veil of paradise, the viper's effluvium was treated for public narcosis. It didn't feel like a good place to be. People in East Bay weren't happy. He could feel the malaise in the air like a bad gin hangover, evil as a serpent's tooth.

When he got back to the paved road, he waited as a burgundy pickup truck drove past with two schoolgirls riding in the back. A pony-tailed young girl flipped her middle finger with a doleful, meaningless, discontented vacant stare.

He passed a trailer with five boats in the yard: a mullet skiff and four power boats of assorted shapes and sizes, none of them operable, a stack of old tires, a large wire pen filled with mangy coon dogs, a fenced-in yard with fighting roosters chained safely away from each other under squat wooden shelters, and an old school bus, rusted, on a weed-choked lot. All but one of the trailers were occupied by a loose-knit inbred clan of cousins, doors open, people sitting, passing time, hell, killing time, on government paid vacation.

The Bay was closed to oyster harvesting because of the heavy rains upriver in Georgia. A government emergency relief agency funded seafood workers idled by the flooding. They were content to collect their money and wait for the light to change. Why 'hit a lick' when they could get the same money paid to Kansas farmers for not growing crops or ghetto blacks for having kids. Their strong suit—pride and ignorance—was a deadly combo.

They were sitting on a dung heap of oyster shells, waiting for the other shoe to drop. A child's rusty broken swing was surrounded by fifteen cannibalized bicycles, junk and clutter everywhere, but the satellite dish was sucking TV shows out of thin air, and this time of year the warm weather had a soporific effect on the living and the dead; they lived in a hypnotic zombie trance. Two slothful old dogs, lounging on a gutted automobile seat, watched *Invasion of the Body Snatchers*.

The trailer at the end of the road was surrounded by Belle Rio Sherriff's Department vehicles and cordoned off with yellow plastic: "Caution Belle Rio County Sherriff's Department."

Matthew parked beside a Florida Department of Law Enforcement van from Capital City. "I'm looking for Officer Yancy," he said to a uniformed peacock. They were proud birds, the Sheriff's boys, and one of them indicated a heavy-set man talking with some technicians outside the trailer door.

"You Macintosh?" Officer Yancy asked.

"McCutcheon. Matt McCutcheon."

"You really want to see this, McCutcheon?"

"I can take it. I've got a strong stomach."

"You got a morbid curiosity," Yancy said. "It'll all be in the report. This is Bill Simmons from the FDLE crime lab in Capital City. He's done a work-up on the physical evidence, and I think he also has some info from the coroner."

"The DA's office will have all this information for you," Simmons drawled, a little put out by overt civilian enthusiasm.

On the flight to Chicago, Matthew reviewed what he had seen at the trailer and the information he had gotten from the crime lab. The inside of the trailer was a bleak, bloodstained tabloid memory of anger and violence, a slow agonizing demise for Betty, who bled to death over a period of several hours, and a swift moment of glory for Larry, who took both shotgun barrels in what would have been the head, only there was nothing left to prove. They had scrapped remnants of his skull from the otherwise unadorned. Modern forensic science could then reconstruct the actual moment of love with magnificent detail. He needed to find somewhere that Roy Rogers could have been riding Trigger or singing to Dale while the common law Betty did most of her dying. If Roy would only help him, he was confident he could dispute the state's case that Roy had killed them both, then he could build a self-defense scenario for the double-barreled demise of Larry, the pervert headless bandito.

In the clouds at thirty thousand feet, the world seemed unnecessarily cumbersome and meaningless—the awesome power of the state apparatus developed over centuries of Roman jurisprudence and English common law, the scientific and technical detailing of sordid facts, the scraping and sampling and intricate measurement of over-wrought passion, the obsession with world order, the fear of euthanasia, the promise of the Gnome project, the beauty of Voyager II's death on Saturn, and the simple joy of March Madness. All mingled together with the droning flight toward the Windy City, which balanced precariously on the edge of the ice-crystal Lake Michigan.

He thought that he preferred the possibilities of the battle-scarred, blood-stained trailer, where the promise and passion of love had to be scraped from the walls with the delicate instruments of a morbid but curious technology, and where there was actual proof that someone loved or hated somebody beyond all measure of reason: and it was for that reason that he hated the law first and foremost: there was too damn much reason when there was no reason at all, and not enough passion when passion was all that mattered.

The train from O'Hare to downtown was finally finished. When he came up from the urban mass transit underworld, the frigid Chicago air took his breath away. By the time he walked the six blocks to the Sears Tower, he was frozen—just like his first trip to Chicago when he interviewed with the Strahorn law firm. He planned to attend the meeting with Robert Strayhorn and make one telephone call.

In the Tower his mind warmed to that first afternoon spent in the *Hubbard Street Hot Tubs* with Tom Strahorn and Diana. Tom told Diana to make the new kid in the office feel at home, and she did. Diana the compliant cocksucker. Diana of the magnificent orbs.

It was frozen that day too, but they went to the hot tubs, got naked and blown away. That night they walked along dangerous frozen streets where stalled cars covered with snow were pushed aside by the too-late-arriving city snow plows that caused Mayor Jane to lose the next election to Mayor McCheese, God rest-his-soul-son-of-a-bitch. But after he had moved to Chicago with his wife, she told Matthew that he was a married man and ought to know better, and although she wished that he were single and that she had met him sooner, she had fallen in love with a black harp player who performed at the *Blue Note Lounge* on Halsted and whose dick hit her G spot in a way his never could. She was candid about that.

Her naked image floated across the conference room where sixteen tense, ambitious lawyers, under the astute leadership of the Senior Partners, drafted the final Restrictive Covenants for the Tupelo Bluff Development.

It was a meeting he could have done without. Being in the Law offices of Strahorn, Stratton, Wartberger & Propinski was as depressing as a waiting room in the foyer of Hades. Now they were dealing with the part concerning the Property Owner's Association being actually controlled by the developers until there was no longer any developer involved in ownership of individual lots which meant that, for the indefinite forever, the standards and regulations of the project would be determined by the attorneys in the Sears Tower, and that the homeowner who couldn't read the fine print would never know the difference, until it was too late.

Why was it that people who opposed government regulations were the same people who lived in tightly regulated residential communities, where you couldn't piss in your yard, much less leave your kid's American Flyer parked in the driveway?

Before leaving, he met privately in Mr. Strahorn's office, something he had never done when he was a young lawyer at the firm, and he knew that because of Francois Taghert's involvement in the project, when acting on Taghert's behalf, he was representing Francois, for better or worse, and that gave him only a small measure of comfort.

While Robert Strahorn talked on the speaker phone to his wife in Palm Springs, he walked to the large windows and stood high above the city. The only passion in this family was dead in frozen Lake Michigan.

He had managed to avoid thinking of Anne for almost the entire trip, but now he could see her in the house on the North Shore. Being diligent. Doing the right things. Picking up the pieces. He didn't want to feel the anger and disappointment that swelled up inside him, but the alternatives hurt too much.

"Well, Matthew, I hope the trip was worth the blast of cold air."

"Yes, sir, I think we covered all the details."

"It's a great project, son. You should be very well set when this is completed. Do you have other plans while you're here?"

"No, sir. I think I'll be headed back to Florida."

Instead, he rented a car and drove up Lake Shore Drive to Evanston and checked into a hotel. He killed three hours in the bar watching the Bulls gearing up for their NBA title run. Once again, he was a stranger in his own skin. His mind had done a total disconnect and although he knew everywhere to turn, and what to say, and what to do, he didn't have a clue about how to go on with the life he had been living.

He summoned the courage to call Anne. The telephone conversation was awkward. The divorce proceedings were already under way.

"Is it possible for us to get back together?" he asked.

"Possible," she said. "But hope doesn't spring eternal."

He asked her what she thought about Florida.

"Florida," she said, "is where people go when they don't like where they are and can't think of anything else to do."

"That doesn't sound very positive. I think I meant, could we…?" He paused to consider the alternatives.

"If you ask me, while there's still hope."

He wondered if he would do anything before it was too late, while there was still hope. Still only a possibility that seemed like an illusion.

So, he didn't ask. And wondered if he had the courage to do anything at all. The silence seemed to last until that was all there was.

Anne was having dinner that night with the Pleasants. That's a real family: The Pleasant Family. Mr. Pleasant did whatever they do at the Board of Trade. He was tall and handsome with a laminated Mickey Mantle in his wallet, the clean-up hitter for his credit card collection. Mrs. Pleasant collected artists, and Anne was on her agenda that season. Anne would be a success. No one deserved it more.

He realized that he was not capable of dealing with her. Not now. At this point. It had gone too far. They were almost over.

"It would be nice to see you again," she said, which sounded only vaguely sincere.

He awkwardly interrupted, "Anne, somehow, deep down, it's always about success, and the money, and what it means…"

"To me or to you?" She asked, and waited.

The telephone line between seemed to go dead for a full two minutes. He knew the connection between them was permanently broken.

She finally said that she didn't really expect him to answer. Or return to their life in Chicago.

He didn't have anything to say that sounded convincing or wouldn't cause even greater trouble.

Basically, he no longer knew what it was all about: that unfathomable cold distance between them. He had nothing to say.

A few years before, as the sun came up over Lake Michigan, the city skyline was a vague silhouette against a bleak frozen mass of white. Together they struggled through knee deep snow in the park, holding onto each other in a blissful stupor. The Miracle Mile cityscape at the end of Lincoln Park was barely visible in the mist and clouds. They fell and lay in the snow. He felt that if he died at that moment, he would be happy for all eternity. It was the morning after his forty-fifth birthday.

The celebration had begun the day before with the filming of a high fashion commercial which Anne had directed. It was her biggest commercial project since they'd been in Chicago and had been a huge success. They drank champagne at the photo studio, then went to his birthday party at Radney's River North Project offices, where they polished off a quart of Chevas Regal and shared an ounce of white powder with a crowd of well-wishers and nose-candy rodents.

Tom Strayhorn was there with his current love affair, a tall dark exotic beauty from Ottawa, Illinois. His marriage was in shambles, and his obsession for the current *femme de photo* and his cocaine habit put his life on a collision course with divorce, death, or both.

Tom and Matthew embraced outside on the patio, neither of them feeling the brittle cold, only a sentimental myopia of self-absorption that passed for love or friendship but had become hollow and maudlin and inescapably desperate and sad.

"I love you brother," Tom kept repeating. "We had dreams, man, and they're going to come TRUE!" Tom was effusively over the top with cocaine induced euphoria.

"Go home," Matthew said. "While she'll still take you. Get yourself straight. She needs you. Your kids need you. You need them. Look at you! Stone drunk and fried."

"Who you talking to, Matt? I love this girl, man. She's life to me. You understand that? Don't you? Please. We don't all have your Pollyanna."

Tom always called Anne that: 'Pollyanna.'

He liked it. Almost as much as she hated it.

"You've got to understand me, Buddy, nobody else ever has. Not like you." They embraced again. Tom pulled back and looked at him. "I love you brother. Happy Birthday." Then he went inside.

Matthew stood in the cold alone. He felt like crying. His emotions were exaggerated. Tom was... Tom was, other than Pollyanna, Tom was, had been, Tommy was his friend, was a brother he never had. More even. He opened a new pack of Camels and smoked in the cold.

After that winter night, Tom got lost. He went on a leave of absence from the firm while they negotiated the sale of the Sears Tower to a group of Saudi investors. Tom traveled to Europe with this photo starlet, who left him in Italy, while she went on a fashion assignment in Morocco, then phoned him from Japan and told him to "get a life." Tom came back from Italy and lived for a short time, not with his family, but at his parent's North Shore estate while they vacationed in Palm Springs. He took the sailboat out on Lake Michigan and never came back.

Anne came out to the patio. "You OK?" she asked.

He had been crying. A sentimental coke emotional overload. They held each other in the brittle air.

"You did great today. Yesterday. Whenever it was," he said. "You're an Art Star."

She smiled, and they kissed passionately but with obscure affection. "Can we go home and make romance?" he asked.

"You know we can." She probably thought she meant it.

"Tom left with his prize and didn't say goodbye. Did you say something to upset him?"

"I tried to tell him the truth. But he said, 'We can't all be married to Pollyanna,' and he's right you know."

"I hate that," Anne said. "Don't call me that."

"Coke's up!" Radney said, sticking his evil head out the door. He was a mad scientist, and Matthew was one of his lab rats.

They used an expensive alloy tube to sniff the lines. It made a clear celestial tingling sound when it was dropped on the glass tabletop.

Radney crooned, "Another angel gets his wings."

They lay in the snow, the Chicago skyline billowing steam in the distant cold dawn. His heart was beating an irregular reggae, not a thump thump thump, but kathumpa kathumpa kathumpa, skip a beat, suspended time. Kathumpa kakathumpa kakathumpa. His heart pounded at a rate that was close to exploding.

"I love you," Matthew, said. "But I think I am going to die." Feeling certain he would die in euphoric bliss, but he didn't.

He should have quit when he was ahead, but he didn't. He rolled the dice again and lost. It was not his fault. He made that argument and he tried to believe it. Bank credit was a revolving door almost as bad as drugs. From inside sources, he had learned that Mayor Washington was targeting the south of North Avenue area as a showcase renewal project, so he went for all the marbles. He bought several buildings in the Near North area that was the Mason Dixon line between urban gentrification and the Cabrini Green ghetto. The south side of the Boulevard was a potential gold mine. Already lavish condos selling for exorbitant prices were spreading along the north side of the Boulevard. The scent of federal grant money was in the air but within months of closing the deal, Mayor McCheese died of a heart attack.

"That son-of-a-bitch," Matthew groaned. "Harold and me were like this," holding up his hand showing two fingers, because on three different occasions the Mayor came into a crowded room, and shook his hand, like they were long lost friends. When Mayor McCheese died, everything came to a halt.

The city mourned with great ceremony. Matthew went downtown where Mayor McCheese lay in state. The Mayor had a frozen grin, but he wasn't happy. Neither one of them was happy.

Civil war broke out in Chicago City Hall. Matthew was over-optimistic and under-capitalized. He wasn't prepared for the sudden death of the overweight Mayor and the market collapse. He was just trying to make enough money to live comfortably beyond his means.

When the market hit bottom in November '87, he was barely treading water. Within six months, he was dead in the water. Debt load far exceeded cash flow, and he was scrambling to find a hose for the exhaust pipe of the car. He could hear the Irish nails being driven into his coffin. The Mason Dixon Boulevard was a battle zone. It started to get ugly and depressing. Nobody wanted to be on the shady side of the street. Everybody wanted to be on the sunny side.

It was the same old song with the banker at lunch: "I'd like to help you, but we're concerned that your cash flow isn't sufficient to sustain your costs. The review board has asked me to …" The supercilious loan officer stopped and straightened the napkin on his plate.

"Hang me out to dry after all the money you've made off of me."

"Show me a business plan that I can take to the board. I went out on a limb for you when you got into this. They said, 'That building is too close to the ghetto.' I said, 'Matthew knows what he's doing.' They said, 'What do you think, Bob?' And I said, 'He's been with us for eight years. He's been a good client. He's got a good track record. He's got collateral. I think he knows what he's doing and can make it good.' They didn't buy it."

"What do you think I should do?"

"Stop the bleeding. Sell the damn buildings. All of them, if necessary. You'll survive. It's only money."

By the time he sold the buildings, his real estate holdings, for all immediate purposes, were a bust, and they were living on money borrowed against borrowed money. His emotional collateral was depleted. He was in rehab from the euphoria that sustained his hope.

He rolled the dice and crapped out: Dum Luk they always called it at the *Dragon Inn*.

He no longer believed Pollyanna when she said it would all work out for the best. That her father could, and would, bail them out. But that was then.

Sometimes there was a memory of what he thought had been love, that wanted to be love. Sometimes there was a feeling that he had failed to, was afraid of, or was unable to, express personal love or express his emotions at all, and that he needed to change or he would flounder and drown in his own silence. The expectations, bitter disappointments, and recriminations between them were excruciation. It was so damn hard for them to be nice to each other. Their relationship had grown from passionate attraction, to simple affection, to several good years of an apparently successful life together. Then the cynical preconceptions, disappointments, and clever sarcastic remarks began to get in the way, and the hard, cold facts crept into the silences and calcified around all the bad stuff, like barnacles that were hard to scrape off, that hurt when you touched them. Every time they spoke, they cut their fingers.

He had learned enough with this Belle Rio sabbatical to know that he had to forge ahead, alone. He could not look back now and become a pillar of salt with a heart of stone. It hurt too much being in Chicago, but he took it like the grown man he was: he fled.

Three weeks after his return from Chicago, on a petulant overcast day in Belle Rio, he signed the anticipated divorce decree. Their marriage had fallen through the cracks. They had finally run out of hope. The money was only an annoying afterthought.

Along with the final divorce decree was a letter from Anne.

Dear Matthew,

My heart is cold tears of stone. I can only trust that this feeling of emptiness will somehow vanish (with time) or correct words well spoken; anything less would only cause more harm and distance between us— dissonance that could never be resolved.

It is very sad for me, and I see that you suffer too without knowing why, without you knowing the depth of the hurt your casual remarks might cause. The pain I felt at the laughter. The sudden intense hatred and fear I had from your response to my, yes foolish, behavior but it was my inside feelings, wanting to become manifest, to express only the joy of my life—and you said 'my ego need,' and I felt insulted & filled the cold void with my hatred for you—tho I had loved you and comforted you, as you me, on occasion. Yes, I hurt you too, in much the same way, before I learned how to hold my speech, which was thoughtless—words rushing from my mouth without first going thru my heart.

I tried for many years to master your volatile, quick retorts that lashed out at my "precious flower thoughts & emotions". You stomped on my violets with your Aristotelian boots. Words often too in inaccurate, meaningless, and unnecessary to refute. So pointlessly spoken, so disrespectful. And I, often halting, frail, and in need of your support. Yet, you stomped and laid waste. I too stomped and laid waste… I learned to be aware, to be quiet, and to be secretive with my passion. But it only distanced us from our need to express, in a quiet voice, what was in our heart & soul. Always so difficult to express. Then you turned the dagger on me, eviscerated my heart and magically disappeared into the fog.

I have felt in much disarray this past year, which unveiled a deep anger that, hopefully, time will heal. Or it will crust over with scars & unresolved resentment, with which, I cannot live.

Either you have no idea who I am or I am jealous of your easy madness: one surprises and disappoints, the other frightens me, but is perhaps less damning. We both compete for attention. Sadly, we have dampened and stunted our emotional life in order to lessen the harsh reality of that competition. We have not always done the best for what is best for both of us.

We have, for appearances, lived successfully our lives together, and, I have felt, have always suspected, at the cost of less individual achievement, on each of our accounts. At the risk of self-destruction, in my case. Yet in yours, I know not what.

You could have possibly gone higher alone, or sank lower with a lesser woman.

And now you are free to stand alone, or go to the one who would take you higher. Or the one who would destroy you. You will discover which is best. I have no idea what you wish for.

Of course, we both know that I have already done what our new freedom now allows. As, I am sure, have you. We have both good memories and lost years of wasted ambition. But still, inside, I am not dead. Neither are you.

You have often burdened yourself with an unnecessary, dark, heavy heart. The cruelty of time and memory. That, at last, brought me to my knees.

My heart bursts to sing out with joy—in love, in anger, in awe & wonder, and probably, sometimes in ridicule. So be it. I must go. If the sea cannot be warm between us, then it will be replaced with a desert.

I wish you peace & all the success you truly deserve,
Anne Sargent McCutcheon.

He replied:

I have offended you many times
In many ways
And always paid the price
In your kindness
You have forgiven my broken trust
And I yours
As for the many thoughtless words:
If I cannot see the offense
You cannot tell me
If you cannot go where I want to go:
(Smokey dark caves)
I will go alone
Do not make your un-pleasure
My fault
Because it is my pleasure
Rather than your own
And Vice Versa

What was the point? He did not ask because he did not want to hear the answer, and he was moving through a viscous ether of unknowing, uncaring, as if both his numb brain and his dull heart were only specimens, the splattered remains on the wall of failure, carefully collected and examined by the crime lab technicians who would report that "Although something extraordinary had happened to him, there were no signs of passion, of life, and he was truly unremarkable."

He could see their past life together— the remains of what they had called love being carefully placed in a bottle for examination under the microscope at the crime lab in Capital City.

And for amusement, he attached a short article from the *LA Times*:

A FAIRY TALE OF LOVE & MARRIAGE

Princess Fahia, who lost her royal title when she married a commoner, was killed yesterday by her estranged husband, Riad Ghali, age fifty-five.

At the time of her marriage to the commoner, the Princess was banned from the desert kingdom by her irate Father.

The glamourous couple settled in California, where for many years, they lived a lavish high society lifestyle; but eventually drained of money, she was unable to supply the necessities for her children and her useless husband.

When they finally went broke, he divorced her. He never paid a penny of child support, and she was forced to work as a cleaning woman.

Her jewels and other family heirlooms were recently sold in Federal Bankruptcy Court, where they hoped to raise at least $500,000. They only raised $180,000.

Her liabilities were well over four million dollars, and the interest payment alone on the family debt was $320,000 a year.

After killing his former wife, Riad Ghali turned the gun on himself. Unfortunately, he botched his suicide attempt. He was taken to Cedars of Lebanon Hospital, where he was listed in fair condition and booked for murder by the Hollywood Police Department.

What me worry? Thinking of you
As Always,
Matthew

CHAPTER TWELVE

Wandering Venus

IT WAS EIGHTY degrees and muggy as he trudged along the beach at sunset; Venus appeared in the western sky and hung like misplaced punctuation beneath the crescent moon. Within hours, it would disappear below the horizon, leaving the constellations to wander in the dark sky.

She walked toward him and stood barefoot in the seafoam and twilight, holding her dress above her knees, in the golden back-light, like some Hollywood siren of cruel desire and wanton pleasure; but there had been so many cheap imitations of Ava Gardner that he had lost track and almost given up hope.

"Hello, you," she murmured. "You walk like a man with a heavy heart. I've watched you out here on the beach, walk, run, and crawl."

"You're right, I wasn't really moving," he said while thinking: she had watched me from afar, unnoticed, how unfair and ultimately Divine.

"You were barely alive," she cautioned.

Liana Cates was not a silent heavenly body after all. Her gaze was simple and direct and unaffected, perhaps misleading, and probably meaningless. She moved with liquid grace, yet unsettled as mercury. He moved with her, and his whole being growled from hunger. She came from the moon, stars, and the sea for this conversation and could have the smooth whole beach and the background singing surf for as long as she desired it, then she would exit with the tide when she was damn good and ready. He exhaled. She sighed, and it turned into the fading twilight. A breeze lifted off the water and caught her hair and moved the loose strands against her face. He wanted her and she heard his desire, inhaled his need without changing expression. Time was grinding to a halt.

"I need your help," she said.

The silent coincidence of Venus and the crescent moon twilight was gone. What remained would be mundane, but they would have to go through it. They would have to talk, and it would be diverting and entertaining, but it would never again be that moment.

"Sure," he blathered, "let's go where you've been watching me from," thinking that would be heaven and he could die trying. It might have to be mundane, but maybe it could be profane as well. Was that too much to hope for?

"Let's go to your place," she replied.

That was an earthly place to start. They walked along the beach, not talking, past the Gulf Beach Road leading back to the highway, and when they passed the motel she said, "I bought the motel a month ago."

That was a surprise to him. Right under his nose. He was appalled at how self-absorbed and inattentive he had been.

"I'm living in the apartment behind the office with Terri, my daughter."

"I've met your daughter at the *Sea Horse Tavern*."

"She's still in high school. Determined to get in trouble, one way or the other."

"She seems able to take care of herself. Either way, they live through it. You did. We all did."

"I was no angel," she admitted.

That had a ring to it. The clear sound of verisimilitude. He wished he could abolish words like that from his vocabulary, his mental *vocabulario*. For though they remained unspoken, they cluttered his mind with unutterable garbage. He wanted clarity of purpose and simplicity, only poetry. To be silently absorbed.

"So I hear," he said.

And she looked at him, disappointed.

"Then you know?" she asked.

"I know nothing," he said. "Only what you tell me will I know, and only what you want me to believe will I believe."

That was better. She liked that. They were back on track.

When he returned from the kitchen with two vodka drinks, she was stretched out on the comfortable sofa like a large cat, her foot undulating slowly. As she accepted the glass, she moved gracefully to a sitting position with her feet tucked under her, without appearing to move, and slowly sipped without talking.

He moved aimlessly, afraid to talk and reveal himself a fool. He finally slumped silently into a wicker chair, and as she breathed, he breathed. He could listen to her or he could look at her, but he had trouble doing both at the same time. So, he alternated between listening and looking, and he spoke only when he had little to say.

During the six months of alternating between listening to Liana or looking at her, but never both at the same time, he had learned more than he wanted to know about Liana, but it all remained unsaid, and when he was with her, it was like he had stated from the beginning: Only what she tells me will I know, and only what she wants me to believe will I believe.

He had learned that Bud Hardaway not only made it possible for her to buy the motel, but also that he held the second mortgage on the property.

She had worked at Hardaway Seafood for years and was often seen in public with Mr. Hardaway. The unspoken general assumption was that they were lovers, but if she said it wasn't true, it wasn't true. She was not having sex with Bud Hardaway. She told him that and he believed it. "He doesn't mind that people think that we do, but it's not so. I've done without for five years since I was rehabilitated."

"What a waste," he blurted from his mouth, and he tried to take the words back from the air, and as usual, she ignored either what he said or what he meant with equal lack of concern, or insouciance he thought, his *vocabulario* racing with nervous sexual energy, while he attempted to remain as calm and disinterested as she appeared to be. But the hunger that had been growing in his loins since Liana came into his life, and the coincidence of Venus rising with the crescent moon, was now becoming painful and undeniable.

At a swanky jazzy uptown supper club in Capital City, Liana ate Tournedos St. Laurent and asparagus in butter sauce with scallions. They drank too much wine, and as they danced to romantic ballads played by the sax quintet, he hummed lyrics in her ear and held her compliant body for the first time. She wrapped him in her arms. He kissed her neck, and the aroma opened his nostrils, and he stiffened with obvious, uncontrollable desire. When they sat back at the table, she casually placed her hand on his leg and walked her fingers slowly up his thigh and came to rest on his lonely soldier, and then she smiled a warm vacant vulnerability. He kissed her full lips, which she opened for him, and his breath sank, and her tongue slipped softly into his mouth and out and they drooled in public. Then she squeezed him and moved her hand back to the white starch cloth tabletop.

"We're too drunk to drive home," she purr-slurred. "We're gonna have to stay in a hotel."

He drank a glass of water and took three deep breaths.

"Absolutely correct. Better sex than sorry." And sorry he was that he had spoken, but she had already handled the obvious and had his full attention.

"The best hotel," she said, as they moved arm in arm across the boulevard to the Governor's Inn, the respectable haunt of high-powered litigants before the State Supreme Court.

Then they were alone together in the dark, rigid from head to toe. He pressed against her sweet hot flesh and feared that she would consume his entire body in her smoldering volcano and not be satisfied. She sank to the edge of the bed, her breast then pressed to his loins, grasping his buttocks, swallowing his sex. He tried to raise her, "Please, no," he stammered, "no." But her Venus lips were hungry, soft, and hot, and she consumed him and drank the milky sweet jism while he clung to the bed post. Too quickly he came in spurts and jolts, and she gasped for air and swallowed and sucked him until he ached then released him with a vengeance that was without joy and sank back onto the bed and curled up in her protective cocoon, covering her face. He took her hands, moist with sweat, sex, and tears, and embraced her smoldering flesh, and threw the covers from the bed, but when she looked at him, it was not the Liana he knew, but an unknown bewildered child, afraid, and he cradled her in his arms and held her. She was no longer larger than life, no longer the barefoot crescent moon Venus goddess, no longer the dreamland Contessa.

He alternatively held her and listened to her as she cried and talked and talked and cried and laughed and cried and finally slept as daylight spilled in through the glass skylight in the bathroom. For the first time, he listened to her and looked at her at the same time, and was touched by her, because it was not the myth, the motion of the planets, but the solitary person, wounded and frail, soft flesh and hot blood and deep pensive eyes, a deadly sweltering passion flower.

It was her sad truth, and what she told him was what he knew to be true; and even if she lied, it was the way she said it was.

"I went there to shoot him," she said. "He was drunk and made it easy for me. I was lucky I killed him and just didn't make him blind or a cripple or stupid and then I would've had to take care of him, and I couldn't have stood that. Not the way he was when he was good, 'cause he was so very very good, but when he was bad," she started crying again, "he was such a bastard." She cried until she laughed. "So, I was lucky, I guess."

It was the story he knew. He had read the transcripts, the depositions, the opinions of Appellate Judges, heard the opinions of every person in Belle Rio who had an opinion about Liana and Tommy Lee Matson, the star-crossed lovers of Belle Rio.

"Terri was living with me that summer. None of this ever came out 'cause I didn't want her to have to go through more than what she did. He kept messing with her and that's what made up my mind to do it. Hell, when I first met Tommy, I was no older than she was. He was just out of high school and he was handsome. He was scary he was so handsome, and dangerous. I loved that boy. He hadn't even seen me yet, 'cause I was a young girl when I first came there to stay with my aunt. Then he got married. It didn't last long. He knocked the girl up. She's married to the Sheriff now. After that, he got married again. I knew all them girls, just local sluts like me. By then, I was starting to get his attention 'cause I was tall, and I was a good looking piece of work. That's when you shoulda knowed me."

Her laugh teased him, "I wouldn't have given you the time a day. I was just a hellcat looking for some stud." Then she snuggled up to him and was quiet. "Matt, you're a sweet man, a decent man. That's what made me cry. I never had a really nice man."

"Thanks," he said sarcastically.

"Were you just hoping I'd fuck you? All the time? Is that all you've been wanting?"

He didn't answer, wishing that it weren't true.

She looked at him almost tenderly and said, "I don't think so. All my life I've been a good judge of bad character, and you're not a bad character. You got other faults, I'm sure, but they're too complicated for me. I like you because I like you. That's why. That's all. I'll shut up now."

They were quiet for a while, and he gazed into the mysterious clouds covering her surface, moving his hands slowly over her soft body. He kissed her but her mouth was cold with necessary words.

"Tommy spent a few years in federal prison on a drug charge. He was smuggling cocaine. He kept his mouth shut and took the rap."

"That's why Bud's nice to you, because you killed Tommy?"

She looked at him for several minutes with uncertainty and apprehension, like she might bolt from the Governor's Inn, flee from Capital City and the simple hell that was Belle Rio, and escape from the laws of planetary motion then wander freely through the galaxy.

"You lied to me. All the time. You said you knew nothing about me, about my life."

There was an element of truth somewhere in that supposition. "I believed what you wanted me to believe; that's true. But I don't care about Bud Hardaway or Tommy Matson."

He wanted her now for some perverse desperate preservation of his manhood, and she still wasn't interested. She sat with her legs folded, holding a pillow across her body like she was at a slumber party.

"When he got home from prison, he was broke and couldn't control his anger. Tommy was really possessive with me, but he wanted to play the fool to any woman he wanted. That's the way he'd always had it. He thought 'cause he was big he could beat on me like he would a man, only he wouldn't fight men. He'd talk tough and flaunt his knife, but Tommy was not a fighter, 'cept against women. He beat me with his fist and burned me with cigarettes. Once, he dragged me by the hair through broken glass and I got all cut up. Then the S.O.B slammed my head inside a dryer at the wishy-washy and messed up my face. Why I took the shit I took I'll never know. I wasn't ever the type to take crap from a man."

She thought about the reason: "I didn't want to be the one that sent him back to prison."

Matthew knew what Tommy Lee Matson looked like from the coroner's report: he was 6'2" and muscular. That he was a reckless cavalier corpse wasn't in the report, but it was obvious between the lines. He had long, curly, light brown hair, and a tattoo on his left arm that boasted two hearts with a penis-shaped sword through them and the words *My Love* burned there for his first wife, who was now married to the Sheriff. On his right arm was an elaborate tattoo of a sea dragon, which had a woman's face swallowing its own tail with *Kundi Liana* scrolled beneath it.

"Keith Moss and I were trying to wind surf in front of the house. I fell off and couldn't get back on. Tommy was on the beach, flirting with Terri. When they went in the house, I got so mad I nearly drowned. I was 'disfuctural.' What do you call it?"

"Dysfunctional."

"Disfucktural insanity," he thought. She had to rub it in. Couldn't leave well enough alone. Silently pleading to her, "Have I got to hit you?" Wishing he could, wishing he could hit her, if that's what it took. But she ignored him.

"Anyway, I was mad as hell. When I finally got to the shore, I went straight in the house and Terri was sitting on Tommy's lap, and he was kissing on her. I got to screaming and made Keith take Terri over to my aunt's house. Tommy beat me, ripped and burned my clothes, threw them into the yard, and told me to get out. I went off with Keith to Panama City and fucked Keith good. I called Tommy from Panama and told him so. Tommy stayed drunk that whole week looking for me, in and out of the bars that would still let him in, calling me a slut and threatening to beat me dumb when he saw me again.

"I called in the morning and told him that I didn't want nothing more to do with him and that I was coming to get my clothes. He crooned, 'You know you love me baby' like he always did. And it was true. I did. But I had to get away from him. He said he wouldn't be there because he was going oystering, but he was already drunk, and I knew he'd be there. So, I got that little gun from Louise, his last wife, and I went to the house. *Price is Right* was on TV."

She had been talking steady, untroubled, but as it got closer to the moment of truth, she faltered and hesitated.

"He was drinking vodka, sitting on the sofa. He started screaming at me. I took the gun out and said, 'I'll shoot you son-of-a-bitch if you ever mess with my daughter again.' He laughed, stood up, and came toward me. He said, 'You don't have the guts, and you probably couldn't hit me anyway.'"

She stopped talked and stared vaguely at her feet, her Charlotte Pink painted toenails.

"I was backing away from him. I didn't want to kill him, because I loved him, even though he treated me like shit and nobody ever done that to me before. I wasn't gonna take it no more. I closed my eyes and shot him."

The coroner's report said: *below the left eye, the bullet transecting the brain and exiting the skull, causing massive destruction of the left terminal lobe. There was also abundant blood within the airway and apparent aspiration of blood within both lungs.*

And other miscellaneous facts: she called the neighbor's house and woke him. Told him that Tommy was after her or that she'd killed Tommy. He couldn't remember which. She was hysterical. Was it five minutes? Ten minutes? Did he hear a shot? He didn't remember. He thought so, but maybe he was wrong. There was a lot of traffic on the highway. He remembered the traffic but not the shot. He didn't know. He told one story the day of the homicide, another to the grand jury, then another on the witness stand. When he got to the house, Tommy was lying on the floor in the kitchen, but he wasn't dead yet. He didn't try to do anything to help him. He didn't like the sight of Tommy's face. Tommy was twitching with convulsions, still holding a lit cigarette between his fingers that was burning his flesh. A broken glass of spilled vodka at his feet. Liana was in the living room crying, holding the gun, saying over and over: "I shot Tommy. I shot Tommy. I didn't mean to kill my baby."

She called her Deputy Sheriff cousin and said she'd shot Tommy, and he was dead.

Liana Cates was officially charged with Second Degree Felony Manslaughter: that she did unlawfully by act and without lawful justification kill a human being, Tommy Lee Matson, and that said killing was not an excusable homicide.

Liana fit the profile perfectly. The daughter of an alcoholic career Army officer, raised a gypsy service brat, a runaway, a wild child, a promiscuous teenager, a rebellious hellcat, a Belle Rio cougar with uncontrolled lust for attention, which she could get anytime she "showed her ass in public" as they said in Belle Rio, where many believed killing Tommy Matson was first degree murder and they said so.

Matthew could name a dozen without thinking, including a sister to one of the wives, and all of Tommy's daughters by his first two marriages. To them, it was premeditated and cold-blooded murder. But ask another group and they would say that Tommy was a bad dude when it came to women. When he got to Liana, he beat the wrong woman too many times.

Tommy got at least what he asked for. He had been busted by Federal agents importing cocaine on shrimp trawlers. The cocaine was shipped north from Belle Rio in frozen seafood refrigerator trucks. If you connected the dots of beer tavern poolroom folklore, *mucho dinero* changed hands in Belle Rio and Tommy got almost none of it. Then he did his time without talking. Somebody owed Tommy. But he didn't know how to get it. It was against his code to snitch, but he wanted to collect from somebody, and as the days and months went by, and beating Liana failed to satisfy his feeling of betrayal, he began telling barroom tales with dangerous implications.

Many were glad to see him dead. They didn't mind saying so. There was no disputing the facts: Tommy was going to die at the hands of somebody, sooner or later. It was just a matter of time.

If Liana were unlucky in love, she was lucky in court. Her lawyers from Capital City were experts in domestic violence disputes. They were convinced Liana could win acquittal in a jury trial. The State feared the same. A Motion to Dismiss was denied because the judge was not prepared to admit that "nothing happened."

Liana pled *nolo contendere* to a reduced charge and the prosecution 'swallowed the gun'. Tommy Matson was just dead. Too bad so sad. Liana Cates was sentenced to three years on probation. She never spent a night in jail.

She was now quiet for the first time since midnight. Matt traced the outline of her face with his finger and moved the strand of hair that always caught the warm breeze. And touched her sad mouth. She took his fingers and kissed them and held his hand down against her loins and closed her eyes. He had said he would know only what she told him and believe only what she wanted him to believe, but he knew too much. He couldn't help himself: still, he believed her.

Liana fell asleep before dawn. Her golden-brown hair spread carelessly across the pillow where they lay close to dreaming in a strange darkened room. A voice sang quietly in the dawn as the morning slipped through the bathroom skylight and warm bodies aroused in the silence came together and her shameless mouth opened to him and slowly, he bathed her smoldering face and neck with his tongue and their mouths exchanged breath and he caressed her soft breasts.

Aroused by the courageous Magellan, probing her compliant, yielding flesh, beneath the once unknown shrouded surface, her passionate mouth uttered a low guttural moan, and as she gave way to desire and need. Her weeping dark eyes burned with heat and her devoted palace guard thighs melted and opened wide, as he worshipped at the Mons Clitoria, hidden beyond ancient Vesuvius, where hot lava flowed and ageless men, rigid with lust and desire, mounted the mysterious wandering goddess and lost their minds.

The waves of the gulf were a surly Yahoo soda, and the sky was moody and unhappy. Liana rode in silence smoking a cigarette. His mind was

111

drifting with the smoldering naked Venus, the angel of love, enveloping him in room fifty-seven at the Governor's Paradise Suite.

He didn't want to care one way or the other that a million stars disappeared last night beneath Venus tears, that lost stranded memories died like fallen monarchs, that dreams cried like angels, that white-caps curled in the wind and rain, that bruised clouds obscured the horizon, that the dark sky fell to the water like a curtain, that for the sweet peace of hell, heaven must be a lie.

Once it finally stopped raining, the sun rays streaked through the clouds, creating an idealized vision of the *Ascension,* an image of allegorical bliss. Swarthy pelican priests perched on weathered dock posts in the vast ocean, drowsy from the morning *Gloria,* the *Sanctus Benedictus.* World without end. Amen.

But some prayers remained unanswered.

"That was the last time," she said. They could be friends, she said, but "that" was over. He was a nice man. She wanted to be his friend. She thanked him again for kicking Billy Goat Gruff off the bridge and kissed him on the cheek.

It was only eight in the morning when he dropped her at the motel and drove away with the rest of his life. He told himself that he was lucky. He told himself that he had journeyed beneath the mysterious shroud of Venus and survived, that he had lived to try and forget it. That he was better off. No matter what.

CHAPTER THIRTEEN

Damn Good Deal

STUMP, SON OF PEG LEG ORVILLE, ordered a smoked mullet and a beer. There was a football game on the TV, but the sound was off. Stadium lights glistened off the slick wet astro-turf, liquid silver with no color except the streaking jerseys of the red team. Players slid and collided out of control, an electronic vision of mayhem.

Stump was a gnarled gypsy, five foot-tall, with a round belly, a full gray beard, and long thick hair that he kept tied in a ponytail. He drove a 16-wheeler most of the year. When he was off the road, he carved animals from cypress lumber with a chain saw. Cigarette smoke curled up around him. His father, Orville, escaped Spain when Franco started rounding up Basque gypsies. Orville came to America with his wife, his woodworking tools, and a brown dancing bear. They settled near Sarasota where he carved wooden horses for a circus merry-go-round until he got hooked up with a traveling show. Stump was the first of his family born in America. He was born on the road in a carnival caravan of twenty-five cent rides, freaks and midgets, and clowns who did acrobatic stunts on little unicycles. The dancing bear died in Charleston the same year a Ferris wheel ride fell on Orville and smashed his leg flat. A doctor amputated the leg and from that day on he was known he was known as "Peg Leg Orville."

When Stump was thirteen, he had a fist fight with his one-legged old man and left the show. He lived alone for many years. Spent time in jail. Drove a freight rig. Said he had over a thousand odd jobs. The year he turned thirty he was working in the Ozarks near the Missouri border and living with a woman whose husband was away on active military duty. They were clearing a line cut across the mountain, setting poles in for power lines, making something less than good money. He took the woman into town where there was a little carnival show, and the ferris wheel operator told him Peg Leg Orville was still running a carnival show and was probably holding for the winter in Florida. He'd had a heart attack and had been in the hospital. Stump quit his job on the power line crew (the woman's husband was due home in a week anyway) and went back to Sarasota with his small savings.

Without being recognized by his brothers, who were young children when he left home, he took a job operating one of the rides. A month went by before Peg Leg Orville returned from the hospital. Stump saw Peg Leg coming down the midway with a walker—now he was on five artificial legs. He was coming to see the new guy who had been hired in his absence. Stump was up on the machine when Peg Leg Orville got there, looked up at him, and said, "When you get a break, son, come up to the office."

His replacement operator came for the night shift, and he went to the office where all the family was gathered. His younger brothers still didn't recognize him. Peg Leg said, "That's your brother, Stump. He's gonna run the show from now on." And he did.

His father died two years later, and Stump closed the show.

Stump's eyes were glazed over, and a Lucky Strike hung on his lip.

"I was living down in South Florida and got in an argument with a snowbird from Toledo. I got so mad I hit him in the face with a fish. Big one too. They took me to court for malicious assault. When I got out of jail, I came to Belle Rio because people take you as you are and leave you alone. You've got to be lost to find this place."

An oysterman from Wakulla County wandered into the Seahorse Tavern wearing white rubber fishhouse boots, grubby jeans, and a dirty yellow T-shirt that had *Cleopatra's Temple of Love* stenciled over a picture of a topless Egyptian dancehall queen. He took his seat at the bar

Matthew bought the oysterman a beer and asked where he could find the famous temple of ill repute advertised by the *Temple of Love* T-shirt.

"It's one them naked dance clubs in Panama City," the oysterman said proudly.

"I'm due an oil change and a lube job" Matthew said.

"You really got to perform to get one a them," Elvis cautioned. "It ain't like getting a high school letter jacket for banging a couple cougar cheerleaders."

"What that shirt say on the back?" Skinny Sherman asked, flashing his expensive set of government teeth.

The young oysterman proudly showed the back of his shirt, which read, "*Cleopatra's Temple of Love, Come Often, Die Hard*" in ornate Victorian type.

"I'll trade you my shirt for that Cleopatra T-Shirt," Matthew said. He was wearing a faded black polo shirt. "And buy you another drink."

"That's a damn good deal for you," Elvis said. "That shirt of Matt's comes from some exclusive man's store in Chi-car-go. It's authentic Ralph Lauren Polo."

A good deal was not to be taken lightly at the Seahorse Tavern, where the patrons could lose their heads at the drop of a pin, even when there were no angels to count.

The pros and cons debated the finer things in life, while the Wakulla oysterman pondered whether or not he wanted to part with his dirty *Temple of Love* souvenir T-shirt, authentic or not. He could always get another one.

At last, the oysterman said, "If that's really one a them expensive Chi-car-go man's store polo shirts, then I'll do it."

Matthew pulled the shirt over his head and showed him the label. The oysterman stripped off the *Temple of Love* souvenir. To applause, they both sat bare-chested at the bar admiring their respective new shirts.

Billy Ray strolled into the Seahorse Tavern wearing a pink, turquoise and yellow California surfer shirt with colorful parrots and a *San Sebastian Caribbean Cruise* logo stenciled on the back.

Skinny Sherman holler'd, "Billy Ray, I'll trade you my shirt for that damn ugly lookin' Margaritaville piece-a-shit you're wearing."

He ripped the buttons clean off his shirt and held it out to Billy Ray, showing off his muscular skinny body.

Billy Ray was momentarily stunned. "What y'all doin' with your damn shirts off?" He was not prepared for this. "Y'all Crazy!" he croaked. "I don't want none of it."

Skinny Sherman was crest fallen. He had just destroyed his one clean shirt and was not to be denied. He turned to Madonna and said, "Madonna, you trade with me?"

She shook her head from side to side.

"Please Madonna, please?" he said, groveling on bended knee. Sherman begged and pleaded.

"No way," she gummed and smiled with toothless splendor.

Five guys were now standing at the bar with their shirts off, flexing muscle magazine competition poses.

"My best Arnold Schwarz-nagger," Skinny Sherman boasted.

Madonna stared at Billy Ray's beautiful *San Sebastian Caribbean Cruise* shirt. It was not a difficult decision: she was eager to trade with Billy Ray, to be swept off her feet wearing the colorful cruise ship parrot shirt.

"I'll trade with Billy Ray," she said proudly.

Everyone shouted, "Take off your damn shirt, Billy Ray!"

Billy Ray didn't want any of this nonsense. Wasn't in the mood. Not about to part with his favorite piece of Margaritaville wardrobe.

"Shit!" Billy Ray said. He headed for the doorway where he turned and said, *"T-t-that's all F-f-f-folks"* like a Looney Tunes Saturday morning TV show and stormed out.

"Pitiful Dumbass," Skinny Sherman lamented.

Crazy Maxwell threw a beer can at the door. He said that Billy Ray was an animated cartoon who only lived while the pages turned.

They all agreed: it was a pity that Billy Ray had the only shirt that caught Madonna's eye.

She smiled her enigmatic Mona Lisa smile, still thinking of the parrots on Billy Ray's shirt and a cruise to San Sebastian, wherever that was and scribbled love notes on the back of Budweiser beer coasters like they were postcards from San Sebastian.

Checking out the classic Madonna bosom, Sherman pleaded, "Just lemme peek, Madonna."

"Lemme have a look too," pleaded Crazy Maxwell.

"Only Sherman," Madonna cautioned.

Holding out the top of her faded sweater, Sherman sighed.

"What you see down there?" Maxwell asked with envy.

"Pure as snow, boys, and white as the seven dwarfs."

It was a night to remember. The jukebox ran through a medley of *A Little Less Talk & A Lot More Action, Mustang Sally was Born on the Bayou, while Louie Louie Eats the Brown Sugar of Honky Tonk Women. If We Get Drunk and Party All Night Long, It's a Family Tradition.*

The Satyrs of Neptune danced with frenzied abandon and the bar hounds hollered for more flesh. Darlene rewarded them, performing her famous topless Fandango. This fabulous night, she forgot her sorry fate and was the dancing queen of Belle Rio.

CHAPTER FOURTEEN

Cleopatra's Temple of Love

BILLY RAY HARDAWAY swung his red Corvette into the No Parking Zone at *Cleopatra's Disco* adjacent to *The Temple of Love* on the strip at Panama City Beach. The rotund rent-a-cop, a local fixture weighing over three hundred pounds, cursed him, his over-heated face dripping sweat. The guard recognized the Corvette, gave Billy Ray the FU gesture and cursed him again

"Tell your boss I'm doing him a favor coming to this joint," Billy Ray croaked, assuming all the confidence he could muster. Billy Ray looked svelte, and he worked to exude confidence and bravado, but he knew he had everything to lose.

"So whatdaya think, honey? You haven't answered my question." Terri the Pirate Girl was talking as she got out of the Corvette. She was dressed to kill in a snug knit aquamarine dress that stopped well above her knees. She looked hot, like the girls of Panama. "You think I oughtta do that dance thing or not?"

"You do what it takes to get what you want, baby, you know that. Percy's a straight dude. We're partners. It's all arranged. And I'll watch out for you."

Billy Ray caught her around the waist and they waltzed toward the disco—four tropical themed bars packed with a rowdy crowd of college beach bums surrounded by huge jungle plants, big TV screens tuned to ESPN, MTV and CMT, with punk thrash rock music blaring through the din of a much too sultry afternoon.

Cairo had cleaned up and looked respectable. He was working the dance club door in the afternoons. At the *Temple of Love* Cairo had become a full-time bouncer, benevolent buffoon and the ultimate protector of the prima donnas, with his Cheshire cat grin that almost never left his face.

Billy Ray and Terri found Percy at an outdoor table by the patio dance floor. Terri ordered a Tequila Sunrise and tried not to feel Percy's eyes crawling over her.

Suddenly, Billy Ray wished he hadn't brought her to show her ass in Panama City. He wished so many things that never came true. Doing business with Percy always made him nervous and today was particularly bad.

Billy Ray owed Percy a grand because a bantam weight fighter didn't fall within the six rounds allotted for the knockout. Tough luck. Billy Ray didn't have the cash at the moment. Cairo had said that he would cover the debt. They needed Billy Ray's charter boat's expanded capacity.

Percy liked to keep the money square, but he was watching Terri Cates breathe. "How many times have I told you not to bet on bantam weight fights or two-year-old fillies," he chided Billy Ray,

"I just put a lot of my money into re-fitting the boat so we can bring in a thousand pounds next month," Billy Ray boasted, trying to stake out some territory for himself.

"Billy Ray, don't talk business around women, and don't gamble if you can't win. You wanna dance, honey?"

She hated being called honey. "You ain't very polite, and my name ain't 'Honey.'"

Percy stood. "I don't believe we've been formally introduced. Billy Ray, introduce me to the lady." He turned his attention to Terri, "My name's Drew Percy."

"Go on and dance with him, Terri."

"Only if he's a gentleman," she growled, then she turned a different face to Percy.

"My name is Terri Cates. My friends call me Terri the Pirate."

"Jesus Christ," Percy mumbled and pulled her from the table to the dance floor where she tried to hold her ground, but pressed together during the Kenny G ballad, he felt her up good. His hands knew where to be. She wanted out of Belle Rio bad enough that a little fooling around wasn't gonna hurt nothing, and Percy was her best shot. Percy was what Billy Ray said he was: not too handsome but dangerous enough. He offered her the opportunity she'd been waiting for.

She had a need for excitement that Percy could not resist. He said "Go on, honey. Get ready to perform. They're gonna make you gorgeous. You're not gonna be happy until you do this."

The Show Room at *Cleopatra's Temple of Love* was packed. Half-naked bodies waltzed through the colored strobe lights. The blonde Chaos from Detroit held center stage. Percy watched the Detroit Chaos with admiration. He still thought she was a bitch, but as long as she entertained the customers, she would keep the cash registers ringing, and he could live with that.

Mia was breaking in a customer who didn't know what to do at the ballet: "If you ain't spending money, honey, why don't you pack your tail to another club. We're working here. Don't come in an' just look. It ain't polite. You buy another drink and put some of them President's faces right here next to my g-spot where they can do me some good."

Tahlia straddled a rabid sports fan who was watching the Seminoles and Gators game on TV. He paid her for the duration of the contest and because the Gators usually won or lost on the last play of the game, she was confident that he would lose his before the Gators lost theirs.

Sybil, a statuesque bleach blonde wearing a black lace jumpsuit, was playing pool with three F-15 hotshot jet jockeys from the Air Base, where they spent their flight time shooting down drones in the target range over the gulf. Stretched over a pool table, she was a fine piece of work. And she was a good pool shot.

Percy watched Angie, the doe-eyed mulatto faun, who managed to hold herself aloof. She didn't want to be with bog trotter rednecks. She walked past him at the bar without a change of expression. She had the nerve to tempt and dare him. Somehow, he would pierce the veil. The mustard mulatto made him crazy.

Mother Teresa announced, "For her first appearance ever at *Cleopatra's Temple of Love*, Terri the Pirate, Goddess!" Terri emerged from the backstage in a golden see-through harem costume. She was ready for action, alive with fright.

Terri mounted the stage to Clarence Carter's *Strokin'* – the funk music routine she had rehearsed in front of her mirror for more than a year. This was her big break. It was not easy to stand out in this hotbed of flesh and alcohol fueled energy, but Terri managed. She had that stormy young aphrodisiac aura that men pay for. The crowd loved to see a neophyte ballerina get naked, the illicit appeal of a virgin dancer. She was graceful with a natural imperious attitude, a spirited unbroken filly; and yet she was still just a girl, an unformed tropical storm, not yet a hurricane. College boys, tourists, beach bums, sailors, and flyboys encouraged her as she slowly aroused herself to her first seductive moves. She flushed hot. Clarence Carter: *"I stroke it to the east, I stroke it to the west, stroke it to the woman that I love the best."* Her flesh glowed moist. The draped chiffon costume could not hide her explosive youth. Ballet aficionados and bar hounds howled. Boisterous celebrants stomped and hollered for flesh, wanting to see her sex act, and slowly the Pirate Goddess became one with the music. She shivered, squirmed, ran her hands over her body, squeezed her breast, head thrown back and finally lost in the groove. She grabbed the pole, wrapped her legs around it, nasty and vulgar, raised herself off the stage, and then slid down the pole. Her mouth made the shape of pleasure and she sang *Strokin'* with Clarence, and the ecstasy of exhibitionism took over.

Now she slowly revealed her booty. Got the response she wanted. Then she was coy and played the virgin prick tease she knew so well. It was all now her world. She vamped around the stage shaking her finger "no no no" to the sailors, then she peeled off the harem gown and revealed her excited nipples covered with gloss, shine and sparkle. She was on her own now, no turning back. She was hot. She slowly removed the transparent harem threads as Clarence Carter sang: *"and she said, if my thing ain't tight enough off you can shove it up my... woo! / Saying Clarence Carter, Clarence Carter."*

Then she exploded with her rehearsed stylish multiple spin move. Dropped to the floor, and lay on her back, legs in the air. Filled with a shameless burning, she climaxed under the hot lights to raucous applause.

Billy Ray was sick, his eyes glued to her, filled with hate and fear and awe of the nightmare he would never lose, but a dream he could never have.

Leaping to her feet, she shook her thinly covered booty in the jet jockey's smiling face and she was home free, taking money from strangers like she was already a professional.

After midnight Billy Ray drove in petulant, hostile silence for more than a dark hour from Panama City, through Mexico Beach to Port Royale, then east toward Belle Rio.

"Was I good, Billy Ray?" Terri just had to hear him say it.

"You like showing your stuff to strangers?"

"Was I good at it? That's what I want to know."

"You got a great body, Terri. What do you want me to say?"

"Was I good on stage? Did I act good?"

"You were great." He couldn't help but sound mad.

"It was just pretend, Billy Ray. I was a dancin' goddess."

Then she told him her secret: about how she planned to go out west and if that got him mad with her that was OK with her. She just didn't care anymore now that she'd done it, actually got on stage and done it. As long as she got past New Orleans this time. New Orleans was as far as she had ever been, and that was with a class trip, she said, and she got in trouble and had to sneak out of the hotel because she was supposed to be restricted, but she was going to see New Orleans, and there wasn't any way they was going to stop her from seeing New Orleans even if they had to leave her there. And they almost expelled her for the remainder of the school year. Like she cared and she told them so. She knew she was gonna get at least as far as Dallas, because she believed it was a real TV show, and then she'd go to Las Vegas because Las Vegas was THE show place. And then she was going to Los Angeles and maybe even

Malibu. Hollywood for sure. Like it was someplace that actually needed her. Had a place reserved for her on the *Wheel of Fortune*. It was her destiny—or her *Dynasty* or her *Knot's Landing*. They all meant the same thing to her, like a trip to the mall in Capital City. She didn't know the difference between reality and reruns. Like she cared one way or the other.

"Thanks, Billy Ray. You were sweet to do that for me. I showed my ass in Panama City and got paid for it. Without fucking nobody. Mama never done that."

CHAPTER FIFTEEN

The Net Ban Amendment

THE GODS CAN BE bountiful, but they can also be fickle. Two weeks of heavy rain and flooding in Georgia had closed the bay for oyster harvesting. The sight of coffins and stiffened livestock floating down the swollen river had not made people feel too good about the water quality. The bay oysters were a mirror image of their surroundings and sucked up all the pesticides and fertilizer from the Georgia soybean and peanut farms, so the bay would stay closed until the Marine Fisheries Commission declared the water free from harmful bacteria and the oysters safe for human consumption.

Adding insult to injury, the Marine Patrol had descended unannounced on shrimpers working in the Bay, issuing citations for equipment violations, and before the morning was over, they had effectively shut down the shrimp fleet. This action was the result of a dispute over shrimp size and body count, which had theoretically been resolved by a State Court ruling that had been considered meaningless and had never been enforced by the Marine Patrol until the shrimp started running big time, and suddenly every shrimp trawler registered from Texas to South Carolina was working off the Belle Rio coast. Then the MFC panicked, blew the whistle, and called in the Water Pigs.

Things would have to get better before life returned to normal in Belle Rio. But on this day in late September, a crowd of irascible shrimpers, out of work oystermen, and craggy-faced commercial fishermen had gathered at the riverfront dock by Hardaway's Gulf Seafood. Behind them, across the river, the brown marsh wetlands spread as far as the horizon. To the south, the bridge arched high above the town against the blue sky, and beyond that was the bay, the islands, and the open Gulf. The desperation and hostility in their voices punctuated the idyllic noonday.

A bearded shrimper with Bruto forearms threatened a newspaper photographer who looked like the urban environmentalist type that was their prototype enemy, along with the Marine Fisheries Commission (MFC), the Department of Natural Resources (DNR), the Marine Patrol (Water Pigs), the Sport Fishermen Association (Sons a Bitches), and the editorial writers for most of the state's major newspapers (Dumb Shits).

The gods were angry. So was everyone else. A voice vote was taken on their willingness to contribute money to hire an attorney to represent them on legal proceedings before the Federal District Judge and to seek a temporary injunction that would allow them to go back to work while the state courts reviewed the MFC regulations. Threats of violence accompanied the voting, most of it directed at the Marine Patrol for enforcing the damned regulations without first warning the locals about what was going on.

Bud Hardaway's oldest son, Donny Hardaway, had called their U.S. Congressman, who was in London for an economic development junket. Then he called their State Senator, who promised his help in the state legislature. He also had a brief conversation with the Governor and stated his observation that "these strong-willed men would resort to violence, if something wasn't done to get them back on to the water immediately." And to get the Marine Patrol off their backs permanently.

Television crews appeared with handsome anchors in tow and circulated among the waterfront crows getting defiant statements from angry shrimpers and other seafood workers. The spontaneous assembly was re-staged for the TV cameras: there was unanimous agreement, a loud voice vote, and a simultaneous show of hands. Today they were going to get what they wanted: their voices heard, their faces on TV, and a court injunction that would get them back on the water.

However, there was general suspicion that the entire event was a devious plot to get them all hot and bothered so they would do something rash and generate some bad publicity that could be used against them by the *Net Ban Amendment Coalition Committee*, that nefarious group of strange bedfellows which was circulating a state-wide petition to put a constitutional amendment on the ballot in the next general election. The amendment, if passed, would severely restrict and/or ban commercial net fishing in Florida waters, a concept that was sweeping the fisheries of America and had strong support in the metropolitan areas of the state of Florida.

The *Net Ban Constitutional Amendment* was going to be a tough fight. It was a well-funded coalition of environmentalists, pleasure boat manufacturers, sport fishermen, tourism promoters, and real estate developers who supported the drive to collect the 430,000 signatures necessary to get the Net Ban Amendment on the ballot. The "Save Our Sea Animals Committee" compared the shrimpers and commercial net fishermen to blood-thirsty buffalo hunters, with glossy highway billboards depicting sea turtle by-kill. They warned that soon the oceans would be as empty as the western plains, and there would be nothing left for the well-heeled vacationing sportsman in his power yacht.

An angry local sea captain asked the cardboard TV anchorman what was "sporting" about a $300,000 yacht with a GPS NorthStar Navigator and a Furno NAV Integrated Data Screen and a computer-enhanced Fish Finder, locating a prize Sailfish, dragging it until it was exhausted and near death, hauling it from the ocean depths for a glossy photograph, then mounting it on the condo wall. Maybe he was just stupid and backward and missed the point of all that fun.

They might win this first battle, but the beleaguered commercial fishermen were just beginning to realize that they would have to fight the Net Ban Amendment against heavy odds. They had not yet realized that they could not win the war, so they had no idea what would happen after they lost.

The following Monday morning, before the liquid sun climbed out of the water and rose over the barrier islands, the bay shrimp trawlers were temporarily back at work, their double outrigger green nets extended over each side like fragile butterfly wings. The court-ordered injunction allowed the shrimpers to continue working without having to re-rig their nets, and they could catch the smaller bay shrimp with the stipulation of a 57 count per pound. The 10% margin of error allowed them to take shrimp no bigger than your baby finger.

Then the weather changed and the MFC opened the bay for oysters the last week of October, just in time for *Festival! Belle Rio,* the yearly celebration of Neptune's bounty from the sea and Belle Rio's rich cultural history.

CHAPTER SIXTEEN

Festiva! Belle Rio

EUROPEAN HISTORY of Belle Rio began with a band of Conquistadors led by Panfilio de Navarez and his aide, the one they called Cabeza de Vaca, "Head of a Cow," because his large head with its ugly features sat cockeyed on the shoulders of his small twisted body.

The Spaniards left from Cuba in 1528 with 400 men, two women, 30 small horses for pack animals, killer dogs, and a dark moor, the personal traveling companion of Panfilio de Navarez.

Landing on the southern Gulf Coast of Florida, the Spaniards wandered northward through the swamps and lowlands and hostile natives until they reached the place they named Belle Rio. Their numbers considerably diminished, they made camp on the bluff overlooking the broad river, where they stayed six months, trading with the sometimes friendly Apalachee Indians.

Using their crude implements to build six small boats coated with pine tree resin, the foolhardy adventurers set sail in late autumn, hoping to meet up with their Conquistador brothers in Mexico City.

Gusting winds and high waves destroyed half the boats before they reached New Orleans.

Panfilio de Navarez drowned at sea, but Cabeza de Vaca and two boats beached on the coast of Texas, where they lived among the Indians for five years as powerful medicine men. Then they pushed westward, half naked, like savages.

Crowds of Indians followed them, fascinated by the strange pale skin of the Spaniards and the mysterious darkness of the moor, who had now become one of the leaders of the wandering Conquistadors.

The unfortunate moor was eventually killed in a skirmish with angry Zuni Indians in what is now New Mexico. Cabeza de Vaca, with a handful of Spaniards and a miscellaneous assortment of Indian slaves and concubines, arrived on the Gulf of California in 1542, the first Europeans to cross the North American continent.

Festiva! Belle Rio was an annual cultural bouillabaisse. Traffic from Capital City was bumper to bumper across the Five Mile Bridge and Belle Rio merchants were eager for seafood hungry tourists, snazzy island residents with money to burn, dull-witted muskrats from the swamps and loggers from the backwoods, hard-working families from the Port Royale pulp mill, cracker farmers and rednecks from the rolling clay hill country known as FloraBama, and the descendants of African slaves and renegade Indians of every hue and persuasion.

The wailing of police squad cars accompanied by the bleating of several fire trucks announced the celebration Parade, with the Grand Marshall, *King Retsyo*, holding an oyster trident as his totem of authority.

King Retsyo was surrounded on the float by the Royal Court of Belle Rio High School beauties. Above them, a huge inflatable plastic Spiderman floated through the air, tethered to a trinket merchant's cart loaded with Mickey Mouse knockoffs.

The Marine Corps Brass band played *The Halls of Montezuma*.

Young *Dance Academy* ballerinas twirled batons and performed their elaborately choreographed streetwalking routine in pink tights and turquoise tutus.

A country music singer belted out her hit single, *I'm Not That Kind of Girl,* from the back of a new Ford pickup.

Sullen, macho twelve-year-old *Pee Wee* football players looked bored, chewing gum; they couldn't chew tobacco in the parade.

Little Miss Belle Rio County, a six-year-old Barbie in a white formal gown, rode on the hood of a new Chevrolet convertible. Her proud, toothless grandmother waved from the passenger seat.

The Flag Corps of *VFW* old-timers repeated "left right left" so as not to forget.

The *Shaddai Temple* Band played hot Dixieland jazz and danced with women in the crowd, while the Shaddai Potentate rode in a silver Thunderbird with the Chief Raban, the High Priest & Potentate.

Marzuk Temple bandits drove dune buggy Hot Rods, reared on two wheels, and screeched figure eights along the crowded street.

Shriner Clowns performed silly balloon tricks. They made old people laugh and children cry.

The *Krewe of Bowleg*s Spanish Galleon float, sponsored by a popular Panama City Beach bar, exploded smoke and confetti from cannons. Cavaliers, wearing red satin shirts and broad brimmed hats with plums and swords, threw strands of pearls before swine and danced with naughty Elizabethan bar maids.

From a neighboring county came the *Osceola High School* Marching Band. The drum major pranced to an Afro-Cuban cadence, with the band members chanting a rhythmic call-response chorus, while the brass section played atonal harmonies, led by a tall thin trumpet player blowing solo with a flashy Dizzy Gillespie horn. Their scantily dressed majorette beauties sang tribal melodies, thrusting and gyrating, as they broke formation, morphed into a snake configuration, and slithered, curving and winding down the street, much to the delight of the crowd from the "Section" who grooved to the syncopated tribal rhythm and freeform expressionism.

Sister Salvation, a Black-Angel Diva, rode in a Cadillac DeVille convertible and belted gospel Motown Soul music. *Sister Salvation* was a comfort to all.

The afternoon crowd gathered at the bandstand, beneath the high bridge, for the famous *Festiva! Belle Rio Oyster Eating Contest.*

Big Huey, the defending champion from Panama City, was taking on the final round of challengers:

The local DJ personality announced the rules:

"Proper etiquette must be observed at all times, meaning what goes down must STAY down. If you regurgitate any oysters, you will be immediately disqualified. If you leave your seat, you are disqualified. If we run out of oysters before the time limit, the contestant who has swallowed the most oysters at that time will be declared the winner. The Judge's decisions are final. The Supreme Court of the USofA has NO jurisdiction over the *Festiva! Belle Rio!*"

"Gentlemen Start Your Eating!"

There was a spontaneous eruption of cheers from those in crowds who mostly came to see the barfing portion of the contest.

Big Huey inhaled the first dozen oysters.

"The world record for Oyster Eating Contest was set in 1975 by a fellow from New York City with a prodigious appetite. He ate 38 dozen and lived to tell about it!

"A total of more than 500,000 oysters have been eaten since the inception of the *Festiva!*

"Sally Osgood, the Smorgasbord Queen of the Panhandle, holds the record for most oysters eaten by a woman. She set the record in 1982. Today Sally owns and operates a brothel in Reno, Nevada."

By the closing bell, Big Huey and Fat Bobby White from Opelika had each polished off dozens of oysters with amazing synchronicity.

But Billy Watkins from Capital City was looking pale. He swooned and nearly fell out of his chair, then started turning green.

Someone yelled "Don't Barf Billy!"

But the crowd began chanting in unison, "Barf, Billy Barf!"

To the delight of the crowd, Billy lost it and began tossing his oysters over the back of the platform.

"Billy has been disqualified," announced the judge.

When the bell sounded, Big Huey stood behind the table looking stuffed and glazed over, but once again, he was the big winner: twenty-nine dozen.

In the twilight, walking away from the crowd, an African American brother from Capital City bragged to his woman on the sexual prowess derived from eating eight dozen oysters. She listened patiently to his braggadocio, but warned him that he had better perform or else she was going to leave *his* fat ass for a man that didn't need to take her to a backwater cracker town for a damn eating contest. What she wanted was a man that would stay home and eat catfish, a man who could keep his steam up all night long, without needing oyster "Afro-dizzy-acts."

CHAPTER SEVENTEEN

Roy Rogers & Bonnie

THE PRE-TRIAL HEARING for Robert E. Rogers' double homicide took place in a room adjacent to the Judge's chambers. Counselor Francois Taghert conducted this criminal matter like he was taking out the trash.

Mr. Rogers had undergone three psychiatric evaluations. The first doctor was not able to draw any meaningful conclusions because Mr. Rogers had refused to talk to him and refused to answer any of the questions on the MMPI, written or verbal. He told them that he didn't like Larry very much, and that was that.

The next two evaluations were conducted by Capital City clinical specialists, and the primary content of the discussions between the doctors and Mr. Rogers concerned the nature of the degree of recognition a fighting cock might have regarding his offspring, or that a young cock might have toward the rooster who sired him. It proceeded to the general theory of whether or not the lower species of animals, as they were commonly called, had any recognition of their "familial connectedness" and were therefore capable of having any meaningful emotional relation to immediate relatives.

Mr. Rogers conceded that the casual relation of "Cousin" was probably meaningless, and almost certainly a second or distant cousin was meaningless, according to his observations. But he was deeply concerned with the primary connection between father and son, or father and daughter, or between siblings, and their degree of awareness of that basic biological relationship, if indeed they had any knowledge of that relationship; and therefore, what emotional bonding, and/or what psychological conflicts, might be present in their competitive interaction, when engaged in a fight to the death with a known or unknown incestuously related offspring.

The hopeful, but somewhat mystified, psychiatrist allowed that recent studies with some higher mammals, particularly with elephants, whales, and certain primate groups, established the existence of a familial bonding which was discernable on a scale that was equivalent, or co-relevant, to human understanding of such relationships.

Primarily, Roy Rogers was concerned, whether or not, his prized fighting cock, was, for example, aware that he had bred with his daughter to produce the young rooster, who was to be placed in the ring, as his adversary to the death. Did the sire rooster acknowledge his daughter as his child and "lover", and thus vanquish his adversary/son as a competitor for the affection of the sister/daughter?

The psychiatrist then asked Mr. Rogers if he were aware of the Oedipal Complex, or the mythological tale of Oedipus Rex. But that line of discussion went nowhere. When the examiner mentioned Doctor Sigmund Freud, Mr. Rogers stated that the only doctor he knew was a pep pill dispenser in Galveston.

Further questioning led to a recounting by Mr. Rogers of his prized fighting cock, Alfredo, who was slain in "gladiator combat" by his son, Pepe, at a Bandera, Texas ranch sporting event.

Mr. Rogers seemed to believe that Alfredo refused to kill Pepe because he realized that Pepe was his son, and he was therefore, killed by the savage young rooster who, possibly, knew no father. An event which seemed to cause Mr. Rogers great sadness.

"We were able to get no information from Mr. Rogers regarding the specific events of the alleged homicides with which he has been charged. It is our opinion, at this time, that Mr. Rogers is not able to understand the proceeding against him, nor capable of participating in preparing his defense for the crimes with which he has been charged."

Counselor Taghert made a formal request that Mr. Rogers be committed to the state mental hospital until they could establish his competency to receive a fair trial.

Assistant State's Attorney, Ronnie Smith, stated his opinion that it was more likely that Roy Rogers definitely had a mind of his own, and that he knew he could bamboozle the court appointed psychiatrists, until he had time to figure out what price he was willing to pay for what he had done. The Circuit Court Judge hemmed and hawed for a full twenty minutes before he granted Counselor Taghert's request.

They rolled into town in a battered Toyota with expired Texas plates. She was a trim-figured sprite who looked about fifteen, but radiated a determined worldly provocative attitude. She needed it.

Her companion was gaunt and bored. He waited for her in the foyer of the second-floor landing outside the courtroom, smoking one cigarette after another beneath the "No Smoking" sign, sitting in the open window across the street from the Victorian Inn, watching the traffic roll down off the bridge. He looked like he had probably been in several courthouse dramas and did not want to audition for a part in this local saltwater production.

Attorney McCutcheon, accompanied by a deputy, took Mr. Rogers up the stairs to a small, sparse room behind the Judge's Chamber, near the courtroom where the girl, woman-child, waited for him.

He repeated to Mr. Rogers exactly what he had told him before: "There's a young woman here to see you. She told me she was your daughter."

"Why'd she come here?"

"She said it was important to her."

"How did she know where I was?"

"I contacted her because she was Betty's daughter. You won't have much time with her."

Even though handcuffed, shackled, and wearing a day-glo Orange County prisoner's orange jump suit, Roy Rogers struggled to maintain his cowboy swagger. His weathered face was now sallow, but he was still proud and defiant.

Attorney McCutcheon opened the door and Roy disappeared into the small conference room, alone, his own hell.

"Are you alright, Roy?" The young girl's voice like shattered glass.

Roy twisted in agonizing silence. He became a pale hollow ghost.

"I'm sorry, Bonnie. You mother..." His barely audible voice dried and vanished.

"I know you didn't expect to see me, Roy. I really didn't mean to come. I don't know why. Your lawyer called and said I could see you... I told him I was your daughter. So, I just come here. I didn't expect to see you. I just come here. I didn't mean to. I just drove here with Jimmy."

"Larry had it coming."

"I don't blame you, Roy. I mean, you shouldn't a done it. Look where it got you."

"I done what I had to do."

"You shouldn't a done it, Roy."

"Did they let her go in peace? Or did that son-of-a-bitch preach the wages of sin?"

"They got buried side by side. You shoulda been there."

"I could do without that."

"She loved you, Roy. I always known that. Larry meant nothing to her."

"Larry begged to die."

"I'm going to Dallas. I'm gonna live with Betty's sister. I'm gonna have a baby. I'm only sixteen. Can I change, Roy?"

"Yeah, sure you can, Bonnie. You can."

"Jimmy wants me to go to California with him."

"But Bonnie…"

"I can't leave until after the baby. Maybe he won't want me then. I can change, Roy. I have to go somewhere. I don't have nobody."

"You have me, Bonnie. I can make it right."

"We can't, Roy."

"I want you."

"Don't you see? It's wrong. It can't ever be right."

"I'll make it up to you. I won't try and hold you. We can move somewhere else, anywhere. It don't matter where."

'It can't work. Not now."

"You can start over. We can start over," he pleaded.

"It's too late, Roy."

Silence surrounded them.

"I won't try an' hold on to you, I promise. … Please, Bonnie. Don't close your mind to it."

"My own mother, Roy. Did you kill her?"

"We can be a family."

"You shoulda been there, with us, Roy… During all those years. You shoulda been there. It coulda been different."

"I want you, Bonnie."

"God…" her fragile voice pierced his desire. "I don't stand a chance, do I?"

"You stand a chance with me Bonnie. I'll make it up to you."

"You shoulda been there."

"I hated to miss it."

"You shoulda been there, Roy … Larry moved in. I was young. It was a mistake … Houston was … What can I do … now?"

"Buried side by side, huh? After all that."

"She felt somethin' special for you Roy. I always wanted you to be my Daddy, Roy. … Are you my Daddy, Roy?" Her voice disappeared in the vast, awkward silence.

Roy was stranded on the road to Damascus, grappling with the damn Angel, the damn Devil. He wanted to hold her, but he was constrained by the shackles on his legs, and he stumbled and fell to the floor, fighting to deny his consuming desire to possess her. He struggled to his knees, hands outstretched in supplication. His breathing stopped. His body drained of all but the desire for her.

He gasped, "I want you, Bonnie. What more can I do? I killed him for you, Bonnie … For us."

"Roy, I can't."

She began to cry, backing toward the door in the sudden cold, frightened, lonely.

Roy Rogers was stranded on his knees, doomed to Hell. He tried to stand, lurched toward her, and fell to the floor.

"Bonnie, please."

But she was gone.

She was gone forever, fleeing past the courthouse guard, past the lobby of milling spectators, to the cowboy Jimmy, who crushed his cigarette with the heel of his boot on the marble floor and followed her down the stairs to the battered Toyota with the expired Texas plates.

They traveled toward Galvaston in a cloud of dark exhaust.

CHAPTER EIGHTEEN

Search for Father

HE HAD SEEN and heard plenty. Her voice reverberated piteously in Matthew's head. "Are you my daddy, Roy?"

Roy Rogers sang "Happy Trails to You." Roy had convinced him that he had not killed Betty, but that he had killed the S.O.B. Larry in self-defense. Cuffed and shackled, he pleaded to young Bonnie, that he had killed Larry for her.

Damn. It was depressing. And he realized that it was a great, misguided passion, not reason, not legal. Not rational. A passion for his daughter, Bonnie. Passion of the young cock, Pepe, who killed his father, Alfredo, because Alfredo refused to kill his son. He loved his son, and the sister mother. Maybe none of this was true. Maybe none of it ever happened. Whatever it was, he needed a break from the law.

Matthew traveled west. He knew that he had been with Attorney Francois Taghert long enough, but he also knew that his time with Taghert was not complete. The hostility between he felt for Taghert left a bitter bile in his gut. But he couldn't blame it all on Taghert.

He was lonely. He had not thought of Anne for more than a year. He had survived a close encounter with wandering Venus. She was harmless, unlike her dangerous daughter. He needed a break from Belle Rio, and he had a longing to connect with himself, somewhere. He wanted a cigarette. He hadn't had a cigarette in almost four years.

He spent the night in a cheap motel west of Mobile, and was alone except for the ghosts that embellished his childhood memories and fantasies. It was the past he needed to keep and the past he needed to let go. Etched in his memory was the war time telegram, and a faded letter: "I'll admit I didn't know as much about your mother as I thought I did before the war, but after I return…" Yeah sucker, when you return you might discover that it was Francois Taghert, Esq. or some other stateside swashbuckler, with a Medal of Devotion to the Spoils of War, that knocked her up.

Margaret Patterson had been a full-bosomed brunette beauty with an easy smile, a teacher, a social worker, a court clerk, a good-looking woman in a bathing suit. And as she told it, a secret lover of the real Tarzan, Johnny Weissmuller, while he was filming *"Tarzan Finds a Son"* at Wakulla Springs, the Garden of Eden, the first magnitude Fountain of Youth. Who could resist Tarzan? The Call of the Wild? Unlikely, the Tarzan paternal fantasy. Though he often wished it to be true. Saturday matinees he sat in the darkened theaters and wished it to be true.

"Boy, Tarzan son. Tarzan man. Tarzan love Jane and Boy."

He only knew what she had told him. And it wasn't that much.

Pearl Harbor put everyone on a short string, and it was the Christmas season. Franklin McCutcheon, was stranded temporarily in Capital City. Margaret asked him to help her deliver packages on Christmas Eve.

When they finished the deliveries, he suggested that they open his bottle of Old Overholt. It was his birthday.

"I thought I was going to drink alone," he said.

They talked about the avalanche of war, the price of nylons, the value of education, and the taste of Old Overholt. It was the December birthday kisses that sealed their fate.

Before he reported for duty in the north Atlantic, he took Margaret to Mississippi to meet his mother.

Catherine McCutcheon wondered out loud what kind of young woman would travel alone with a man, to whom she was not married. He told his mother that he was planning to marry Margaret, but that he had not asked her yet. Certainly, Margaret was not the kind of woman she wanted for a daughter-in-law.

Franklin left for training without asking her. But in December '42, he wrote and asked, that if it were not too inappropriate, would she meet him in Washington D.C. He enclosed a train ticket.

When they met at the train station in D.C., he thought he would turn to stone if he didn't get the words out of his mouth immediately, and then, suddenly they poured out, stumbled and bumbled and confused and awkward, while they gathered her luggage. She responded, "Yes, you silly sailor." They kissed again and it was nobody's birthday. They got married that weekend.

An emergency blackout was declared as the simple civil wedding service ended. The lights went out throughout the city. In a cold drizzle rain they walked the darkened streets to their hotel, where they were given two candles at the front desk and told to keep the curtains closed.

They made love to the wailing sirens, and she sang the Jimmy VanHeusen hit, *Darn That Dream,* with her mellow contralto voice in the flickering candlelight, *"Darn your lips / darn your eyes / lift me high above the stormy skies / I tumble out of paradise / darn that dream /... you say you love me and you hold me tight / but when I awake / you're out of sight... Darn that dream."*

With the winter morning light coming through the shuttered windows, on a single bed in the small hotel room she said, "Sweet man, please come home to me."

Standing on the train platform in the darkened tunnel, she wanted to cry. She tried not to say goodbye. A little bird had once told her that words were dead sentiment, and so it was hard to say anything at all. But she quietly said, "Your touches, your glances cannot steal my heart's treasure." And finally, she said to him, "Please don't leave."

Then he left, and she cried. Certainly, she hadn't meant to cry. She prayed that she would see him again, no matter what.

She only saw him three times after that night. Slowly, surely, the make-believe world caved in, and only the dream lingered on. Then it faded from memory, like the dream it was. Maybe it was better that way, that there was only the melody to remember.

One thing was for certain, she had told herself before the marriage—that she was a tough modern girl and that neither love nor death could take her for a ride. But despite her promise to herself, her legs had been knocked out from under her. She truly believed that the painful rainy night of romance would never come again, as she waited through the many nights that followed. When a familiar song was played on the radio, or raindrops fell, or an evening breeze stirred the trees, it would bring a cruel smile to her lips.

Her mind refused to come up with a new dream that could satisfy her need, because he had gone and nothing had taken his place.

"Love was such a disappointment," she said.

Late in the afternoon Matthew was lost on a county road north of McComb, Mississippi, where he remembered that his father's family had settled sometime around 1830. There was only a vague recollection of the old cemetery plot which he had visited, years ago, after Mardi Gras, as he meandered from New Orleans to Nashville, using the hand drawn map his mother had scribbled with her uncertain memory.

He couldn't find the Bogue Chitto Primitive Baptist Church which was his guide post. He stopped to ask for help from a taciturn old farmer who was standing by the side of the road, kicking his dog. The old man admitted that he couldn't read a map, even if he had one. Matthew made a joking comment about "his arms being too short."

The farmer just looked at him without smiling. He couldn't read and it was no laughing matter.

The man said, stone serious, "Listen to me carefully. I ain't gon tell ya this but once. Go down past tha holler an over the crick, and when ya crest up over the hill, they'll be a sign that says 'Chew Tobacco'. Then ya veer to tha lef at the crossroads, not the paved road but the dirt 'un. Then when ya git to tha river bottom. If ya pass the soy beans, you gon' too far. It's right there somewhere abouts."

Matthew thanked him and went looking for the sign that said *Chew Tobacco* and he veered to tha lef'. When he got to the river bottom, before the soybean field, he drove slowly. He didn't want to go too far. Not after what he'd been through. And sure enough, down in the holler was the Bogue Chitto Hard Shell Baptist Church.

He pondered the difference between 'Primitive' and 'Hard Shell' as he wandered through the small cemetery. It was not what he was looking for. Not a McCutcheon in the ground. The afternoon was quiet and still except for a mockingbird high in the poplar tree. He thought, that if he waited long enough, there would be a gravestone somewhere with his name on it.

An elderly man parked at the church. He had come to visit his wife. Matthew asked if he knew where there was a small family plot near a different Bogue Chitto Baptist Church, not this one, but another one. And he told the man that it had been his father's dying wish that he make this pilgrimage to the family plot. The friendly old man tried his best to figure out where that might be, but he could not think of another Bogue Chitto Church. Finally, he said, "I wish some of the old folks was around who could help you, but most of 'em's already dead."

Matthew went back to the *Chew Tobacco* sign. This time took the paved road, and less than a mile he stopped at a little crossroads store. He asked the clerk if he knew of any grave sites off in the fields or wooded areas. He told the clerk, "at least three generations of the McCutcheon family were buried somewhere in the county. My great great grandfather had owned half the county around 1830. Or so I have been told."

The clerk said that he had heard of such a place on the good-looking widow's farm, but it was not near a Bogue Chitto Church. Since he was closing, he said he would be glad to take him up there.

The widow was on her riding lawn mower when they drove up and she was glad to stop. She wasn't that good-looking but she was glad to have company. She said that over the years a variety of McCutcheon people came and wandered her woods looking for the burial site. She said that the logging company would've torn up the grave site, but she made them leave the hill alone where the old McCutcheon family was buried. They had a cup of coffee and chocolate fudge while she failed to located a copy of the abstract, which dated back three generations. The widow was glad to talk about that, or anything else. She had little interest in other people's grave site, and none in her own.

It was cool on the hillside, which was still covered with tall oaks and sweetgum. There was a view of the rolling countryside fading in the dusk. In the slowly fading afternoon, they went tromping along a rutted road, thru what had been pasture land, and the big fellow said that he was a wanderer at heart. He used to drive a Peterbilt to Omaha and back, once a week. He said he missed being on the road where every damn body didn't know where he was every damn minute of the day.

His granddaddy had built the store at the corner of the road to McComb. Then his daddy had run it, but he was dead. Now there was only him and his Ma.

Years ago, all this had been the McCutcheon family dairy farm. It had grown back in timber and the uplands hardwoods had been logged out.

Just before dark, on a hillside that was a mess of scrub tree rubble and bulldozer tracks, they located five grave markers, inside a wrought iron fence. Barely legible: *Alister McCutcheon, born 1800* etched beneath the Masonic emblem on the tallest stone. *Died 1880.* And beside him, his wife, *Elizabeth 1812-1850.* A crumbling stone for *John, born: 1832 died 2001.* And a stone for *Angus McCutcheon: Born 1848 – Died 1865. In a pointless Calvary skirmish in North Mississippi.* And two markers for children, crumbling beyond recognition.

Matthew closed his eyes but nothing happened and he was relieved.

They drove back to the corner store in drowsy silence until the big fellow spoke in his soft Mississippi drawl.

"Like I said, I been on the road most of my life and never cared what the old timers knew, but now I am one. I guess I better learn some of it. Used to be when I was little, I could go sit on my grand pa's knee when I was hurt or had a question. He had the answer and could make it right. When he died and I had a problem, I would go to my dad. Now I got nobody. Just me. I'm the old man. And I aint got any kids to look after me. I still want somebody to say, 'Tom, you done good. Everything's gonna be alright.' Hell, I don't know the answer to anything." They rode a while in silence, then Tom said, "Aint that pitiful."

In McComb, Matthew parked along the curb in front of a faded Victorian style house in an old residential neighborhood. The house was in need of repair, having surrendered years before to both forgetfulness and benign neglect.

An elderly man carried a ladder from around the back of the house. His walk was erratic and clumsy, and he struggled to get the ladder up against the roof of the house. He staggered back out of sight, then returned, carrying a bucket and a toolbox.

Matthew walked from the car toward the busy man and asked, "Is this Catherine McCutcheon's house?"

The man stopped dead in his tracks. His body began a slow steady tremor, and he glared at Matthew suspiciously and mumbled something mostly unintelligible, then turned awkwardly to his ladder, angry with someone, and spastically began adjusting the ladder against the house.

Matthew waited for a reply that did not come. "Thanks," he said and walked to the porch, knocked on the screen door, and waited. He knocked again. There was low static music coming from a radio inside. Soon a slight, trim elderly woman peered at him from the shadows.

"We don't need any," she said curtly.

"Is this Mrs. Catherine McCutcheon's house?"

"Well, what if it is? She doesn't need any either."

"My name is Matthew McCutcheon, Franklin's son. I called earlier and left a message."

"Is that so?" she said with her face pressed against the screen. "Who did you say you are?"

"Mrs. McCutcheon's grandson. Franklin's son."

"Franklin's dead."

"Yes Ma'am. He is... is Mrs. McCutcheon home? Could I speak with her?"

"Well, if you know Franklin."

"I'm his son."

She cautiously opened the screen door. "Well, aren't you a sight. You're all grown up. I didn't recognize you. Come in here."

He followed her into the darkened foyer. The smells of the past were suffocating, when combined with the actual presence of old age, illness, and death.

"You don't remember me?"

"No Ma'am." He had never seen her before.

"Well, if you are Franklin's son, I am your Aunt Victoria." She straightened up and stood proudly. She wanted that to sink in. She really was a tiny woman. Not five feet tall. Her hair tightly wrapped in a bun.

"Catherine's husband's sister. I'm ninety-four years young and getting younger every day." She spoke with a soft broad Mississippi old south accent. Then she yelled, "Elli! Elli! Get in here."

A black woman, every bit as petite as Victoria, came in from the long hallway. Dressed in what was reminiscent of a maid's uniform.

"Elli, get this young man a glass of cold tea and tell Miss Catherine that she's got a visitor. Come into the parlor. Franklin's son. I do declare."

He followed her into the parlor. It was the only room that retained any semblance of cleanliness and order, and that still left a lot of clutter, photos, books, an old upright piano, a threadbare couch, and several over-stuffed chairs layered in cloth unaccounted for. He stood awkward and uncertain. Now that he was actually in the house, he had no idea why. He was felt lacking in the social skill of dealing with these aged relatives. Margaret had not included them in her life, so he was meeting perfect strangers, who could not have been more strange, than at this moment.

Victoria maneuvered her prim little figure graciously onto one end of the sofa, folded her hands in her lap, and smiled pleasantly.

"Did you meet your Uncle Charlie?" Outside the parlor window, the wooden ladder leaned against the house, and Uncle Charlie labored with his bucket of tools to the roof.

"Yes. He was working with the ladder."

Victoria said proudly, "I'm Captain Scott McCutcheon's sister. He was the pride of the U.S. Army, and a bit of a rogue in his time." Her eyes twinkled. "The boy was a fine young man until the Great War when he ran off and enlisted following his brother, Robert. He followed him everywhere. He died in Europe too. Both of them. Scotty was my favorite boy, but I've already lived longer without him than he did. I raised them all after mother died birthing Scott. Mary Lynn wasn't good for much, but Daddy liked her."

Catherine McCutcheon was wheeled into the room by Elli, the nurse. She was no bigger than Victoria and less alive. She was mostly blind, and her faculties were diminished by age and disappointment.

"Catherine, this is your grandson."

"I'm Franklin's son, Matthew," he said. He took her hand and held it, not knowing if he was supposed to kiss her or flee. And this was after many years of trying to take care of his mother. The cloudy cataract eyes revealed nothing, but her hand squeezed his with a strong grip that was more frightening than comforting.

"Franklin's dead," the small voice quivered.

"He knows that, Catherine. Franklin drowned against Japan."

"I had five children. Four of them are dead."

Elli entered carrying a dark silver tray with three tall glasses of tea and little napkins. "Y'all gone want anything else?"

"Elli, you go and tell Charlie to come down off the roof," Victoria said firmly. "He knows he's not supposed to clean those gutters."

"Yes, Ma'am."

"Charlie's all I got left," Catherine said. "And he's got the chorea."

"You've got a fine grandson, Catherine. This young man came all the way here just to see you."

She still held on to his hand. "He came with that woman. She was a Jezebel."

"Catherine, she was the woman Franklin loved. She was very talented. You remember her. She sang so pretty and played the piano. Franklin brought her home before they married. Before the war. Young man, you favor her, I do believe."

"Franklin was like your brother. Liquor and Satan's music."

"Then you straightened out my Scotty, Catherine?" It was a question with more than a small portion of pique. "It's time you faced the truth old gal. My brother died in a brothel in Italy."

"You like to say that. Scotty was a war hero."

"Yes, he was. But he died in the arms of a, what do you young people call those women? Truth is what we want it to be. It's easier to remember that way."

There was a noise from Uncle Charlie on the roof. The hammer dropped. And the bucket of nails rolled off the roof.

"Get him down! What's he doing?" Catherine was agitated.

"Elli! Elli!" Victoria screamed.

Through the window, Elli could be seen hollering and gesturing at Uncle Charlie.

"I never knew my father." Matthew said. He wanted to say something meaningful, but it was neither the time nor place.

"He never should've divorced that nice girl."

"His sister died the same year."

"She was sick."

"Mother said."

"A sinner that woman. Marrying a divorced man. What could she say about that? Franklin never should've married two women. I told him so.

Elizabeth was my daughter when we lived in the Philippines. I told Scott if we kept on, the kids would never have a home. That woman lied to Franklin. She may have sung like a bird, but he never should've married her."

"Catherine, you know you lived in the Philippines before you met Scotty. Carrying the gospel."

"You cannot ignore the way of God, Franklin. Scott was a hero. But he was always at war. Victoria, you must make him go. My other son was only six. He died. All the McCutcheon men died in France and Korea. Victoria knows all about Korea. She knows and won't tell." Catherine became even more agitated. "Go away! I can't see you now."

"Yes, I'm sorry, Mrs. McCutcheon," Matthew spoke softly.

Uncle Charlie fell from the roof with a loud crashing of ladder and tools, Elli screaming at him as he came flying backwards holding onto the ladder, waving his arm, flailing the air.

"Charlie! You idiot," prim little Victoria shouted.

Matthew rushed out into the yard where old Charlie lay stunned on the ground. As he struggled to stand, convulsive movements contorted his body, his arms swinging wildly out of control.

The fall could have killed an ordinary person. Brusquely, he refused help, then he stumbled drunkenly, twitching, banging against the side of the house while he continued making unintelligible threats and gesturing toward them until he was at the far corner of the house, where he turned and yelled, "I don't need you! None of you! Now get your butt outta my damn yard!"

CHAPTER NINETEEN

La Coquette

WHILE THIN LAYERS of pink chiffon clouds floated motionless in the evening sky, hordes of insects swarmed the lights over the football field like something the Pharaoh saw in his worst dreams, seven years of nightmare visions fading in the twilight. Cougar cheerleaders jumped and tumbled and strutted along the sideline beneath insect laden mercury vapor lights, their squeaking hoarse voices chanting in singsong unison, without knowledge or concern for the outcome of the struggle being waged by the warriors on the field of glory behind them. This was football country, where they got their butts kicked early, coaches yelling,

"This ain't supposed to be fun! This ain't church! You ain't gotta be nice! Kick their butts before they kick yours!"

Matthew and Liana had gone to the high school Football Jamboree because that's what there was to do, and then she was staying over at his house because the roof leaked in her apartment at the motel and they were remodeling the motel, and there were a litany of reasons for them being together, but mainly it was nice to have companionship, so they had developed a comfortable but boring, cozy but frustrating relationship, where they cooked and ate together several times a week, and she slept in one of the upstairs bedrooms while he used the other, although they would occasionally sleep in the same room like an old married couple on the twin beds that were pushed together and made a rambling, comfortably safe double bed. And he still wanted what he could not have.

Liana had fallen asleep in the front upstairs bedroom with the light on, covered with unread magazines. She worked hard at the motel and was exhausted by the time she got to bed. Reading was a pretense she had learned in rehab.

He turned out the light, opened the shutters, and lay down on the bed beside her. She mumbled something, and he acknowledged that he was probably better off well-fed than well-loved. She had been true to her word: there was no spark, no flame, no fire. They had become friends. They didn't mess around.

He got used to the darkness and silence, then he could hear her breathing, then the wind picked up and the waves sloshed against the beach, like water spilling over the edge of a large bowl. The half-moon was late rising, and it filtered through the shutters across the room. The famous forbidden planet was snoring. He suspected that somewhere in the universe she was still the wandering, mysterious Venus.

The wind was blowing, and the palm trees were snapping like palace guard dogs. When it started to rain, he drifted off to sleep, not unhappy, but he slowly disappeared into a cyclonic dream. Each moment produced an erotic reverie. Belle Rio nymphs, exhibitionist Cougarettes in pink and turquoise tutus, swirled and frolicked around gnarled tree stumps at low tide. The image became the young wife he could not forget. No, no don't tell me. Let me guess. They were riding in a gondola on the Chicago River, winding between the cold steel and shattered glass, with an aria from an Italian comic opera. The gondolier was passionate in expressing his love for Pollyanna, a perfumed Courtesan, displeased by exotic French cuisine. All the baritones were laughing while the chorus of sopranos sang Mozart's *Requiem Mass*. The slow, sad song became the familiar wartime songs that played on the radio. The young Lieutenant McCutcheon left, never returned, and his mother cried. He thought he was sweating, but it was raining instead. Uncle Charlie was banging on the roof. He did not know why. Who were these two old women? The little maid brought iced tea. Grandfather Scott was a war hero and died in an Italian brothel. That makes sense. But not: who exactly was Uncle Charlie? A son of his father's mother? Or the younger brother of the woman married to the Lt. McCutcheon's mother? And what was he doing in Korea that made him fall off the roof? That makes no sense. Did he have the chorea? He was so herky-jerky. The old soldier Scott becomes grotesque. In a bright empty room. He grimaces in pain, open and closing his mouth like he is eating something distasteful. Meaningless sounds escape his throat. Repeating garbled phrases in repetitious litany. A bewildered face fills his vision, the wild uncomprehending stare, frightening, young Matthew wanting to escape from this nightmare. Emptiness glows through the old man's eyes like a victory celebration. He struggles to speak, words slurred, unintelligible "… sssweearr … it … uuu… noooottt mmmmyyy ssooo…nnn." To the soundtrack of *Love is a Many Splendored Thing*? Or was it *From Here to Eternity*? Which became the overture to Harry Truman's famous *Macabre Mikado for Violin and Genetic Mutation in D Minor*. It was a military symphony; the U.S. suffered heavy casualties to subdue worthless Okinawa, then it was time for "Nuke 'em Harry" to take out Hiroshima and Nagasaki and let history decide what price glory and shame and honor and infamy went with a tough call. The buck stopped with Harry. His picture ought to be on money! But it was just the black and white *Movie Tone News:* General Douglas McArthur smoking his pipe in a Popeye the Sailor Man cartoon, then the Saturday afternoon matinee, where Tarzan discovers Jane and the naked Zulus dancing to the mating pandemonium of elephants.

Matthew woke up from this crazy jumbled dream and lay in the dark. A truck passed along the highway in the distance. He slipped away from Liana, as she mumbled something about the dessert menu needing a French twist. He couldn't have agreed more. And went downstairs to get a drink. It was still raining, and the wind was blowing hard, and the old house creaked and shuddered. He heard voices coming from his office across from the kitchen. He opened the door and wished he hadn't.

"So, were you making mama happy?" drawled Terri Cates, lounging on the sofa in a pair of Levi cutoffs, smoking a cigarette with the TV getting poor reception of an old black and white movie. Liana's daughter, Terri the Pirate, was a dangerous caricature, a pent-up fold out.

"I didn't know you were here," he stammered, standing in the doorway, not quite middle-aged heavy, held in thrall by an undeniable, impending catastrophe.

"Yeah, well I knew Mama was here and I got in a fight with that stupid dumb ass Billy Ray and I come over here, and the door was open so I come in. You don't mind, do you?"

"No, I don't mind."

"I was just gonna sleep on the sofa."

"What happened to staying at Crystal's house?"

"They was fighting over there, and I needed some peace and quiet."

"You came to the right place."

"Yeah, right. I thought you slept in the nude. Those some funky jammie bottoms."

He didn't really know what to say. It was prelude to being road kill.

"You want a beer?" he asked.

"I got one already," she stated.

"Yes, you do. Make yourself at home then."

"Hell, why not. Mama did."

"We're friends."

He went into the kitchen and poured himself a shot glass of Stoli from the bottle in the freezer and opened a beer. Against better judgement, he walked back into the study. He didn't go back upstairs like he knew he should. Feeling reckless but vulnerable, unable to flee, he sat in his swivel chair by his desk across from the sofa.

"That Billy Ray is such a dumb shit."

"He's maybe a little slow on the draw."

"Not with his pecker he ain't."

"I wouldn't know about that."

"I just let Billy Ray hold his own pecker."

"I bet that makes him happy."

"Not really. Like I give a shit."

"What do you give a shit about?"

"He's got a nice car. He took me to Panama City and introduced me to some fancy club people."

"That sounds impressive."

"Yeah. Means I danced naked in front of some drunk sailors and old farts and college boys. I showed my ass in Panama City and didn't have to fuck nobody. It's a damn site better than changing the bedpans in that damn motel one more day."

"Sounds like a new career to me. Liana works hard too."

"Like a damn wetback!" She tossed her beer can at the waste basket, but it missed and fell lopsided against the wall.

"Missed. Mind if I have another?"

"I'm not your mother."

"No, and you ain't my father either," she cautioned as she sauntered toward the door to the kitchen, barefooted. Her cutoffs barely clung to her hips. "So don't get no curious notions 'bout me," she challenged as she disappeared into the kitchen.

He moved to the edge of the sofa near the TV and surfed the three black and white channels, wishing he had cable, wishing he didn't feel so hungry and defenseless, wishing he could flee. He sat staring at an old Lana Turner movie with a square-jawed leading man, and again he thought he should get cable; there would be more to watch. He knew if he were gone when she came back, it would be over. But he wasn't.

"I could work at that club in Panama and make lots of money," she said, posing provocatively in the doorway.

"You could," he almost drooled. "Yes, you could." Who needed Lana Turner on late night black and white TV, when this was in lurid color.

"Why can't boys be more like real men," she said. "Billy Ray's just a boy. I mean, he's older than me, but he's—"

"The best shot you got."

"Bingo." She pointed her finger at him like a pistol and shot him. Drank her beer. "And I like his car. And now I know an important person in Panama City that likes my style."

"And I bet he's rich."

"Nobody's rich in Belle Rio. I mean really rich."

"Mr. Hardaway does alright."

"*Alright* ain't good enough."

"What would be good enough?" he asked.

"A man," she answered, pausing for dramatic effect while she thought about it more seriously, then added, "a man with money, lots of money."

She was perched on the arm of the sofa facing him. He was helpless prey.

"I guess you know all about Mama?"

"I know enough," he said.

"Tommy was her man, but Tommy made her mad."

"That's what I hear."

"And you took his place."

"Not exactly. I wouldn't want to end up the same way."

"Lightning don't never strike twice in the same place."

"That so?"

"Was you up there making Mama happy?"

"She was asleep. She seemed happy."

He could feel the air dry up in the room. She was inhaling it and it was condensing in her and making her wet.

"You could make me happy," she said barely audible.

His throat clenched and he swallowed. It was probably getting noticeable. He twitched and it was the only movement in the otherwise unmoving, unbreathing room.

"You're a *coquette*," he said, stalling for time. It was his best shot.

"A what?" Her body odor exuded a sweet-tinged mixture of Wal-Mart perfume, alcohol, and stale cigarettes that hung in the air with reckless availability.

"A *coquette* teases men."

"Spell it."

"*Coquette.* C-o-q-u-e-t-t-e. Coke-ette, like a ma-jor-ette."

"She twirls batons."

"You're getting close."

"A *cock-ette*? You mean like a prick tease?"

"That's right, but it's pronounced *coquette*—it's French."

"She plays with men's toys. A growed-up Tomboy."

"That's correct, she plays at sex without love."

"This ain't about love. I don't really know nothing about love, you know, because my dad was Terri the Pirate, that stupid shit. He left Mama before I got enough love, and now I can't get enough."

"Enough what?"

"Sex without love. Like you do with Mama."

"Not exactly. We don't engage in… sex… often…" He said it quietly, awkwardly, formally, like he was proud of it, but it sounded stupid. "Actually, we don't have sex. We're just friends."

"Say you love her!" She waited.

He stared blankly at the corner of the television beyond the rim of his vodka, and he couldn't say it.

"I know you want to fuck her. I've watched you look at her the way all them men look at her. It's their first thought, if you want to call it that, outta their tiny dick brains. Say it. At least say you want to fuck her."

He couldn't say that either.

"What I'm trying to say," he said, "What I'm not saying… that we're not, that I, that you, you're not. I'm sure you're good at whatever it is. Do you call it making love?"

"It's just sex," she assured him. "When I let them. Which ain't very often."

He should have moved but he was held in place by the inevitability of sex. She slid from the arm of the sofa effortlessly onto his lap, straddled him, and pulled her shirt over her head, her breasts in his face, daring him with hard eyes and flagrant mouth. He kissed her scented nipples and she swooned and pressed down against him. She grappled to open his shorts. His mind was lost. The fragrant odor of sex consumed the memory of faith and trust, the unfulfilled desires, the failure of love, the constant presence of death. She whispered "hard hard" while he kissed her and she writhed against him, and he actually thought that he could

161

be tempted and resist, because he had learned that it was rarely worth the trouble.

"This is gonna be worth it," he thought she said before her mouth covered his.

And then the sun rose from the void where nights and days run together. The water along the Belle Rio coast was murky with wind-curled whitecaps. The sky was turbulent, the wind still blowing a moody passionate lament. Overhead in the thick clouds, he could hear the insistent droning of the X-15 fighter jets that were hidden in the clouds far away, but the dull drone still pervaded the air. Roadkill pizza littered the highway at Whiskey Creek. Raccoons that came down to the water to feed in the night failed to make it home. It was the last supper. It was that kind of night—Judas hanged himself.

Heavy thick clouds opened and the rain fell in torrents, driven by the southwestern squall, and he was unable to see the city up ahead, or the island across the sound. Palm trees on the causeway leaned and snapped in the wind.

The distressed faded logos of bankrupt seafood companies added to the desperate morning. A tattered oyster boat lay half-submerged in the cove, useless and forlorn in the shallows.

Giant concrete legs of the high-tension wires stalked across the bay against the moving tides like aliens. They were doomed as war machines. The Kamikaze pterodactyls would take them out in no time.

The swollen river emptied its pesticide laden flood water into the bay, where it mingled with the changing tides, before it was swallowed by the brackish salt sea water, the source of life, now polluted with lust. The smell of sex on him. He would think almost anything to not scream, to not feel ashamed, and glorious.

In the office, he spilled the coffee filter pack, then poured water onto his pants. The unfinished remodeling of the law office of Francois Gellot Taghert & Partners made it hard to find anything. The fresh cut juniper wood paneling smelled tangy. He sat in a straight back chair with his head hung between his knees, his hands covering his face.

He decided he would terminate his relationship with Taghert. He had to start somewhere. He needed a break from the non-stop absurdity of life in the sewer with Francois Taghert, Esq. His own sewer was sufficient.

Struggling through the depositions in the Tater Godfrey case, the truth was stranger than fiction: Wil Meeks, the owner of a charter sport fishing business, that bought and sold shark fins on the side, had carried a small tape recorder in his back pocket and recorded his own death. Meeks got into an argument with Godfrey, an unemployed deck hand, over some missing electronic equipment. Meeks was stabbed repeatedly in the back with a kitchen knife and his client, Mr. Godfrey, had been charged with aggravated assault and second-degree murder. Godfrey claimed self-defense, but the tape recording of the argument, the ensuing fight, and the dying man's pitiful voice asking for mercy before he was killed was an unforgiving witness for the prosecution. Tater Godfrey was up the creek. There was only so much he could do.

Then Liana called. "I never heard you leave."

"It's just as well," he said.

"Terri was asleep downstairs in your office."

"So I noticed."

"She looked like she'd been done, but good."

"I'm sure she gave as much as she took."

His life was out of control, like a hog on ice. And he was trying to forget to savor every moment, every smelly orifice, every thrust into her tight wet sex, and remembered to not remember what happened after she landed spread-eagle on the sofa Anne had selected from the furniture showroom at Burdine's when she was excited about decorating the beach house. He knew, he remembered, he had said "no," in no uncertain terms. But his throbbing memory was not to be denied, and he filled her with his second effort at resistance, and her teeth bit and fortunately, finger nails clawed, or unfortunately, his shoulder and his memory was not what it used to be and he could see the hickey in the bathroom mirror and the memory of her, and he tried to not remember her churning mouth, her hard scented nipples, her squirming butt, her breasts, they were, he tried not to remember, to not think of her, to not want her again, because he knew it was dead wrong, and because, if Liana had walked into the room, he knew he would be dead now, no matter what he remembered. The pit of his stomach felt like hot acid lava. And he knew that Liana would kill him if she discovered that he had dallied with her teenage coquette—for sex, with or without love.

CHAPTER TWENTY

Dominickers in the Wilderness

AFTER LUNCH, MATTHEW drove through the Section on his way out of town. *No Trespassing* signs nailed to gutted wooden houses painted in muted pastels made perfect picturesque poverty. Groups of black men gathered on street corners to pass the time. There wasn't much work for them in Belle Rio. They either worked for the Gulf Royale pulp mill thirty miles west, or had manual labor jobs at the county landfill, or with the Department of Corrections.

Colorful shotgun shacks and unpainted, dilapidated houses with windows broken or missing, doors askew, lined the paved and unpaved streets. Elderly grandmothers sat in the shade on the porch. Yards were strewn with furniture and old rusted appliances. There were burned cars. His favorite, a rusted Olds Eighty-Eight, with no hood and no tires, rested on concrete blocks.

The rundown city park had four basketball goals with bent rims and no nets. Their nets had already been banned, by too many people congregating on hot summer nights.

At the concrete picnic tables under broken shelters, two black men and a high yellow woman drank beer from quart jars. Under the oaks, several men listened to some booming gangsta rap and talked jive.

Big Lou's green Lincoln was parked down the street next to Sister Salvation's Cadillac DeVille Christ Mobile, with her shiny plastic Golden Crown of Jesus displayed on the front dash.

There were plenty of drugs in the Section, and Big Lou had been the Main man. Anybody in Belle Rio could smoke all the pot they wanted, but crack made people hostile and dead. Big Lou sold crack and pills to shore-leave shrimpers and local hop heads from his ramshackle house near the park. A petition circulated to clean up the drug mess, and after several undercover buys, the Sherriff's department raided the crack shack, arrested Lou and four other black men. The next morning, the fat lighter shack, which had no electricity or running water, caught fire and burned while volunteer firemen trained their hoses in the opposite direction of the blaze and practiced close order drills, to the shouts of angry black women.

That's how the Sheriff dealt with blacks in Belle Rio. Bust 'em, plead 'em, snitch 'em, put 'em on probation, work 'em for the county until their time was up, then bust some more. The Sherriff promised to have the cause of the fire investigated, but he was personally convinced that "arson was not likely."

Big Lou died unexpectedly, of natural causes, when he fell down two flights of stairs at the jail and broke his neck, just after he named all the white girls that had exchanged sexual favors for drugs during the past three years. A broken neck was the best he could have hoped for.

Bad as it was, the Section was certainly as appealing as East Bay. There were lots of poor blacks, but no transient white trash, fish head cowboys.

The reluctance to change ran as deep and true as the intractable separation between the two races, and what held them together was what drove them apart: the deep intertwined roots of families, a bouillabaisse of Crawfords, Demetris, Faircloths, Hannahs, Hardaways, Matsons, Millers, Olivers, Fergasons, Picketts, Robertsons, Shermans, Talmadges, Whites, Blacks, and Browns.

Matthew Pine Road drove north past Hardaway's Dark River Fish Camp to where the railroad line crossed the river, then followed the railroad line up to Sumatra through the National Forest. The storm had blown over, but the heavy clouds hung low overhead and moved reluctantly eastward.

Late in the afternoon, he turned on a narrow sand road and followed it through the Gulf Royale Forest, through wild hammocks of saw palmettos and scrub pines. He traveled along the meandering Chipola River, that poured from an underground spring fifty miles north in the hill country of FloraBama, until he reached the most isolated corner of the Lake Wilderness, where the river met the low swampland, dense with large trees, oak, magnolia, sweet gum, tupelo, and towering cypress draped with long gray shrouds of Spanish moss.

The road stopped dead-end at a cluster of dirt-stained concrete block houses and weathered cypress shanties on a low bluff overlooking river.

A ramshackle vacant dry goods store that was long closed, useless, rusted, forgotten, and slowly being reclaimed by the inexorable vegetation, was covered with hand painted signs: *White Mule Sold Here. No Gun & No Knives Allowed! Anyone Shootin' a Gun will be Fined $5.00! If You Fight You Will Go To Jail!*

Four black men were playing cards beneath the sign that said *No Wemen Loud Here* in front of a two-pump gas station. Half-naked children ran in the clean-swept yard of a clapboard shack.

They stopped and watched Matthew with caution. They didn't see many white men. A bare-footed old woman, her head wrapped in a faded turban, sang while she tended her patch of greens. A blue heron floated down into the marshy reeds of the cypress swamp that spread from Dead Lakes to Tate's Hell on the flatland side of the river.

Matthew stood from the car and was drawn into the almost suffocating stillness. Then a battered pickup truck rumbled slowly, noisily past him, the afternoon quiet broken only by the excited voices of the children who ran beside the truck along the pack of curious, barking hounds. The truck crawled to a halt at the end of the dirt road where several men had gathered.

In the back of the truck was a primitive creature more than three feet across, with a massive neck and head. His powerful scimitar mouth was poised to tear an arm or hand from a careless spectator. Its cold predator vision had no respect for its captors, and eventual diners. The kids were laughing and hollering and poking sticks at the alligator snapping turtle which had righted himself in the back of the truck. With his powerful jaws it broke off the end of a stick held by one of the half-naked youths. The youngsters screamed and jumped back in fear.

Several ropes held the animal by the three legs. Quickly a noose was slipped over its thick neck, and another on the other hind leg. Then, with a metal bar, he was flipped again onto his back where he struggled to right himself while the children shouted "killa killa killa."

Talmadge Hannah was Possum Hannah's oldest surviving male relative. He was close to ninety years old, give or take a few, with a once proud carriage that defied his age. He had a mischievous glass eye, and walked with a limp and the use of a cane. He claimed a swamp gator chewed off part of his foot, and no one had been around long enough to know, or dared to tell otherwise.

Matthew sat with Talmadge in the twilight, amid a jumble of voices, laughing children, barking dogs, and the mumblings of the memories Talmadge drew from the shadows, stories told to him by his ancestors that were the legend, myth and folklore of his extended family.

"NanNaw, my common law wife, an' I, we both Dominickers."

Talmadge Hannah's colorful legato speech was a complex melody, mixed together with the constant chewing and spitting of tobacco. The sound of sucking the juice and spitting added a rhythmic punctuation to the "hem naw an' holler'n" speech.

"We all cousins, an' we different color. Some Dominickers black as night, some like tha boy over yonder white as you is. We mixed up blood fa sho, but we is all colored an' black folks, 'cept the ones dat go north an' pass fo white. They's callin' us 'Dominickers' long time bafo I's borne to dis world. Da truth be tellin'.

"Long ago they's a peckerwood farmer in tha county north a here an' he's divorcin' his white woman, after he'd don kilt tha colored man she went with, an' he say she been messin' with tha colored man, an' he say she didn't have no discrim'nation in her sexual appetites 'tween black an' white, jus' like she's an ol' Dominicker chicken. An she weren't tha onliest one – man or woman. An' since I can 'member, all a us up here in tha woods been called Dominickers."

A few Dominickers, like Talmadge, had lived down near Belle Rio; some worked at Port Royale, but most of the Dominickers had never lived in a town other than this loose collection of buildings near Dead Lake swamp. They were on no government census. They farmed greens, they hunted, they fished, they played can-can, and drank White Mule. They dealt with the white devils as little as possible. Some had been in the woods for generations, descended from slaves on the large plantations in the red clay hill country of north Florida or south Alabama. Some had not been slaves since the day they escaped into the woods, long before

Lincoln proclaimed them free, and joined the renegade Creek Indians and fought against Andrew Jackson, the most hated of all white men.

It was dark now, and there was a fire in a barrel over by the gas station. The men were drinking and playing cards again, joking about the Pensacola Mardi Gras poontang, the black Jesus on the Mardi Gras Parade float, and the bolita numbers they busted when they used to play against the Big House.

"Jones say you gonna help get Possum outta jail," Talmadge said.

"I'm going to try. With his help. And if what I have been told me is correct, I feel I've got a reasonably good chance of being successful."

"Well, tha last lawyer didn't do us no reasonable good a tall."

"I'll do the best I can. That's all I can do."

"He's gonna have to come back here to stay. He don't know nothin' 'bout livin' in town."

"He might by now. Jail is a lot like town."

"I hear that."

"You spent some time down in Belle Rio?"

"I usta live down there."

"And Jones is your grandson?"

"We all related. He's my nephew by my brother's son."

"Do you think Possum could stay with Jones? Have Jones look after his parole. They're going to want to know where he's going to be. I don't know if he can come live here without approved supervision. They won't know what to say to this."

"You know da boy dat play football. He one of us."

"Which boy?"

"Da one on da Suga Bowl team. Da one de calls the 'New Deion.' He come here from Belle Rio. But he a Dominicker. His daddy's a white man an' his Mama's mixed. She lived right over yonder." He pointed to the night, somewhere outside the circle of fire light. "She went way up north. I heard she got killed up north. They is some sorry niggers up north."

"White folks, too."

A man brought over a quart jar, and the three of them had a drink of White Mule. It kicked hard, and they had another. The man left the jar with Talmadge, and went back to the card game.

Possum's grandfather, who was named Abraham, took his wife and daughter into the turpentine camp with a promise of big wages. One day he was loading the wagon with the barrels of turpentine, and he was called by God, because he had a powerful gift, and he quit the turpentine business and moved to Pensacola. He took up preaching. Had a little church, and people would put money in his Bible, and he would intone the names and message of the prophets,

Talmadge smiled toothless in the firelight, "an' I do mean *profits*," he said, grinning and rubbing his fingers together, feeling the cash, "him preachin' with tha low boomin' voice dat was God's gift, an' a ritual of singin' an' layin' on hands, dat could heal de sick, an' damn near bring back da dead, if they was 'nough profits involved."

He had a laugh at his own self.

They sat and got kicked a couple more times. "He died there. His heart so big it busted plum open, an' his Mama brought Possum back home. Dey moved down near Belle Rio. Dat's where he got his trouble."

Talmadge sat quietly for a while, then he started humming. From the nearby darkness came a sound like a Jew's harp, another humming and a hand slapping, and Talmadge, feeling tha spirit, sang a turpentine blues in his gravel-scratched throaty voice:

Where ya gwine nigger? Where ya gwine? /
I's gwine to Flarda, t'work dat turp'tine.

The pre-dawn village was quiet except for the lusty mad crowing of roosters and the chatter of chickens. The chicken house was a vacant cedar frame house with the screens ripped from the porch. Roosters and hens wandered in and out. Part of the house had already fallen down. A gutted jon boat was turned on its side against a tree with a duck decoy balanced on the rail. A rotten fish net was piled on the porch steps.

The yard was full of roosters, and they ran wild, fighting each other and chasing the white and brown hens around the sandy yard. They quarreled and fought and scratched. Screaming with gusto, the biggest rooster strutted and preened. It was early morning and there was nothing else to do. He abruptly flew from the porch, landed in front of a speckled hen, and chased her around the car where Matthew was laid out across the front seat of his Buick. Just as the sun broke through the trees Matthew, his head throbbing from a White Mule mugging, woke up to the victorious screams of the boss rooster.

Possum Hannah was a large black man with an easygoing smile, but a genuinely suspicious nature. Before Possum went to jail, he'd spent his life in remote poverty, so when he got to jail, he was overwhelmed with convenience and luxury. He had suddenly moved uptown. Jail had flush toilets, running water, electricity, and television. There was enough excitement in the new surroundings for Possum to like jail for the first few years, and by the time he reached his full size at six foot five inches, he was a celebrity on the basketball court, the Moses Malone of the Florida Correctional League, a legend in the prison yard. For the last six years, he had been a trustee and all-star power forward on the Correctional League basketball team.

When Possum Hannah was seventeen years old, he killed a white boy. That was thirteen years ago. Possum killed the white boy because the boy, along with two others, beat his younger brother to death with a

172

piece of picket fence. Possum found his brother's body in a shallow grave in the woods, but nobody cared. The sheriff deputies weren't very helpful, and his mother couldn't afford the fifty-dollar coroner fee, so the cause of death went into the records as "congestion of the brain."

Possum took the matter into his own hands. He caught one of the white boys walking home alone and broke his neck, almost twisted his damn head clean off. At age eighteen, he was tried and convicted of first-degree murder and sentenced to the electric chair. Disagreements about the morality of capital punishment and his awesome slam dunks had kept him alive.

For the last five years, Possum's Warden at the Liberty Correctional Facility had the best Won-Loss record in Correctional League Basketball, and he was not happy about losing his power forward now that the young republican candidate for Governor in the November general election was calling for a house cleaning of the Death Row cells, and Possum's name had come up as a prime example of the failure of the Criminal Justice System, i.e. the salary cap had to be applied to achieve parity in the Correctional League standings. It was sure going to fry Liberty's chance of a Threepeat.

Possum was either going to get out of jail or be electrocuted. And as the discussion of his possible execution began to sink in, Possum got woeful, then angry. Standing in the solitude of the closed cell, or working the fields of the prison farm, or finishing the three-on-one fast break with a slam dunk, the murmuring pine trees kept coming back to him, calling him home in a thousand whispering voices saying, "Possum, get yo black ass outta jail."

Matthew had gotten a call from the Warden to either keep Possum alive in jail on the basketball court or have him released on parole or, if necessary, have his initial court trial reviewed and the conviction overturned due to procedural irregularities. It was a rare combination of self-interest and simple gratitude for multiple championship seasons.

He and Possum sat in a small room next to the Warden's office.

"If you say that you'd do it again, they won't let you out of prison. If you say you want to find the other two and kill them, they won't let you out no matter what the ruling is on the constitutional question, or who gets elected Governor."

"I'd do it again," Possum said gravely, still without remorse. "If I could find the other two, I'd kill them too."

"That may be, but if you say that, you won't ever get out of jail and you'll probably be electrocuted."

"So, what do I gotta tell tha Judge?"

"You tell him that it was an accident, that you regret what you did, and that you have learned to be a good citizen."

"That's a mouthful."

"You find a way to say it convincingly, like you mean it."

"I gotta think 'bout that." He thought about it then said, "There's not a day gone but I wished I coulda killed all three of them boys."

"Think about something else to say. If you want to get out of prison, don't say that you wished you had killed all three of them. I promise I'll do the best I can to make this happen, hopefully without you having to say anything at all."

Matthew drove back to Belle Rio through sixty dark, lonely miles of pine woods without passing another car. He knew that he had to make a decision. His life had to change. He was depressed about the Tupelo Bluff real estate deal. He saw trouble looming with the *Net Ban Amendment.* Belle Rio was going to change, even if tourism was a four-letter word. Attorney Taghert was not pleased with his involvement in the Possum Hannah business, particularly a controversial *habeas corpus* petition, or anything else that might cause trouble for real estate sales.

CHAPTER TWENTY-ONE

Percy Travels South

"HOT TEA," Percy mumbled. "Come with me and make it."

The mulatto waif surveyed the room, as if listening to little birds sing. His collection of birds was a small choir. She walked through the house with the same expressionless vacant stare he'd seen from her ever since he picked her out of the dance lineup at the Mustang Club in Detroit, where the manager thought she would be great for visiting Japanese design engineers vising the Ford Headquarters in Dearborn. Percy only saw her dance once and knew she had potential. Exotic little animals weren't for everyone, but he collected them

They crossed to the kitchen. He found the tea bags and boiled water on the stove top, and she made the tea while he fed the parrot, Collette, and talked to her in jumbled nonsense.

"Why do you talk to the bird that way?" the tan, doe-eyed waif asked.

"I don't want her to say anything that can be used against me in court. Say something, Collette, say something stupid, stupid."

He splashed bourbon in a small glass.

The parrot responded, "Stupid stupid stupid."

"Enough," Percy said.

"Enough," said Collette.

"Say goodnight Collette."

"Goodnight. Goodnight Collette. Goodnight Collette."

"Jesus, shut up!" Percy said.

"Praise Jesus," Collette added. "Praise…"

"Enough," Percy interrupted, as he covered her cage and she quit.

"Collette is a true parrot, a Psittacoidea."

Collette could not pronounce that.

Angie followed him, carrying her little cloth shoulder bag, dressed in slacks, a man's shirt, and sandals, through the house to the bedroom. There was not much in the room, a king bed partially made, an expensive Turkish rug, chest of drawers, clutter, and an oversized chair with a lamp. There were no pictures and no music. She sat on the edge of the bed. He sat opposite her in the worn velvet over-stuffed chair. They were both quiet—just the sound of sipping tea, his sound of slow breathing, and the faint, muted singing of little birds.

He downed the drink, took off his clothes, and dropped them on the floor. He went to the bathroom and took a shower, then stood in the bathroom and dried off, looking at her while she sat and watched him. She didn't have to look at him naked, but she did.

He was thin, but he was chiseled and muscular. He learned in prison: don't eat, exercise. Besides the scar on his neck, he had a tattoo of the Jack of Diamonds on his right arm, and on his left arm was a pair of dice, snake eyes, under a "Good Luck Sucker" banner. His one-eyed monster knew she was in the house. It generally hungered indiscriminately without being satiated, but it had reverence for certain small animals.

She had not moved from the bed. He wrapped the towel around his waist and sat next to her on the bed.

She laughed. "You have elephant ears, large elf ears."

His hair was plastered to his head, combed, slicked back.

"They are way too large," she said.

"But they are pointed, see." He pulled them at the top.

"Mine are too, if I do that," she laughed like a young bird.

"I used to be an elf," he admitted. "When I was little, I was an elf. I wore funny little curled-toed shoes."

"With a bell?"

"Yes, with a bell, and I lived under a toadstool."

She studied him. Maybe it was true.

"That's why I like you," he said. "You're an elfin. We're the same, only I'm grown up now. I'm a bad elf. I can eat little elfin."

She studied him some more. It was true. She was going to get eaten. The color changed on her neck. She finished her tea, stood, put her shoulder bag on the straight wooden chair, pulled her oversized linen shirt over her head, and dropped it to the floor. She was only a morsel, he delicate perfect breast with dark nipples punctuating her cinnamon complexion.

She stepped from her trousers and skimpy panties and walked to the bathroom. He watched her disappear into the shower. Her body was fragile, delicate, like a porcelain doll. He swallowed hard. His curved one-eyed monster stretched and opened its eye to look. The shower ran hot and soon the bathroom was filled with steam.

He went through her cloth bag. Cotton bra, pair of sandals, several containers of nail polish, little mirror, emery boards, and wallet with driver's license: *State of Michigan. Expired 1998. Angie Fellows. DOB 6/10/72. Hair Blk. Eyes Brown. Wt 105. Hgt 5'2". Address: 25 Tyler Apt 3. Ann Arbor, MI.* Twenty-five dollars cash. A picture of a little girl. Maybe a sister. Or a child.

Percy sat on the bed and watched her dry her body in the mist. She came to the bed and stood facing him with the towel covering her. The towel dropped to the floor, and he gazed deeply at the object of his desire. He patted the bed and she sat facing him, cross legged on the bed.

His monster had a mind of its own and the beast was stirring, barely under control. He took her foot and began stroking it gently. He held it up to his face and rubbed it against his cheek. They were perfect angel's feet, innocent, blameless.

"Tell me a story," he said.

She was afraid of him. "What story do you want to hear?"

"Tell me why you are unhappy. Why do elves dance?"

She struggled inside as he kissed and licked and massaged the bottom of her feet. "Perfect little piggies." He kissed them. "Tell me a story," he said again, distant. He was totally intoxicated.

As she relaxed, her insides began to warm from the feet up until her whole being was smoldering, glowing radiant.

"I was the third child of my mother, but with each of us there was a different father, and there were five of us all together. Three of my fathers died. One of my brothers died."

"Was your mother black?"

"Yes, mostly."

He put her toes in his mouth, slowly caressing her delicate ankle and lower leg with his hands while they talked.

"And your father?"

"Two of my fathers were white and three of my fathers were black."

"Why do you call them all your father?"

"Because my mother called them 'our father.'"

The warmth became a glow, and the feat from her foot spread to her loins and to her breast, and she swooned.

"Who made you an elf?"

"My brother, the son of my first father, came into the room at night and played with me. He taught me things."

"What things?"

"That men are strange."

"They are strange. They crave mystery and beauty. Then destroy it."

"I always loved to dance."

"I love the smell of your body."

Her sex had come alive beneath its downy cover, and he could hear it inhaling in little gasps.

"I ran away. Many times. And they always found me and brought me back. My last father took me to a woman who taught me the sex dance. I became exotic."

"But not a whore?"

"I was protected by my father's woman friend."

He nibbled her toes, and she exhaled a muffled little noise. Breathing deep, she sighed, then quivered. The petals of her lips drooled, and her neck flushed crimson on her brown creamy skin.

"And she loved you too?"

"Yes."

"But she never kissed your feet?"

"No. No one." She squirmed and laughed hesitantly, then she lost control, and because now she felt no danger, laughed and laughed until she cried. Then she became pensive, blissful, and once again she was the silent little animal. She watched him curiously as he took a bottle of nail polish from her bag, and one toe at a time, painted her toenails a bright cherry pink. Then he kissed each foot and put them down and sat naked facing her. She was like a little bird singing. Her throaty little voice deepened and she began making low guttural sounds, and she transformed herself into a little animal, and she slowly arched her body and purred, taking no space at all on the bed, like a prized aristocratic honey-brown ferret, lay facing him, purred a guttural hunger and took his aching monster in her delicate hands and wrapped herself around him.

Before dawn, she woke up frightened. Two men were standing in the dark shadows of the doorway. She woke up Percy, who usually slept on nails with eyes open—that's why he was still alive—but he was out cold.

A large black man yanked her naked from the bed. She screamed, and he slapped her across the face, growled "shut up bitch!" and threw her like a ragdoll into the bathroom and slammed the door shut.

Delgado was swarthy and muscular. He wore dark slacks and an expensive dark shirt open at the neck with a single gold chain across his hairy chest.

"You've been taking it easy, Drew."

"I was making a new friend. You guys forgot to knock."

"We got places to go. Things to do."

Spit-fire Angie waif screamed insults at them through the door.

"Be nice to her," he motioned to the door, "she's my pet."

"Looks like you got too many pets already."

Percy got out of bed and walked naked around the room until he found his cigarettes. He lit a Camel then went for his pants.

"Jesus!" he said. "It ain't even five."

"I'm leaving town and we got work for you."

"You still got Chi Chi?"

"Yeah. I got a pet too."

"Keep her in a cage, otherwise she'll fly away."

"She likes my personality."

"She likes your money."

"I got a big stogey."

Delgado limped around the room. He had been a Jai-Alai star but broke his leg when, chasing a pelote traveling over a hundred fifty miles per hour, he crashed into the wall and his career was over.

"Judge Traynor's going to be called before the grand jury. He'll sing like one of your damn birds. The Judge don't want to stay bought after he's been paid. What a jerk-off. He either got cancer of the brain or got Born Again. Either way he got stupid."

"You want him not to testify?"

"He can shut up and be happy, or be dead."

"What do you think I am, Delgado, a hired killer?"

"What I think you are, besides a whore-monger and child molester, is immaterial and malevolent."

"Try irrelevant or something you understand," Percy said.

"I meant what I said. Whatever I said. Do what it takes. Dead is probably better. He took the money, but it's against his nature to shut up and be happy."

Angie was banging on the bathroom door.

"Until last night she never said a word," Percy shrugged.

"Do something about that cooze. I can't think."

The black muscle disappeared into the bathroom; there was brief scuffle, then a whimper, soft crying, then silence. The muscle came out the door and Percy could see Angie on the bathroom floor.

"If you deliver on the Judge, we'll be even."

"You'll never leave me alone, Gato. It's not like you."

"Mr. Traynor has not been reliable. You, on the other hand, I trust."

"Thanks, I'm sure."

"It should be something sympathetic, like suicide. Call me when it's done."

"Thanks, Gato. Don't do me any more favors. I don't ever want to see you again."

"That's too bad, Drew. I'm your own personal guardian angel."

They disappeared like they arrived, silent as the flapping of angel wings.

The faun's petulant mouth was bleeding from a busted lip and one side of her face was crimson and swollen. She was lucky to have her teeth.

"Sorry, my elfin," he said, holding ice to her soft, bruised doe-eyed face. "Someday I'll get even with Gato for you, and it won't be pretty."

"Those two got no manners," she grimaced.

Percy left Panama City and drove east through Port Royale toward Belle Rio. There was a late rising moon over the water, and it was a quiet and distant world. He had started feeling comfortable with his life, which was just next to being dispensable. Disposable, Momma said. Either way it was an unnerving feeling. He was not indispensable; he knew that. But he was trapped by that damn Delgado and the whole Miami crowd. Nobody else would do what he did. That had to change. Somehow.

He knew Judge Traynor: rotten ten years ago rotten today, a self-righteous son-of-a-bitch, state prosecutor in Miami, then a federal prosecutor, and all the time taking cash, never missing a beat, heavy on black hopheads without a clue, sucking up to paramilitary Cubans, stuffing gambling, drug, and whore money in his wall safe. He was a TV show all on his own. Now Delgado expected him to kill the chicken-livered Judge. Actually he did feel disposable. himself. It was a tough call.

He connected with Cairo in Three Rivers, and they drove east to U.S. 27, then south through Dixie County. Cairo had a Miami Dolphins hat pulled down over his new buzz cut.

"Chief, I like that new hairdo."

"I feel like a dumb shit without my hair," Cairo grumbled.

"You look like a gentleman," Percy smiled.

They drove for hours, just the hissing drone of tires on pavement.

Then Percy got talkative to settle his nerves. "I was dealing cards at the Bordeaux Club in Nashville and after midnight this well-oiled silver-headed country singer was playing at my table. He was deep into the house bank, and when all the chips were on the table, I dealt him the card that saved his damn ass. That's how I got to be his personal manager, bodyguard, chauffer, drug supplier, guitar tuner, and pimp. I traveled with that country singer two years, doing state fairs. I went along to keep the singing cowboy happy: drink with him, if he wanted to drink, listen to him talk all night, if he wanted to talk. Buy him shit when he wanted to get stoned—speed going up, when he needed emergency inspiration, then, whatever I could buy, to bring him back down.

"Anyhow, we were in Dubuque. 'Debauch, Iowa' we called it. I got him two plump underage Dubuque chickens and we was back at the motel after the show, and he had both of 'em naked in the shower when his wife showed. She'd drove all the way up from Nashville with her girlfriend. I was stalling her in the room next door, but she could hear what was going on. She kept calling his room, you could hear the telephone ringing through the wall, and then, finally, I opened the door to his room. They were all naked, the two Dubuque chicks running around with their heads cut off, looking for clothes. The wife grabbed that expensive famous silver hair and they fought all over them two rooms, until the road manager showed up with his shotgun and fired two shots into the ceiling. Damn countrypolitan singer fired my ass right there on the spot, and I was glad of it. I'd been screwing his wife for a whole year. She was one wild woman, but I was getting tired of her. He didn't never know 'bout that, but he was sure as hell mad at me."

He laughed nervously in the dark and sang, *"Let by-gones... be George Jones..."*

Nashville was the best Percy ever had it until a federal gambling investigation ruined the sport book and took all his money. He walked away clean, but it was a big disappointment. Like knowing Hank Williams was dead.

When he got to Miami, he was broke. He knew some hot shot players who got him involved in the Jai Alai racket, where he worked directly for an international banker who had a substantial financial interest in the outcome of the individual standings. Part of the job was to entertain clients and pay off a District Attorney to take care of cops on the vice squad.

Then things went sour. He shot a cokehead Cuban courier who had misplaced a bundle of cash, and he served the rap for a reduced plea. He did the time. Called it his Club Fed Vacation. He remained silent, otherwise Delgado would have killed him for certain. Somebody tried and he still had the scar on his neck to prove his Big House pedigree. Until now he was feeling comfortable. Too comfortable. Disposable, Mama said. Gato would get him killed sooner or later, or he would have to kill Gato to stay alive. Maybe it was time to move on. He couldn't stay in Panama City much longer.

It was already too late for Judge Traynor. He thought a judge should be smart, but after what he saw in the newspaper, he wasn't so sure anymore: four north Dade Judges hoarding enough cash to build a new civic center, money stashed like Easter eggs, twenty thousand in the closet, twelve behind the volumes of Federal Appeals cases, another ten in a bathroom safe. The Feds could always find money when they wanted to. Criminal indictments listed over two hundred thousand dollars paid out over the past year by the undercover Feds to buy Judges.

Judge Traynor had been bought by everybody. It was hard to tell the undercover cops from over-the-counter criminals, street drugs from pharmaceutical cocktails. Delgado must have known the Judge was getting paid by the Feds too. Traynor was taking money, suppressing evidence, and disclosing confidential information to anyone who paid. He set bail for a scar-faced, cold-blooded killer at only fifty grand, then denied bail for frontal nudity on a public beach. Judge Traynor was a dead man.

Driving into the sunrise Percy said to no one in particular, "I hate this."

Orlando was crowded with pilgrims who prayed every night to a midget in a mouse costume. They located the dark blue Dodge van with bogus plates at the Orlando International long term parking lot. Inside the van was another set of plates, two uniform shirts, and a hand-painted sign for the van exterior: *Prestige Lawn Care Specialties/Landscape Consulting & Exotic Plants— "We Make Your Home a Paradise"* with a seven-digit south Dade address and a telephone number that only gave you a recorded message: "Your call cannot be completed as dialed. Please check the number in your directory."

At nine in the morning, they arrived at the gates of the private residential community. The Security Guard checked his clipboard and said they were expected. They drove along the tree-shaded boulevard of the exclusive enclave, past tile-roofed Spanish architecture with manicured lawns. Percy had a nervous hyper twitch beneath the Ray-Bans. The two sides of his face looked like they belonged on two different people. The left side of his handsome, un-scarred face was agitated and regretted being there. The convicted felon, beneath the long scar, was confident and cruel. They turned into the curved driveway that led to the ornate Mediterranean style villa.

A dignified Cuban maid opened the elaborately carved heavy wooden door. She led them across the tile floor through the courtyard toward the Judge's office. Cairo put a hammer lock on the maid and wrapped her up good. She scuffled and kicked, but with her mouth tightly covered, she was reduced to silent thrashing, and he dragged her off down the hallway.

Percy was moving fast. He was almost on Judge Traynor's desk before he entered the room. It was a large room with a high arch-beamed ceiling. The aroma of lush tropical flowers and the melodic birds of paradise filtered in through the courtyard window. The adrenaline rushing, his head was so clear it startled him. The smell of anything surprised him.

Judge Traynor was seated at his desk. A heavyset man in his late fifties, he had been a dapper prosecutor and couldn't get enough newsprint of himself. He reached a hand to the telephone. Percy showed the Italian .44 caliber from behind his back, and it was clear what was happening. Traynor's hands fluttered to rest on the top of the desk. Then he moved to stand, but Percy knocked him back to his seat. He had hoped Traynor would do something to make him angry. It would be easier to kill him.

Percy stood facing the Judge like he had done years before. Traynor had been more lenient with him than he would be with the Judge today. Now the shoe was on the other foot. He wasn't bought the way the Judge had been. He was paid, but not bought.

Traynor recognized him even before he took off the Ray Bans.

"I certainly didn't expect you, Mr. Percy. I assumed you had moved on to more civilized endeavors." The Judge would make him mad. Just let him talk. He didn't look like a man preparing to die, but there was still time for him to get scared.

"I expected somebody, the way things were going."

"Nothing ever changes," Percy said.

"I assumed Delgado would change his plans after the Federal Sting was revealed. What could Delgado want with me now? My being dead won't make his life any safer. Surely he knows we've all been compromised."

"I'd say Delgado doesn't know what he wants besides some Cuban Chi-Chi. I asked him, 'What kind of judge won't keep his word?' and he said, 'A dead one.' That's the trouble with the world today, people who ought to know better, they don't know when to wait quietly in the wings. Where's the lovely Mrs. Traynor?"

"Shopping and then to golf. But she should be home soon."

"Not soon enough. She'll be glad she missed this."

Judge Traynor was a sorry bastard, but either he was not easily intimidated or he had resigned himself to ignominious fate. He lamented that Delgado was scum and Percy and the lot of them, himself included, must be scum, since they all swam in the same cesspool. The Judge had arrived at a profound revelation of character. Judge Traynor was being brave, and that wasn't making what he had to do any easier.

"Four Judges are under investigation by the Grand Jury. At least one of them will make a deal that will hang all the others, and everybody else involved."

"Somebody always talks and walks, Judge. You know that. We're not all equal before the law."

Percy cursed the day he met Delgado. He couldn't talk to Judge Traynor anymore.

The Judge refused to deny he was guilty. He was prepared to die. What he faced alive was worse. He wanted it to be clean. Traynor could see the handgun blow a fist size hole in the back of his skull and then tear away the flesh of his face. He imagined the clear sharp vivid burst of red-splattered brains and skull fragments over his bank statements, diplomas and certificates, letters of congratulations, pictures of his attractive gray-haired wife playing golf, the happy children of successful children, photos of political and judicial accomplishments. Gurgling bubbles, he would die, face down in his own blood, at his own desk.

Cairo stuck his head in and said, "Conchita travels with the Judge."

The room got real quiet. Percy was a raw nerve.

When Percy turned back to Traynor, he caught the trailing movement of Traynor's hand as it whisked something into his desk drawer and closed the drawer slowly, as if he had never moved.

"Write it down, Judge," Percy snapped.

Judge Traynor didn't move. The awesome hands of a long dead eternity were beginning to suffocate him.

"Take a piece of paper and write what I tell you."

Traynor put a legal pad on the desk before him.

"Write this on stationary. Good stationary."

The Judge carefully selected a clean sheet of official stationery.

"Write: '*To my dear wife and family. I have lived a full life and have been blessed with a wonderful family. I deeply regret that I failed to uphold the trust,*' WRITE! Damn it! Write! '*I deeply regret that I failed to uphold the trust placed in me by my family, friends, and fellow citizens. In my heart I have paid for the failure a thousand times. I love you all very much. Please do not think unkindly towards me.*' Write!"

Traynor was writing, but he was getting sloppy.

"Quit sniveling! Write: '*Life is sometimes difficult. Sometimes we make mistakes.*'"

Judge Traynor was trying to retain his dignity. It was touching. It made Percy want to vomit. "Write: '*I pray that God Almighty will have mercy on my soul.*' Now sign it."

Traynor slowly finished writing and signed his name. His handwriting, which had begun in a controlled print style, had degenerated into an emotional, unrecognizable script.

Percy was angry. He could feel it coming. Unholy Joy. Like the stabbing pain of a raw nerve. Strike the match and let her blow.

Hank was singing *cold cold heart.*

"Now put it in an envelope and address it to your wife."

Traynor struggled through folding the letter and addressing an envelope. Percy's black-gloved hand snatched the letter from the Judge's trembling hand.

"I'll mail it for you."

Judge Traynor stood abruptly from the desk and threw himself against Percy. They fell to the floor, the heavy judge on top, struggling, violently and desperately, for one last chance to survive, or die trying.

Cairo suddenly appeared in the room, embraced Judge Traynor in a head lock, pulled him off Percy, and held him upright. Traynor groaned, breathing heavy. An arid smell of fear and urine pervaded the room.

It was coming now. Percy slammed him across the face with the barrel of the Italian pistol. Traynor sank to his knees, and as he went down, Percy took the garrote from under his jacket, wrapped it quickly around the man's neck, and choked him, pulling harder, tighter around his throat, as he struggled, breathless, and tried to stand, his hands flailing at the air, thrashing, falling, eyes bulging, guttural grunts, color flushed, then he ceased struggling, sagged, and slumped in the floor, dead. A pall of death spread silently throughout the room.

"Son-of-a-bitch Gato is next," Percy said.

Delgado owed him big time for Traynor's inability to testify. One of the song bird judges was bound to chirp: Del Del Del Gado Gado Gado. Delgado Shitbird. Fly away home. And Gato would chirp: Andrew Jackson Percy.

Working fast and quiet, he checked the drawer and took the squiggly scrawled note that said *"AP killed me"* from the drawer and shoved it in his pocket. They straightened the mess, wiped and polished the office. Cairo carried the carpet crumpled heap of the Cuban maid and threw her in the back of the Dodge van. They deposited the lumpy Judge, wrapped in a drop cloth, beside her.

Chief grunted, "I broke her neck."

Percy said, "Diablo."

They were moving now, driving away from Casa Cielo, but it seemed to Percy like the world was in slow motion. It was quiet, the world streaming by like a silent waterfall of blurred cascading automobiles, except for the relentless pounding inside his head. They were on the Florida Turnpike to Disney World, when he finally smiled with the pleasure he took from Judge Traynor's suicide letter, thinking no one would believe the asshole killed himself, no matter how glad they were to see him dead. He would burn the letter with the body.

Caravan north. Percy in the Lincoln. Cairo in the Dodge hearse with Ohio plates. Prestige was gone. Anonymous killer gargoyle headed north on I-75 against the flow of traffic. They turned west over to Crystal River, then drove U.S 98 north past Cedar key.

They were traveling west again, toward Steinhatchie, going steady through the scrub oak and palmetto, through the pine barrens of the coastal swamp. Looking for the dead end. Following Chief, who was running wide open.

It was dusk, going to dark, Hank singing *Long Gone and Lonesome*.

About a mile off the paved road, they turned left on another road deep in the palmettos. At the creek, they turned onto a sand road that reached dead end at the water where they pulled the heavy, bulky Judge Traynor and the innocent Cuban maid from the Dodge van.

Cairo heartless, necessary, grisly, ghastly. Traynor decapitated, headless, hands hacked off. Two bodies consumed in the unifying flames, the marsh palmetto swamp flickering in the dark moon night.

The Lincoln throbbing with the soundtrack of Judas Priest for the living ghouls and the stench of gasoline-soaked burning flesh. The remnants gathered and smashed with sledgehammers, skulls crushed, teeth disappeared.

The Dodge van doused in gasoline, blazed in glory.

Chief waded into the marsh carrying the crushed, charred remains, a lonely, isolated burial in the bayou of gulf coast salt marshes, where they would never be discovered, and if discovered, never identified.

There was nothing left of the self-righteous Judge Traynor and his innocent Cuban maid to float to the surface somewhere, with the flesh gone, the eye sockets empty of all but the maggots of decay. No mouth full of gold teeth. No shard of bone. Just dust to dust—nothing for the state's famous forensic anthropologist to identify.

There would be no "Alas, poor Yorrick, I knew him well" revelations in the courtroom for Judge Traynor's skull.

CHAPTER TWENTY-TWO

Riviera Club Brawl

THE *RIVIERA CLUB* on the coast highway just south of Capital City was packed this hot humid Friday night with a boisterous crowd—a volatile mixture of brash party animals drinking beer with the bravado that comes from overheated hormones and fake IDs. Frat hounds and sorority foxes mingled with die-hard Fishheads, rowdy South Georgia rednecks, belligerent Dixie County loggers, overzealous Hot'lanta tourists, and a large contingent of the Sugar Bowl Champion football team from the state university, out for some serious rest and relaxation after an exhausting day of academic weight training.

Billy Ray Hardaway and Terri Cates, with a boat load of Belle Rio refugees, including Crazy Maxwell and Keith Moss, with Darlene and Chad along for the ride, often came to party at the Riviera Club.

Terri Cates wore her new threads from the Capital City Mall, a little dress that flared out just below her ass, and her shapely bronze legs hummed *Stairway to Heaven* when she walked.

The house band was kicking out some raucous hillbilly heavy metal, Guns & Roses mixed with Tupak Shukar, and the crowd was riding a scary thrill-a-minute roller-coaster, becoming increasingly chaotic, drunk, and disorderly. Raw excitement made the nerves twitch.

When Drew Percy saw Billy Ray's Corvette, he swerved the Lincoln Town Car into the *Riviera Club* parking lot. The Capital City crowd of local Crackers and university Blacks would be welcome comic relief from the smell of burning flesh, which prolonged an agony that could only be released by a throng of nameless faces and drunken oblivion.

It was a momentary lapse of reason, a simple twist of fate. And it didn't take long before Percy had Terri the Pirate on the dance floor.

"You really want me to perform full time at the *Cleopatra?*" she asked, living her dream, spinning through the clouds of smoke with a real man.

"Sure, baby, be nice to the boss," Percy replied, smooth and hungry, unfazed by the tension and danger around him. He was seeking release. It was a reckless moment for a man who almost never let his guard down.

"Maybe when I get to know you better," she purred confident and coy. At long last, she was gonna get what she wanted.

A large contingent of Sugar Bowl celebrities from the University in Capital City were out to prove to anybody and everybody that they did whatever they damn well pleased: like where do two thousand pounds of offensive linemen dance, drink, and piss? Any place they want to, and tonight it was the Riviera Club. Kate Hardaway, a raven-haired hellion, her father's daughter, brave and reckless, danced the Dirty Dog with Cleave Thomas, the fleet-footed wide receiver, defensive free safety, and kick return specialist, heir apparent to famous Deion.

"I ain't gonna have him puttin' his hands on my sista," Billy Ray blustered, surrounded by his group of swaggering "fergit hell" hotheads.

He called Cleave Thomas the worst kind of S.O.B.—even if he was the big shot Sugar Bowl hero, and even if he had the whole muscular offensive front line to protect him.

"Looks like it's yur sista's got her hands on him, Billy Ray. She's acting like a common slut," Cairo said.

There a was a break in the dancing and Billy Ray stormed across the dance floor to where the Sugar Bowl Champs were holding court.

"Kate," he sputtered, agitated and out of control. "I wanna talk to you."

"Billy Ray, this is Cleave Thomas, who you probably know because he went to Belle Rio High School. He graduated the year before me, if I'd stayed in school in Belle Rio, instead of going to that awful Episcopalian Chattanooga girls' school … And this is Levon, Charlyne, Dumont, and Daymiunne and Latisha."

Nobody was shaking hands.

"I wanna talk to you," Billy Ray growled through clenched teeth, and angrily pulled her away from the table. Cleave stood up to stop him, but Kate motioned him to be still.

Billy Ray hustled Kate to the hallway by the bathrooms.

"What in the hell you doin'? Huh? What the hell you doin'?"

"Billy Ray, first, get your damn hands off of me!"

He let her go, and stood glaring at her through a violent, red-eyed mist of anger and fear.

"You calm down, little brother, or you're gonna start trouble here, and maybe get yourself hurt."

"I ain't your little brother! And you already started the damn trouble."

"Billy Ray, this is the twentieth century. Leave it alone. Leave me alone. Leave us alone."

"It ain't right! Kate!" He spit it out, "Schmoozing a black boy. It don't matter what century it is."

"For your information, Billy Boy, he's only half black."

"God dammit. Don't matter. That's enough! An' you ain't going back over there."

"You can't stop me, Billy Ray. I'm different than you. And I'll do what I damn well please, with whomever I damn well please, and you don't have a damn thing to say about it."

"Kate, I'm taking you outta here." He grabbed her arm, but she pulled away. "That's why daddy sent you to that Chattanooga school, Kate, so you wouldn't have to be around them… all the damn time."

"I've known him since I was fifteen, Billy Ray. A lot of the girls in Belle Rio knew him. He was cute. He had a nice personality. He was a nice boy. I liked him. You're jealous, Billy Ray. He's a star, Billy Ray. What are you? … Huh?"

She walked away from him.

Poised on the brink, The *Riviera Club* was ready to explode, waiting for that impetuous moment when the frenzied action, and destructive cultural momentum, would carry them across the River Styx into the maelstrom of Hell.

The band played ear-splitting loud, heavy stabbing decibels. The crowded dance floor, bathed in streaking colored strobe lights, became aroused until there was no point of view but rhythm, pulse, beat, no rational world, no sense of order in the swirling bodies that blurred into unconnected moments of random violence.

Cairo, putting his arm around the honey-brown poontang cheerleader, made the wrong move, and the burly black pulling guard, a graduate of Don King High School, Noneck, New Jersey, bounced him against the wall and busted his nose. He shouldn't oughtta done that.

Dancing, Kate squeezed herself around Cleave Thomas.

Billy Ray went berserk, called his sister "a wild whore," and stomped onto the dance floor screaming, "If you're gonna fuck him, by God, fuck ME!" He fought his way through the surging dancers and aggressively pulled Kate away from Cleave Thomas.

Cairo came off the wall in a rage. They could all die now. Cairo cracked a mug of beer on the Noneck lineman's head. And the blood began to flow. Fists were smashing faces, bottles, glasses, tables, and chairs were flying across the dance floor.

The amphetamine driven band belted out heavy metal lyrics with no hidden meanings: just the blatant blood lust satanic chorus, chanting: "Fergit Hell/ Kill Rednecks/ Go Home Yankee Blackass Motherfuckers! / Die Crazy Cracker Peckerwoods!"

The Riviera Club was total chaos.

Protected by the famous two-thousand-pound offensive line that won the Sugar Bowl Championship, Kate Hardaway escaped with Cleave Thomas, the New Deion, in his silver Mazda, just before the County Sheriff Department's vehicles came squealing and screeching into the parking lot, follow by three units of Florida State Troopers who arrived just in time to keep the *Riviera Club* from being totally demolished.

There were more people to arrest than there were local law enforcement officers to do the job, but after an hour of random head knocking and face bashing, the disturbance was quelled by enough physical force to ensure that every patrolman's little woman could get herself royally screwed when her patrolman climbed into the sack with his emergency violent hard-on, in the pre-dawn half-light, wanting to calm down, and finally get some sleep, the encore rhapsody to the police officer's all-night wet dream brawl at the *Riviera* Roadhouse.

The left tackle from Badass, Pennsylvania, the Fudgeman from Monster Hill, North Carolina, the Power I Fullback, Black Thunder

Willie Steamboat Harris, and the pulling guard from Noneck, New Jersey, along with the honey-brown cheerleaders, after being singled out for disorderly conduct and the malicious destruction of private property, were escorted by State Troopers back to the University, where they were met by officials from the Athletic Department who hoped to paper over the incident to insure that the student athletes maintained their eligibility and did not further endanger the on-going NCAA investigation of the Alumni Scholarship Fund.

After midnight, as dark clouds drifted across the face of the moon, the surviving cracker warriors who escaped the *Riviera Club* gathered at the beach on Ochlockonee Point and tallied up the score.

Cairo led the celebration with an uncharacteristic war dance around the bonfire. Keith Moss got Darlene to dance naked and then slipped off with her to the woods. Crazy Maxwell goaded Billy Ray with non-stop insults about the Sugar Bowl hero, the gold chained Deion, having his way with Billy Ray's whore sister.

A host of furies drove the cause of hate and blind drunk stupidity. The intoxicated celebrants became dead-of-night conspirators. They cursed the enemy, seen and unseen, the uppity Blacks, the Commies, the cops, and the whole damn world north of the Mason Dixie Line. They consumed alcohol from a quart jar and smoked the Gulf Royale weed.

Cars came and went from the *cul du sac* at the beach. The Sheriff Deputy's radio squealed and squelched and repeated that the silver Mazda was headed west bound from Sopchoppy.

The lost cowboys bragged of revenge. As the night got uglier and dragged into the hollow hours, the conversation lapsed into unintelligible silences, broken by threats of mythic revenge on all Sugar Bowl heroes: past, present, and future.

Andrew Percy, his over-charged libido racing on violence and death-drunken ardor, finally achieved his road weary release with Terri the Pirate, even though she failed to impress him with her French abilities. She played at sex. She wasn't all that good at it, but he'd had worse. And at that particular moment, he didn't care anymore, one way or the other, about anything. He had at last, temporarily, forgotten that Judge Traynor had ever lived. He was more than drunk.

Cairo was now driving the Lincoln, trying to keep up with Billy Ray's Corvette, his vision blurred with the oncoming headlights. Terri, in the back seat, crying, scared at last. The Chief running wide open as they raced along the coast highway, turning back, east at the Highway 98 junction, then speeding recklessly toward Sopchoppy.

The Lincoln swerved onto the gutted McIntyre sand road, still following the red Corvette, and sped along the pine forest toward the river. Percy, callous and heartless, lost in oblivion, riding shotgun. Then suddenly, at the dead-end intersection, the Lincoln, spinning out of control, crashed to black.

The moon was now lost somewhere behind the swirling clouds, and in the dark of night, the heavens wept. When the last bucket of tears had fallen from the sorrowful sky, the stars were silent.

CHAPTER TWENTY-THREE

Andrew Percy in Hades

THE HUNGRY BUZZING of yellow flies broke the morning silence. The summer furies ate away at the torn flesh on his forehead and gorged themselves with blood. In a cesspool of confusion and delirium dreams, Percy lay in the sand, about twenty yards from the Lincoln, by the side of the road.

The narrow sand road went for miles in either direction, through pine forest, going nowhere. He could see the car down the road where it had swerved, spun around, and slammed into a ditch. His head was lacerated from where he had shattered the windshield, his nose busted, right arm probably broken. When he tried to stand, his knee gave way, and he fell back to the ground. His head, caked in dried blood, felt like it was being crushed in a vice grip, jackhammers shattering his skull with every beat of his heart. His brain was blinded by throbbing pain, unable to think clearly. He was barely able to move. One arm was useless.

He thought he remembered trying to walk down the sandy road, cars passing. He was still wet from a heavy rain, but in the heat his clothes would dry soon. He had been lying in a pool of dark water. He dragged himself to the edge of the road and made himself stand. It was still morning, but already the sweltering big sun glared in the clear blue sky. He collapsed to the ground and just sat there. The sun screamed.

He was pissed at Cairo. That was his first complete thought. The half breed son of a bitch had left him. Must be bad juju. All trouble was bad. What was good trouble? What was juju? He wondered if Angie fed the birds.

Images and sounds from the night reverberate in his head. There is a noise like a crack! Pop! Voices yelling off somewhere. The crack! Pop! Silence in the dark. A car drives past. Another car passes. Where is he? In the ditch. Dumb. What is he doing in the ditch? In the water? His arm hurts bad. Face hurts. Two cars go past. But now, he knew he could stand. His leg ached, bruised, but wasn't broken. His right arm just hung like it was dead.

Remembers: voices, cursing, Cairo screaming, "Run wide fuckin' open!" They hit the dead end, crashed into the ditch. He's sprawled out on the road, out of the car. Cairo cussing. Pirate girl crying. Then nothing. Out cold. Last thing he remembers he was in the car. Other cars pass. Voices. Rain rain rain. Flesh eating savages. Heat. The pit of hell. He stood at last and limped slowly toward the car, dragging himself through a dense fog in his head. It was bad. Like stupid. If I ever find that renegade Chief, he'll be a dead half-breed Seminole.

Lincoln smashed in the ditch. Blood splattered the windshield. Keys dangle from the ignition. He struggles into the car and pulls them out with his left hand. Opens the trunk. Curses the missing briefcase. Damn stupid half breed stole my money and my favorite Italian pistol. Caught reflection in mirror. Nose swollen. He was ugly. Bright red blood oozing through caked dark dried blood on his lacerated forehead,

Sand logging roads go nowhere. Yellow flies eat his flesh. Head hurts. Arm hurts. Hotter 'n Hades. No way out of hell woods. Tried to picture where he came from. Creature, where did I come from?

He started limping on sand road. Away from the wrecked Lincoln. Deeper into the woods, past clear-cut acres of devastation on both sides of the gutted road, pools of dark stained rainwater soaked through the bulldozer tracks, the rubble.

All roads looked alike. World turned topsy turvy.

Gambler's instinct: Odds always favor the house. Get out of the house. Cards have numbers. Roll the dice. Life is all chance. When he was right, he scored. When he was off, he lost. Nobody loves you when you're down and out, baby, when you come up short, crapped out. He had always followed his hunch, like animals smell dear. Sometimes he suffered the consequences. Endured. Survived. What chance did Sister have? What happened to Sister's mind? Random chance. He was lucky: when he played by the rules. Respected the law of chance, hit or miss: Reggie needed only one in three to be a star. I need a perfect game just to stay alive. Delgado: kill or be killed. Chief 100% dead, if I ever see him again. Gone back to reservation. Never to be seen again. Chief must be dead already, or he'd be here. Or, I wouldn't be here. Stumble mumble bumble. He hated the word: humble. Who wants humble pie? What a stupid thing to eat. If you must, eat crow, it's a lot better.

House Rule: dealer wins all close calls, making his present condition a matter of self-inflicted misfortune. Damn stupid of him. Judge Traynor dead, gone forever. He did the world a favor. Next, get even with Gato, then Chief. Terri the Pirate, cheap color reproduction. Probably gone to Vegas. Cairo let me down. Fooled me. Fuck him. Both of them. This ain't funny. Pain getting me down.

Intersection: straight ahead goes forever. Pine trees all the same, forever, scrub brush under-growth, yaupon bushes, palmetto black burnt desolation. Other direction: road got small, narrow; grass grew tall. Must be close to river. Go to the river. Second thought: Don't go there. Last chance. God's will, Momma said: to be washed in the river.

Small people surround trucks. Monsters devour forest. The saber-toothed beast hoists mouth full of timber, spits it onto log truck, swings away and growls in his direction. Logging trucks. Pickups. He staggers toward them. One good step for me dragging, one dead left foot …

Remembers: they walked away, leaving me for dead. He fell from the door of the car onto the road, crawled, dragged himself free. Watched them as they disappeared into the dark. Tried to walk, bleeding from his head, down his face, into his eyes, cloudy. He stumbled, fell unconscious into the ditch.

Percy opened his eyes to Nurse Kelly's cherubic face looking down at him.

"Well well." She sounded like a blue bird. "You can open your eyes."

One giant lizard. His right arm wrapped in a plaster cast held aloft by a sling. His left leg wrapped in some synthetic support brace.

He couldn't feel his face, but the doctor peered down at him: Dr. Ashish Malhar Bilaskani, the new doctor from Pakistan at the Belle Rio Community Hospital.

"I see you are like accident looking for place to happen. Ah, you be very lucky to be alive and in the very good hands of Doctor Ashish."

He had been dead.

"In maybe three weeks' time, you be like perfect. Look to my eyes."

Doctor Ashish peered into his eyes, shined a light into his soul, and examined him with exaggerated curiosity.

"I see you be a very lucky man. Be happy. You rest. Soon you walk like new. The arm be okeydokey in few weeks. The head take many stitches. But after cosmic surgery, you be handsome like new. I have cousin doctor in Oklahoma. He does very good what you call 'cosmic surgery.' He can also fix old scar on neck. You be like new. You very very lucky. Nurse Kelly take very very good care. I can tell you okeedokey, because you so mad. You mad mean that you do okeedokey."

"Damn," Percy said. It was painful to be alive.

CHAPTER TWENTY-FOUR

Aftermath

DUSK, SATURDAY. Nearly dark, the hour of mosquitos. It was hard to tell what traffic had been on the sand road. The torrential downpour that broke an hour before dawn had dumped buckets of water over the coast and washed away almost every footprint or track or stain that could have been evidence. From what was left of the skid tracks, the Lincoln in the ditch must have been traveling at a high rate of speed, failed to navigate the turn at the dead-end intersection, went into a skid, slid sideways, then crashed into the ditch.

Deputy Shaver called in the license number. The Lincoln registered to *Andrew J. Percy, Jr. Panama City, FL D.O.B 2/11/51. Port Royale, FL.* Then he called Major Wallace.

Early Sunday morning, before dawn, nobody was there when Billy Ray drove out to the fish cabin in Darlene's car. He parked just off the highway, trying to be smart, keep his wits about him, and with a high beam flashlight, walked along the side of the road, in the weeds, almost a mile back to the cabin He even wore shoes that he would throw away.

There were new tire tracks in the soft sand. Somebody had been on McIntyre Road since it rained, at least as far as the Lincoln, which was still in the ditch; then the driver turned around and went back to the highway. The car had not continued on to the fish cabin. His stomach was wired tight, nauseous with fear.

Outside the cabin, he located two .44 caliber shell casings. There were others he couldn't find. The FDLE could look for bullet fragments lodged in the cedar exterior wall of the cabin if they knew what to look for. He hoped they would never look. His light shining through the misty air, he dragged a tree bow across the brown dirt around the cabin door, scuffed it with the boots he would throw away. Dragged back and forth over the path down to the water. He didn't want to go into the cabin. His courage was gone. Yellow, he thought, coward.

He went inside. Overturned furniture and broken dishes, door busted, windows knocked out. Broken glass on the ground. Wiped and scrubbed but could not concentrate. His mind was skittish and jumpy. He wanted to vomit. He took a can of spray paint and covered the dark stained walls with nonsense graffiti inside and out. Broke more windows. As he had been told: 'Vandalize the cabin'. He was there maybe an hour. Longer than he ever spent cleaning his apartment on the island. He hurried back to his car, almost running, past the Lincoln, oblivious to his foot tracks, and continued on McIntyre Road out to the highway.

Country Sheriff Walt Tatum got a telephone call late Sunday morning from Bud Hardaway whose voice sounded tired and restrained. He told Walt that his daughter, Kate, had been beaten and raped by the football player Cleave Thomas, Friday night after the fight at the club in Wakulla. He said they drove from the club to Sopchoppy and then went up the McIntyre Road. It was apparently one of those date rape situations: she said "no" then he beat and raped her. Thank God, he didn't kill her. He drove off and left her out there. Billy Ray and Maxwell found her walking on the highway when they were driving home from The Point.

Bud said he wanted justice. But, for the sake of his wife and daughter, he wanted to keep this incident under wraps as long as possible. They could talk to Billy Ray. Get a statement from him about what happened. He was not ready to file a complaint. It was just too soon. He needed time. And he wanted Ronnie Smith under control, no matter how much pressure he might get from the university, or whatever. Avoid an unnecessary scandal. He said his daughter, Kate, was in shock and under sedation in a South Georgia private hospital. Bud's aunt lived up there in Georgia, where her husband was a physician. She was in good hands, but traumatized. He had taken her there early Saturday morning.

Bud was definitely upset and was none too happy about her being with the boy in the first place. Even if he was who he was. He didn't want the world to know what happened to his daughter. But he was prepared to file a complaint against Cleve Thomas when the time was right. He would go the distance. He wanted the Thomas boy to pay for what he'd done.

Sheriff Tatum assured Bud that he would have a talk with State's Attorney Ronnie Smith, but that he would not discuss the violation incident until Bud was ready to proceed. When it was appropriate, became necessary, they would issue a warrant for the arrest of Cleave Thomas on charges of rape, kidnapping, and sexual battery, based on a sworn testimony and formal complaint.

"This won't be pretty, Bud. And if you decide to proceed, it won't be a private affair anymore. It won't get any better and it won't be easy."

Sheriff Tatum thought: they should've arrested the lot of 'em over there in Wakulla after they tore up the club, but they just let'em all go, and escorted the football team back to the university. They could've stopped all this from happening.

He wished he'd retired or not been re-elected. He didn't have the heart for this kind of thing anymore. He took medication that kept him awake and gave him headaches. Twenty years ago, when he was first elected Sheriff, there was hardly enough crime to fill the ledger book, and nothing serious at that: bad checks, second degree felonies, assault, battery, thefts against property, mostly modest beach vacation homes, the usual trouble with the Blacks in the Section, knife fights and repeat offender domestic disputes. Lewd and lascivious conduct between adults and underage nephews and nieces were everyday local events.

It started to change in the late seventies: miscellaneous drug possession for personal consumption gave way to possession with intent to sell and distribute, first cannabis then cocaine, and, and that went deep into the community, deep enough to keep getting him re-elected. Then after the hurricane ripped up the bay in 1985, they started growing more and selling more marijuana, importing from South America. The Tommy Matson problem could have brought down the house, but didn't. And recently more bigger houses on the island, more to steal, more environmental problems that affected the bay, and that caused more problems with the out of work itinerant water rats in vacant trailers in East Bay.

Then the crack shit and heroin: more violence, more trouble with assault with intent to commit murder, more trouble with all of them, armed robbery and homicides, rape, mayhem, first degree felonies.

He could still see that most of the killings took place at the fringes of the county and involved non-residents, like the skull-licking creeps from Wisconsin that brought their victim to Snake Bend Road, blew his head off, and dumped the body for the dogs, and then they came back six months later, took the skull to a party, bragging about how they had killed "the snitch," kissing the skull, threatening to kill anybody who told.

Creeps and lost kids. Too many drugs. Too many rich new residents. And too many poor. Now the criminal activity filled two ledger books a year. It was time for him to collect a pension.

This could only be trouble for Belle Rio. He had grown up with Bud Hardaway. Like everyone else, they were cousins to some degree by marriage and claimed or unclaimed love. His wife, the mother of his second set of children, had been married to Tommy Matson when she was young. Tommy could have got them all in jail, but Tommy was no snitch.

It was all too damn convoluted and spiraled down into a mess that always went back to Bud Hardaway, who had the guts to act when others walked away. Bud often took risks when others had already decided it was time to quit. If Bud wanted to take this to the limit, Bud had it figured so he'd win. Bud never walked away from a fight. He always did what he had to do. But he wished he hadn't called Bud Friday night.

Damn times moved too fast. He could only hope for a good outcome. He was too old. He wished he was already collecting a pension.

CHAPTER TWENTY-FIVE

Billy Ray's Statement

MONDAY MORNING the Sports sections of the *Capital City News* contained a two-column story about the potential harmful ramifications resulting from the melee at the *Riviera Club* in Wakulla. The University Athletic Department was already under NCAA investigation for recruiting violations, sports apparel endorsements, and players' improper contact with agents for NFL contracts. The Capital City paper did not usually feature Friday night mayhem at a Redneck Riviera night spot; but this story could fan the NCAA flames and had potential marquee value: one small insert today, one giant scandal tomorrow.

Matthew had barely finished reading the morning newspaper when the telephone rang.

"McCutcheon. This is Bud Hardaway." The dark smooth voice sounded troubled.

"Billy Ray's going to give a voluntary statement to Sheriff Tatum this afternoon regarding the incident over the weekend. I assume you've heard of that incident."

"Yes, sir. Seems like a fun time was had by all."

"I've already talked to the Sheriff, and I intend to press charges against the Thomas boy, when the time is right. I hope to be able to keep my daughter's name out of this, as much as possible, you understand, but I'm afraid if this thing blows, it might get outta hand. Billy Ray's statement should make it clear what happened after the altercation at the Riviera Club. But not go off the deep end. He was still pretty upset earlier this morning. I want you to talk to him. Help him get his head straight. He'll answer questions that are directly related to what he knows, but he needs to be prepped, so that he doesn't get himself all confused. You know my boy. If anything, unusual comes up, call me in Georgia."

He repeated the Georgia area code twice and stumbled through the telephone number.

"I told Billy Ray to call you. You get with him ahead of time."

"Yes, sir, I can do that."

"Taghert suggested you handle this with Billy Ray. I know he's comfortable with you. I'm confident. This is all lawyer client privilege you understand."

"Yes sir, I understand."

There must be a good reason, somewhere in the universe, that Attorney Taghert would now send him something of this potential magnitude.

Francois had said that the Possum Hannah petition and the request for pardon of a convicted killer were not only time consuming, but also bad for business. He didn't believe litigation of this sort served any useful civic purpose. Matthew said that he had been looking over county records and that there was every indication of a grievous miscarriage of justice. Taghert said that Possum Hannah broke the white kid's neck. Matthew said that wasn't the point. Taghert asked, if that was not the point, what was the point? Matt said, doing what was right. Taghert said he thought Matthew was getting useless and moral.

Prior to this, Taghert had said he thought it would be best if Matthew concentrated primarily on their real estate development projects, such as the Tupelo Bluff project, which was coming before the zoning commission next month. Matthew had replied that he hoped all the real estate projects in Belle Rio went bust. Taghert said, "Son, you've gotten useless and moral on me. In that you are just like your mother."

It was the wrong thing to say to Matthew, who impetuously responded that Francois was an "ass hoile." He tried to give it a French lilt, but it sounded more like bad Peter Sellers.

Francois then repeated something about him being a pious and self-righteous twit, ridiculously naïve, who, if and when, he ever came face to face with true evil, would, no doubt, tuck his tail between his legs and run the other way.

Matthew replied that Francois was a pervert and a pedophile, and then he turned his back on Taghert and blurted, "But sir, I show you my ass."

Dropping one's trousers and showing a full moon to the likes of Vlad the Impaler was risky at best, and probably not a good way to leave his association with Francois Gellot Taghert, Esq., Attorney at Law. It was a spontaneous response to the old crustacean, ignited by the reference to any relationship Francois, may or may not have had, with his mother.

In typical Belle Rio custom, Francois Taghert's embellishment of the incident became a courthouse legend.

After leaving counselor Taghert, Matthew rented office space across from the Courthouse. He had a small reception area, a round conference table, and a place to read and write. The office was cluttered and messy,

His filing system was incomplete at best. He needed secretarial help but hadn't gotten around to it. At least, now he was Florida certified.

For the past few months, he had been working on a legal remedy for Possum Hannah, and he had spent considerable effort in Capital City trying to work out a direct pardon from the governor. He had realized that he would never get an official hearing until after the November election, much less a parole hearing for the Correctional League power forward.

Crime was a hot item on the political agenda. Executing death row inmates was a vote-getter. Possum had been tried, convicted, and sentenced to death. It was going to take time to establish the systematic exclusion of blacks from the grand jury process in Belle Rio County. In the time he had been in Belle Rio, he had only seen one black called for jury duty. This was the potential political hot button that gave him some room to maneuver.

He took the direct approach and wrangled an appointment with the Governor, whose father had begun his political career as a down state legislator, and at one time had been a political crony of his grandfather Patterson.

The Governor wouldn't promise anything, of course, but he said that after his aides reviewed the case, that all things being equal, blah blah blah, don't hold me to this, of course, et cetera etcetera et cetera, said that when the dust settled, he would help, as best he could, assuming he got re-elected, of course.

In the conference room at the Belle Rio County Sheriff's office Billy Ray looked frazzled. He sat at the table next to Matthew and smoked nervously.

"I ain't slept much since Friday," Billy Ray said. "This damn thing just got way out of a hand. I ain't been thinking too straight," Billy Ray smiled sheepishly at him.

"This is not about you, Billy Ray. I understand from your father he set up this meeting. Keep it simple and to the point. Don't answer what's not asked. Don't say any more than necessary. In other words, say as little as possible."

Major Wallace, Sheriff Tatum's top man, entered the room with Assistant State's Attorney Ronnie Smith.

Major Wallace said, "Didn't expect to see you here, Mr. McCutcheon. Billy Ray doesn't need an attorney for this, but I understand. We're just trying to clarify a few details for Sheriff Tatum – in response to a possible accusation by Mr. Hardaway that his daughter, your sister Billy Ray, was raped Saturday morning, after the incident Friday night in Wakulla; and that you have the most information on what transpired that night. And there is request for information from the University Athletic Department, regarding the whereabouts of the young man, Cleve Thomas. All this, of course, is confidential. At Bud's request, there are, at this time, no specific criminal charges. Only a lot of confusion mis-information and indecision. Consider this a curtesy for Mr. Hardaway."

"Nor did I expect to be here, Major. I'm just lending some moral support, at the request of Mr. Hardaway, who asked me to accompany Billy Ray. ... Afternoon, Mr. Attorney Smith, good to see you again."

"This could be a circus," Ronnie Smith said with a mixture of gloom and anticipation. "We're just trying to get the facts."

Attorney McCutcheon smiled back. He shared attorney Taghert's opinion of Smith: that he was a braggart whose ego would run wild given the opportunity. But State's Attorney Ronny Smith wasn't stupid.

Major Wallace said, "Can we do this while Billy Ray is still awake?"

Major Wallace and Prosecutor Smith often had different agendas. Mr. Smith brought a self-aggrandizing zeal to the Prosecutor's office that Major Wallace could do without, especially considering what he saw coming down the pike. And Bud Hardaway was his uncle by marriage. And on occasion, he went fishing on Billy Ray's charter boat.

Major Wallace took the lead. "Billy Ray, I understand that you were at the *Riviera Club* in Wakulla this past Friday night?"

Over the next hour Billy Ray recounted the events that transpired at the *Riviera Club*: yes, it probably could be said that he started the brawl at the Riviera, but he said the university athletes really caused the trouble by coming in there, flaunting their garnet and gold shit, and messing with the white women the way they were doing. Actually, it was Cairo who started the fighting.

No, he'd never met Cleave Thomas before. He was already over in Panama City when Thomas attended High School in Belle Rio. Yes, of course, he knew that Thomas was a hot shot. No, he was not aware that his sister had been seen with Thomas before, and didn't believe it today. Kate was hardheaded and sometimes did things that could make people crazy. She'd always been that way. Them damn Sugar Bowl players nearly tore the *Riviera Club* to shambles and they got a highway patrol escort back to their dorms. That's some basic, fair American treatment for you.

After the brawl, they continued drinking on the beach around a bonfire at the Ochlockonee Point. He heard Cairo and Andrew Percy say they was "gonna kill somebody. But they was talkin' 'bout that Cuban guy in Panama City that worked owned the Cleopatra strip joint.

Early Saturday morning they all left the Point and was driving home. He saw his sister, Kate, wandering along the highway between the Sopchoppy bridge and Highway 98 junction. He always drove the

Sopchoppy route to Belle Rio. She was in shock. She'd been beat up and possibly, probably raped. He only knew what his father told had him.

He took her to his father's house at St. Cecilia, about 3 AM, then he went to his apartment on the island. It rained like hell. He fell asleep and didn't wake up until the late afternoon. Yes, he had on occasion gotten real drunk. No, he did not drive up to the fish cabin Friday night. Yes, they was all gonna go to the fish cabin, but he found his sister walking along the road. He took her to St. Cecilia instead.

Why was he going to the fish cabin? They was going up there to fish. That's why you go to a fish cabin. No. We was piss drunk and wanted a place to finish the party, then sleep it off. But we did somthin' different when we got Kate walking along the roadway. I was not 'xactly sober but that sobered me up. I had to get her home.

Yes, he thought Andrew Percy and Cairo could've drove on out McIntyre Road toward the cabin. But there was nobody out there so they must've jus left. Yes, the cabin had been vandalized about six months ago, but they didn't report it 'cause there was nothing Sheriff Tatum could do about it anyway. They would just gonna have to fix it up again. It wasn't the first time the cabin was tore up.

Billy Ray said that he stopped at the all-night Quick Stop in East Bay before he went home to the island. That was sometime close to six o-clock, when it rained so damn hard. He wasn't exactly sure of the time. Maxwell was in the car with him. That about summed up what he knew about who was running loose Friday night after midnight.

"You picked up Kate on McIntyre Road? At the intersection where the road dead ends and the turn goes off to the cabin?" Major Wallace asked.

"No, it was just a little ways up the McIntyre Road. Before we crossed the Sopchoppy bridge, we turned on the McIntyre Road. That's where we saw Kate. Walking along the road. She was at the highway."

"Then what happened?" Ronnie Smith asked.

"I stopped the car and got out. Kate was all beat up. Crying. Hysterical. She had walked out from the cabin after that S.O.B left her there. I put her in the car and took her to my dad's house in St. Cecilia."

"She walked from the fish cabin to the highway? How far is that?

"Maybe he drove and left her near the intersection. Maybe they never went there. He was gone by then."

"Why would he leave her there?"

"Hell, why would he do anything he did. Ask him."

"We will. … How far is it from McIntyre Road to St. Cecelia?"

"Not far. Maybe three to five miles."

"Maxwell was with you?"

"Yeah."

"The three of you in the Corvette?"

"No. Maxwell was drunker'n a skunk. I told him he could get his ass out and walk. I let him out, then I picked him up again. Maxwell will tell you the same as me, if he can remember any of it to tell."

"Which direction did Mr. Thomas turn when he left McIntyre?"

Billy Ray went blank. His eyes glazed over. He looked at Matthew. He waited a long time. They sat like stones at the table.

"He left before I got there. I don't know which way he turned. I'd know his car if I saw it. I didn't see it. So he must've went back toward Cap City."

"Did Kate tell you that she was raped by Cleve Thomas?"

Billy Ray didn't know whether or not to answer. He had been told not to talk about that. It seemed like a trick. He glanced at Matthew. He didn't answer. They waited. Major Wallace tapped his pen, then lit a cigarette.

"I told you she was beat up. Maybe she had been. I don't know 'bout nothin' else. She probably was and that's why he disappeared."

"Who was in the cars that went up McIntyre Road?"

"I told you. It was Cairo and Mr. Percy from Panama City, and I think maybe Terri Cates was with them."

"You said there were a couple of cars. Is that two? Three?"

"I don't know how many cars. Keith Moss and Chad and Darlene was at the Point with us, but they took out and went home. … So, there was just one car that went up on McIntyre. … Mr. Percy's Lincoln."

"Did you know Mr. Percy's car wrecked up the McIntyre Road, at the intersection, where the logging roads intersect?"

"I don't know nothing about that. I never got up that far."

"Did you see Cleave Thomas' silver Mazda any time that night?"

"I never seen him or his car after he left the Riviera Club. He was gone after he dumped Kate. Before we got there. I got no idea where he went."

"Do you know what happened to Cairo Thorne and Terri Cates?

"I don't know nothing about them. I just know my sister was beat up an' … I 'd been drinking, but I got sober in a hurry. I took her to my daddy's house in St. Cecilia, and he took her to my uncle Harry who's a doctor up in Thomasville, Georgia."

"Where do you suppose Mr. Thomas went?"

Attorney Smith abruptly interrupted. "He has not been seen at the University?"

"Ain't no way I'd have a clue 'bout that. Me an' him aint exactly talkin'."

State's Attorney Ronnie Smith had an incredulous look of face. "Billy Ray, that Mazda left and three people went up McIntyre Road. Two didsappeared. That's crazy. Something doesn't add up."

"It was a crazy night."

"How did Cairo and Terri Cates get to wherever they are now?"

"… I ain't got no idea. Where do you think they are?"

"When was the last time you were at the fish cabin?"

"Huh? … Damn, Wallace. It ain't been recently. Six months? Last year? That place is always a damn mess."

Major Wallace said, "OK, that's all today, Billy Ray. Looks like you could use some rest. I'm sure we'll talk again before this is over."

CHAPTER TWENTY-SIX

Crazy Maxwell

IT WAS ALREADY ninety degrees in the shade, and there wasn't much of it. The bright glare of recent events was making Billy Ray blind. He felt stupid in the hot sun. He'd already smoked one joint and rolled another to try and clear his head, but his brain was confused, over-burdened. They had partied last night at Cat Point near East Bay and he was trying to sort out all the lies he had told and re-told and tried to believe himself, so that the pieces fit together and the whole thing wouldn't come unraveled. Billy Ray and Darlene had spent the night together. Both of them felt so bad in the morning they went to the East Bay *Quick Stop* and got egg & cheese biscuits and a six pack.

Billy Ray hadn't slept much since the trouble in Wakulla and it was making him crazy. His father had told him to take the boat out and do some fishing, but he didn't think he could stand to be alone out there on the water. He was trying to stay out of sight and sober, but he was walking three steps forward, two steps back, carrying a case of beer, with Crazy Maxwell walking ahead of him like he was leading a lamb to slaughter.

Maxwell got named "Crazy" after a knife fight in a movie theater back when there was a movie theater in Belle Rio. He told the Sherriff's deputies that drove him back and forth to Capital City that he spoke at least seven foreign languages, then he babbled nonsense that was his example of German. His French sounded exactly the same; so did his Spanish, Hindu, and Chinese. He refused to divulge information regarding his personal life and claimed that he was an undercover FBI agent, posing first as a construction laborer, then a backhoe operator, a logger, or bay oysterman. He said he experienced "permanent memory block" while talking to a court appointed psychiatrist because the Sheriff's deputies transmitted telepathic signals that interfered with his mind. He was crazy paranoid and suffered loss of memory when it suited him. Even comic books confused him. He looked at the pictures, but they were all jumbled up; the words were different than the pictures. He didn't get it. He could add and subtract single digits, but multiplication was a foreign mystery and whatever division was, it was totally unnecessary.

The Capital City psychiatrist had said that he was a reckless, impulsive, short-sighted pleasure seeker, with a long history of being unable to control his selfish, immature, indulgent, often violent impulses. All this was clearly stated in the written psychiatric evaluation when he got put on probation for the knife fight during a Clint Eastwood spaghetti western movie.

After Maxwell and Billy Ray had gone down to the pond, Crazy Maxwell came back. Floyd was up under the truck and covered with grease. Maxwell asked for a cigarette. Floyd tossed the pack out from under the truck and told Maxwell to hand him a 9/16 socket wrench from the tool chest. Maxwell smoked while Floyd tightened bolts, then

Floyd crawled out from under the Ford and lit a cigarette himself. Maxwell had put on a clean shirt and said he was going to town, then he walked off toward Mr. Lannie's trailer.

Everybody took advantage of Mr. Lannie and he didn't have no life of his own. He wanted this and he wanted that, but he got nothing because he was too easy to take advantage of. Darlene was staying at his trailer with Chad Mosser, and since that killin' business, Billy Ray was hanging around all the time. Chad just moved over when Billy Ray came around. He was like Mr. Lannie, who didn't want to cause no trouble and had to make do with what was left over.

When Maxwell and Billy Ray came by with a case of beer, Mr. Lannie was working on the boat in his yard; so, they went into the trailer to drink beer and paw on Darlene. At one time or another, Darlene had gone with all of them, except for Maxwell, and there were just too many times she'd had her legs open for her to pretend how innocent she was, even though it was only Billy Ray she wanted. But he never really wanted her. Maxwell kept trying to feel her up on the sofa. She told him to quit. But she liked having people want her, and she wanted the beer Maxwell kept promising her for what she wouldn't do. Billy Ray told Maxwell to keep his damn hands to himself. And to go fuck his own self and leave her alone. Maxwell allowed as how that's exactly what he planned to do. They could watch and see.

Mr. Lannie got tired of hearing all the vulgar talk wafting out the trailer door. Mr. Lannie didn't like 'em hollering and talking about something he couldn't get none of anyways, so he came in and told Maxwell and Billy Ray to leave. They left, walking off down the road, talking real loud. Then after a while Darlene left after them. She wanted another beer.

Crazy Maxwell was Charlotte Jones' first husband's cousin. She had known Maxwell ever since he moved there to be with his sister. Late that afternoon, she watched Billy Ray and Maxwell stagger down the sandy road toward her house. She thought to herself that Billy Ray was dead drunk, but she'd seen Maxwell drunk, and he wasn't drunk now. They stopped at the house and talked with Warren and Ed Leroy. Billy Ray was acting spooked, and he said something to Warren that she couldn't understand through the window. Warren got mad. She could always tell when her husband was mad.

Billy Ray was a goofy boy. They had all watched him grow up, and they didn't expect much out of him. He was usually polite, even if he did have too much money and he was involved with the drugs that was going around. Warren told Charlotte that Billy Ray was a "no count piss ant" and that Maxwell had told him that they was going swimming at the pond, down by Maxwell's trailer at the end of the road.

About an hour later, she and Warren returned from the store and saw Maxwell walking back up the road by himself, walking fast. And he had on a different shirt. Charlotte remembered thinking "where in the deuce is he going?" She had never seen him move that fast.

Soon the Sheriff Deputies were showing up all over the place and that night they had the whole dang county, it seemed like, over at the jail for questioning.

Ed Leroy didn't have anything good to say about any of them: especially Darlene, though it weren't her fault. He'd known Darlene since he moved there, when he was twelve. He used to work for Darlene's father, but he didn't run with that crowd, because her brother got him sent to jail for selling stolen property. Something happened over there after Darlene's mother died. They all assumed they knew what it was. They just said Darlene's daddy wasn't a nice man, anyways, but he minded his own. Sometimes maybe he minded them too much, especially Darlene.

Darlene had been drinking steady since she was in high school. That was more than ten years ago. It wasn't that she was an alcoholic; it was just that she stayed drunk most of the time. And because she was mostly drunk, she aggravated people and they didn't like to put up with her. It wasn't even that she drank an unusual amount, she just drank all she could drink. Besides drinking she lied. She'd say one thing one day, then she'd say something different the next day. She couldn't remember what she'd said. She didn't pay attention, because people ask you a lot of questions and you give so many answers that it gets confusing. Darlene didn't know if Darlene was telling the truth or not.

She'd been Billy Ray's girlfriend since they were in high school. She couldn't keep Billy Ray and she knew it. Billy Ray was in trouble now. But she couldn't help him. Billy Ray was mad at her because he knew she fucked Keith Moss after the fight at the *Riviera* and it wasn't nothing she could deny.

Every place has rules, no matter how strange they are. She got tired of being treated like used clothes. She couldn't remember the last time Billy Ray was really nice to her. She used to live at his house on the island but that was a long time ago, before he started pimping her to out of town fishermen. She hated him for that. But he had been nice to her when she ran away, after her daddy. After her daddy. That's as far as that thought ever went: after her daddy. She tried once to think beyond that but her mind went dead, and after that, there was nothing to think that she wanted to remember.

Young Bill Cody was fishing at the pond near the hand painted sign that said *Risk Your Own Life* when Maxwell and Billy Ray came walking down the path carrying what was left of the beer. Maxwell took off his shirt and waded into the pond. He was a wild man, nasty as a hog, unshaven, his long graying hair unkempt. His arms were tattooed with lizards. Maxwell and Billy Ray were arguing about who was going to win their first big pussy eating contest and Maxwell asked Cody if he'd like to participate. Cody was only twelve, and he didn't think that he was likely to win the contest that afternoon. He said that, anyway, he had tried it once, and didn't think it was anything all that special, or anyway, that's what he'd heard.

Maxwell said "too bad for you" and went on over to his little trailer near the pond. Billy Ray tried to get Cody to drink some beer. Cody said he had to go home and left. Then Billy Ray just sat there on the bank drinking beer and tossing stones in the water.

Darlene wanted another beer. She wandered bare-footed down the sandy road toward the pond and got cockleburs in her feet. There wasn't much else good to hope for in this life besides another beer. When she reached the end of the road, she could hear them yelling and cursing and as she came out of the trees, she saw them wrestling, both half naked. Bewildered by what she was hearing, she approached them, pleading for them to stop. Billy Ray pushed her away. She thought there was a knife with a pearl handle, like a switchblade. She felt it cut across the back of her thigh and blood was running down her leg.

Maxwell cursed Billy Ray and cut him across the chest. He growled with a heavy voice, "I'm gonna kill you son of a bitch! Since you was a kid. Goddamn you!"

Billy Ray yelled, "Run Darlene Run!"

She was running. Then there was silence from the pond. When she turned, Maxwell was standing over Billy Ray. Searching for her. She ran out along the path to the paved road, ran past her daddy's trailer thinking the whole time that Crazy Maxwell was after her, and she was afraid of him. She ran for her life, but would never go to her daddy to be safe.

Maxwell showed up not long after she got to the trailer, wearing a different shirt, and he asked if he could see Darlene. Mr. Lannie said "no, she was inside with Chad." And he told Maxwell to leave her alone, because he'd already told him once before to quit foolin' with her. He'd had enough of Maxwell an' didn't want no more.

Inside the trailer, Darlene played with the little gold crucifix around her neck, while Chad bandaged the cut on her leg. She was engulfed in a dark nightmare. Her mind was filled with awful things: Crazy Maxwell standing over Billy Ray screaming like he was the Devil himself. Holding Billy Ray's head back, he cut deep across his throat. Billy Ray's mouth opened in mute agony as blood gushed into his windpipe. His head fell listless to his body, which dropped like a dead weight to the ground.

Then she cried.

Maxwell said, "Everything's taken care of."

Mr. Lannie said, "Well, still, I ain't gonna let you see her."

And he said again, "Everything's taken care of."

Mr. Lannie said, "What do you mean 'taken care of?'"

And Maxwell said, "I killed the son of a bitch. He aint talking to nobody. Never again."

Mr. Lannie just looked at him, thinking he was as crazy as they said. And Maxwell hung around, smoking cigarettes, nervous and fidgeting, twitching the way he does, while Mr. Lannie worked on his boat, ignoring Maxwell talking nonstop nonsense to no one.

J.T. came over to Deputy Shaver's house. He had spent the day up in the woods cutting trees for poles. When he got home, he went around the back of the trailer and saw a case of beer sitting beside a person who was laying on the bank, empty cans scattered around. Something strange struck him that the person was dead, and he got suddenly scared, his heart pounding. He walked away in a hurry and drove up the road to Deputy Shaver's house and said there was a dead man at his brother's pond, down the dirt road past the little houses, and the trailer where Maxwell lived by himself.

They went back to the pond, and sure enough, the man was still dead, the face pale, bloodless. The throat cut clean through.

"That's Billy Ray," said Deputy Shaver.

Deputy Shaver called into headquarters. Soon Deputy Guyton arrived, and they went down to the pond where Deputy Shaver said again, "That's Billy Ray."

Billy Ray was naked from the waist up, laying on his back, arms out wide. His hair stained a reddish brown. There was a jagged, superficial slash across his chest, but his throat was cut clean through. There was a dark stain where the blood that had poured from his neck had been absorbed into the sand. He was stretched out beside a half empty case of beer, his bare feet hanging over the bank in the water, his eyes frozen in horror. Nearby, his socks were stuffed neatly into his shoes.

The deputies drove up to Mr. Lannie's trailer and stopped when they saw Maxwell standing in the yard talking to Mr. Lannie, who by know, knew something strange was going on, but he didn't get the whole picture.

"What's going on?" Mr. Lannie ask. "Where'd Billy Ray get to?"

"The only place he was going to," Deputy Shaver said, "was the morgue."

That told Mr. Lannie something he could understand.

Deputy Shaver turned to Maxwell and said,

"Maxwell, I want you to come over here so we can talk to you. Come on easy now. We just want to talk about what happened to Billy Ray."

Maxwell stared at them like they was all crazy but him. Crazy Maxwell had been in jail before and had said that he wasn't ever going back.

He started screaming at Deputy Shaver,

"Yall trying to make something outta nothin! You gonna have to take me," he yelled, just like he was on TV, and bolted and knocked Shaver to the ground.

Deputy Guyton lunged at Maxwell. But Maxwell was swinging wildly with a knife and knocked the deputy into the vehicle. Deputy Guyton's face was bloodied. Maxwell grabbed the officer by the throat, and strangling him until he was gasping for air, they danced in a circle, until Guyton's face turned blue.

Then Maxwell released the deputy, his arms extended out over his head, and growled like some monster in a cheap horror movie.

Maxwell screamed again, a crazy howl that was just an awful noise, not meant to be heard by humans or animals or any living creature, but only demon spirits, unafraid of death and hell and dying.

Deputy Shaver's magnum blew a gaping hole in Crazy Maxwell's chest.

CHAPTER TWENTY-SEVEN

Gathering for Billy Ray

IN SPITE OF BUD HARDAWAY'S desire for a private service, his wife, Nancy Markham Hardaway, insisted on a public graveside preaching.

The funeral service was a melancholy, depressing affair in a steady drizzle rain, attended by the immediate family and friends, so that by the time they all gathered, there were at least seventy-five to a hundred cousins, nieces, nephews, the many children of Bud's four sisters and the ten husbands between them, plus another hundred or so friends of the family, friends of Billy Ray, and the employees from the Hardaway Seafood Company.

Elvis led a contingent from the Sea Horse Tavern. Darlene was there with Chad. She was too far gone to ever cry again, and she still wasn't sober, but she swore it was her last drunk. Skinny Sherman escorted Toothless Madonna, dressed in black. Dr. Zeus had spent the last of his Fantasy Lotto money on a shiny suit. Stump, son of Peg Leg Orville, lost in a cloud of cigarette smoke, brought a carload of gypsies, midgets, and carnival misfits. There were also some workers from the fishing lodge near Dead Lake and the Three Rivers Alligator Farm, the buxom Real

Estate Mogul with her employees from White Hope Realty, Sheriff Tatum and the off-duty Deputies, Judge Kidd from the Circuit Court with his wife, a distant relative of Bud Hardaway, members of the County Commission, the publisher of *The Belle Rio Times,* Francois Taghert and the courthouse gang, and others from surrounding counties who knew the Hardaway family by reputation and thought they should be there.

The whole atmosphere of Belle Rio was pervaded with a somber mood that was worse than anybody could remember, and there was the unspoken expectation that more trouble was coming, that Billy Ray's untimely death was just the beginning.

They had all known Billy Ray the charter boat Captain, the clown, the party animal. They laughed at his inane jokes and his Bugs Bunny and Elmer Fudd cartoon voices, smoked his pot, ate the catch from his fishing trips, and enjoyed his never-ending search for a good time. It was true that most people in Belle Rio got along and got by. They fought, they fished, they fornicated, they forgot about everything else when it was hunting season, time to go up in the woods and shoot at something. They drank, they laughed, they loved each other, they married each other, they buried the dead. Some of them cried, some of them prayed. Sometimes it was necessary to forget, and this seemed to be as good a time as any, to forget as much as possible.

Three of the four children born to Bud and Nancy Hardaway had brought them sadness and grief: an infant son who died at three months, Katherine drugged unconscious in a private hospital in Thomasville, and now, Billy Ray dead at twenty-eight.

Eldest son Donny Hardaway was doing his best to hold together what was left of four generations that had suddenly gone haywire. Their world was being attacked by disgruntled fate, bad luck, and amendments to the state constitution. Donny knew more than most about what was in store for them, and even he wasn't sure what they were going to do after they lost the *Net Ban Amendment* vote. He looked out over the crowd and saw almost everyone that he knew. They would sink or swim together.

Nancy Markham Hardaway was a walking corpse, gaunt and weightless, her white hair pulled severely against her temples, covered in black. She was convalescing from the sickness that accompanied her chemotherapy, and her only solace was that the cure would kill her.

She took some comfort from her flowers which came back every year, never disappointing her, and all she had to do was water them, talk to them, love them a little, and they offered their quiet beauty in return.

Nancy had no family of her own living now, except for an estranged cousin, that she hadn't seen in years, who had been raised as her older sister, then disappeared from her life. She had lived in silence through long years of emotional suffering after the death of her infant daughter, who lay in the sandy ground next to where they were going to put Billy Ray.

Her husband had never been any comfort to her; instead, he was the primary source of her deep unending pain. She had survived years of a failed, loveless marriage because of her faith in God and her fervent hope that, indeed, there was a better life in the world to come, better than this life had been for her.

Donny walked beside his mother, supporting her with his left hand on her elbow, his right arm around her waist. He was practically carrying her. The Methodist preacher assured her that Jesus could wash away the sins of her family, that his death on the Cross of Calvary would heal the suffering in her soul, and that Billy Ray and her already departed little angel would be in heaven, waiting for her. And if there were enough blood, Jesus could even make her daughter Katherine whole again. She prayed with all her heart that there was enough blood for all those things to be made right.

Wilbur "Bud" Hardaway, consumed by opaque despondency, stood beside his wife. He thought: that his life was nearly over, that his son Donny was a good man, and that he would somehow make the best of the family business; Donny is as determined as he is dull. It will take a sturdy man to get through the times that are coming.

Standing unnoticed at the edge of the crowd was Sara Markham Percy, a small gray-haired woman with her hair in a bun, wearing a plastic raincoat, holding an umbrella over her daughter Allison. They were both dressed in black, the small woman clinging to the bigger one, while the awkward large one swayed to and from and hummed off key as they sang *When the Roll Is Called Up Yonder.*

As they prayed for the departed soul of Billy Ray Hardaway, there was never any doubt that God was merciful.

Two months after Billy Ray died and all the other business that had destroyed the tranquility of Belle Rio was settled down, Charlotte Jones found a bloodstained, rusty, twelve-inch kitchen knife in a woodpile on a sandy trail running from the pond to the paved road. Billy Ray had been Charlotte Jones' second husband's first wife's nephew. She remembered what others had forgot: about twenty years before, when Billy Ray was just a boy, Billy Ray had been a witness in court against Maxwell. They had been out in the woods in an old logging road—Maxwell, another man, young Billy, and her young boys. The boys were about thirteen at the time. They were all drinking, and the men got to fighting, and Maxwell picked up a log and hit the other man from behind, near about caved his head in. Billy Ray testified in court against Maxwell, and Maxwell spent two years in the county work camp for

231

aggravated battery. Maxwell swore he'd get Billy Ray for that day in court.

"Someday I'm gonna get that son of a bitch, Billy Ray, even if I have to play the fool for him, an' wait a hundret years. I'm gonna get him in the woods an' kill him."

Maxwell played up to Billy Ray and waited his time. Maxwell was crazy like that. After a time, everybody but Maxwell forgot about Billy Ray's testimony in court.

When Charlotte Jones found the knife, she remembered what Maxwell had said, but it didn't matter now. Not after all the things that happened. The way it turned out. She threw the knife in the pond and tried to forget about it.

Crazy Maxwell disappeared without ceremony. He did not have any friends, and was only survived by his estranged sister who lived in Dixie County. She sent word that Maxwell could be cremated at the state's expense; after all, they had killed him.

CHAPTER TWENTY- EIGHT

Cleve Thomas Discovered

MONDAY MORNING before sunrise, two fishermen put in at the Sopchoppy bridge and went up the McIntyre Narrows where the Crooked River joined the Ochlockonee River. The cypress railroad trestles had been rotting in the water for seventy-five years, ever since the BR/T&S Railroad went bankrupt.

It was their favorite spot to catch large-mouth bass. There was always a good chance of catching a large-mouth at the narrows, and it was damn sure better than listening to one at home.

Casting his spinner over against the cypress stumps in the grass along the banks, one of the fishermen hooked the bloated, decomposing body of the Sugar Bowl hero, Cleave Thomas, the New Deion. He had not been seen at the university since the brawl at the *Riviera Club*.

By late that afternoon, McIntyre Road was swarming with law enforcement, where an Italian made .44 caliber hand gun was found in a palmetto thicket near the wrecked Lincoln on a sand logging road leading from the Hardaway fish cabin at the McIntyre Landing.

On the following morning Judge Kidd of the Florida Circuit Court issued a probable cause warrant for the arrest of Andrew J. Percy based on the information supplied by State's Attorney Ronnie Smith.

There was a sigh of relief in Belle Rio now that the state had a worthy perpetrator to go with the celebrity homicide victim. Andrew Percy looked like a sitting duck. State's Attorney Ronnie Smith swore that he would proceed with caution and diligence. He guaranteed that, beyond the arrest of Mr. Andrew Percy, he would arrest and convict any, and all other, persons responsible for the reprehensible homicide of the local-boy-made-good Sugar Bowl hero, Cleave Thomas, now deceased.

There had only been a secondhand speculation of a rape charge against Cleve Thomas, which was now irrelevant. There never was an actual complaint, only the off the record conversation that he'd had with the Sheriff, based on an accusation by Bud Hardaway.

Andrew Percy was placed under house arrest at the Belle Rio Hospital for the murder of the triple-threat university athletic star Cleave Thomas. He was the most logical and convenient suspect for the homicide. Two Belle Rio deputies were stationed at the hospital. The highway patrol was on standby alert should trouble arise in the Black community.

Suddenly, Andrew Percy wasn't going anywhere. Before he could move on, he was under house arrest. He was still enjoying the drug bliss of Dr. Ashish's IV drip. It had been like a vacation. He had a dream, or a hazy memory, that Momma came to visit him, babbling something about family relations, and God knows what else. He was tired of God's will. Or whatever got him in his present condition: he could barely walk, his right arm was in a temporary cast, he had a broken rib and stitches in his head, which was partially shaved.

Percy wasn't really worried about that. He knew he did not kill Cleve Thomas. But it still felt like thin ice.

He called his over-priced criminal attorney in Panama City.

"Get your ass over here," Percy said dryly. "Now."

Predictable attorney response, "Damn, Drew. I can't ask 'how high?' every time a client says 'jump.' It sounds like you got yourself in a fine mess. At the moment this is an explosive event. Very explosive! ... Stay out of the newspaper. Stay off TV. Youe told me, you were unconscious when this occurred. Stay unconscious until we can confirm what evidence they have to the contrary. What else do you expect *me* to do?"

True, he had not been thinking all that clear. That was certainly evident. He felt no urgent need to just get up and walk out, even if he could. He hadn't worried about his car, abandoned on the forest road. He correctly assumed that Cairo had taken everything of value.

He might never see the Chief again, damn half-breed Cairo hung him out to dry, and could rot in hell for all he cared. Percy assured himself that he would never go to trial for this murder. He sure as hell wasn't going to jail for a murder he did not commit.

At this point, State Prosecutor Ronnie Smith had a high-profile homicide victim. He had the weapon. He had the potential trial of his dreams. Obviously, there were still too many loose ends. He needed more information before he could move toward the legal Circus Maximus.

There was now a national APB "suspect dangerous" warrant for the apprehension of Cairo Thorne. But anyone who knew the Chief, knew that he would "run wide open" and that sooner or later, would turn up somewhere, John Doe, DOA.

Most importantly, for the citizens of Belle Rio, the potential indictment of Mr. Percy, a low life strip club operator from Panama City with a criminal record, took the glare of the spotlight away from the public and private character of Belle Rio, and for the time being, that made most respectable people comfortable, even if it were not true.

Blacks in the Section believed that two of the guilty white devils had already gone to their final judgement. They were happy with that. They preferred them dead, as opposed to a Belle Rio whitewash or a hung jury verdict. But they also needed some retribution, or at least some final judgement and comfort. Few believed Andrew Percy would provide any of that satisfaction.

CHAPTER TWENTY-NINE

Rescue Terri Cates

TERRI THE PIRATE called collect just after ten o'clock.

"Where are you?" Matthew asked.

"Boga something." Her voice sounded small and afraid.

"Where?" he asked again.

"Over by New Orleans," it still sounded somewhat mystical.

"How'd you get there?"

"I got away from him before New Orleans."

"Got away from who?"

"From Cairo. In a truck stop. I got a ride with some guy that sells equipment stuff. We drove to this motel."

"What town?" There was some muffled confusion while she asked someone to tell her where she was.

"Bogalusa" she finally answered. "Am I in trouble?"

"Depends on what you did."

"I didn't do nothing. Was Percy bad hurt?"

"He seems his jovial self."

"I didn't have nobody else to call. I called Billy Ray but nobody ever answered. That's why I called you."

"Billy Ray's dead," Matthew said without inflection.

"Oh." That was all she said.

"He was buried today."

"Dead?"

"Crazy Maxwell killed him. Maxwell's dead too."

"Oh." The line was silent.

"I talked to your mother this afternoon."

"I don't want to talk to her. Don't make me do that."

"Call your mother. She's worried about you."

"I can't go nowhere. I ain't got no money."

"Where's Cairo?"

"New Orleans, I guess. That's where he was headed. We stopped for gas and I got out and hid. Then he drove off. He was glad to be rid of me."

"I doubt it," he said. Sarcasm would be wasted on her. There was only static and silence on the phone.

"Consider yourself lucky to be alive. But you're missing all the fun," he said. "Why don't you come home?"

"How? I ain't got no money, and…"

"And?"

"I don't know what to do. And I don't want no trouble."

"Is your salesman expecting you to repay him?"

"Ain't that what men expect?"

"Make him give you enough money to get home."

"I ain't gonna screw him for money to come home."

"Why not? …"

The line went silent. "Why call me? Call your mother."

"I want you to come get me. I didn't have nothing to do with the killing."

"What killing?" he asked as disinterested as possible.

"Oh." The line went silent again, like she had hung up.

"What killing?" He asked twice.

"I thought…"

"You thought what?"

"I thought they killed him." She started to cry.

He waited until she stopped crying. … "They did."

She said again, "I didn't have nothing to do with the killing."

"Then you better come back."

"Am I gonna be in trouble?"

"If you don't come back, you're gonna be in trouble. Where are you now, this minute?"

"In the motel office. In Bogalusa."

"Put the manager on the phone. I'll pay for your room. You go to your room. Keep the door shut, and locked, until I get there. Tell your traveling salesman friend that 'you already gave at the office.' He'll understand what that means."

"I don't understand… what any of this means."

"Put the desk clerk on the telephone. Then go to your room and lock your door," he said, thinking: she understands less than she knows.

"I'm sorry Billy Ray is…" she paused, couldn't say it.

"Dead," he said. "Yeah, it's too bad."

He was on the highway by midnight. Passed through Panama City Beach at two in the morning. It was the way of the weary world. Terri saying "I didn't have nothing to do with the killing" buzzed in his ear.

Once again, he was losing his faith in the natural cosmic order. Some awful power had taken wandering Venus from the sky and parked her at the White Sands Motel at Belle Rio, then captured the young Pirate Girl and stashed her at a low rent motel in a smelly pulp mill town.

He told smoldering Venus that her daughter had just called from Bogalusa, Louisiana and that he was going to get her and bring her back so she could talk to the law.

Liana asked, "Is she in trouble?" but didn't express any interest in how she got there. Liana seemed dull and listless, probably from Dr. Zeus' Quaaludes.

"It's her own damn fault," Liana said before she told him that Bud Hardaway had decided to sell the White Sands Motel to a corporation from Tampa, and that she would be moving back to Capital City.

"Maybe we could get together sometime," she said. "For old times' sake."

"Yeah, maybe," he said.

He cruised through Destiny Beach after midnight. At three AM he parked in a Pensacola hospital parking lot and slept fretfully for two hours. A confusing, incoherent crazy dream, in distressed black & white, combined the highway speed with the turbulence of memory dread: *His convoy split at Malta, with half going to Naples. 50 ships up the coast the other half around the tow and up the coast to Bari. German planes came in low under the radar and sank all 50. Picked up British soldiers in Africa. Took them to Naples. Left for Atlantic before Anzio Beach. Storm blew us off course. Arrived Norfolk. Then home. Margaret looked radiant holding baby boy. I am still the lucky one.*

Left for South Pacific to follow McArthur wherever he went. Pacific lagoon with over 200 ships. Collected coconuts and watched the native girls swim. Peaceful.

The distant crashing waves mixed with the static babble of early morning AM car radio. He saw again the telegram that haunted him:

Tuesday October 1944
Aboard ship Pacific Theater

Dear Son, God willing, we'll get the best of the Japanese before too long and I'll be home with you and Mother. Until then, take care of Mother & give her a great big hug and kiss for me.
Your father, Lt. Franklin McCutcheon, USN.

There was nothing peaceful in the droning sound of Japanese death squads. The battle of Iwo Jima was a bloody mess. Admiral Nimitz said, "uncommon valor was a common virtue." American soldiers killed thousands of Japanese defenders, but as the Americans approached Okinawa for Easter, 1945, the House of the Red Sun threw every kamikaze pilot they had at the Americans. It was one of those death squads that carried away Franklin McCutcheon and sixteen other sailors when it crashed into the deck of the carrier and skidded to a fiery conclusion.

That was just what it was: dumb, ugly bad luck—that's all. Matthew wanted something he could not have, and he was unable to get beyond it. By the time he realized what he needed to know, that she needed to tell him, it was too late. Her health had broken.

She survived only with a steady supply of wonder drugs from an endless stream of doctors, and from the useless miracle treatments she endured, with diminishing results and increased illusion. Drugs for every purpose she carried in her turquoise travel bag; and that he took every chance he could. She was the first drug addict that he ever knew, and she was a saint. She finally succumbed from a liver ailment and diabetes, from the endless miracle cancer therapies, and ultimately, from a confused mind and a broken heart. By then, there was nothing he could do to help her.

He couldn't take care of Mother. He had to live with that.

His father had died, damn him, as fate would have it; and so, it wasn't his fault that he could not take care of Mother.

It was just dumb bad luck.

He woke up with a headache. The dream was gone now, and only the silence of the whispering pines remained.

His mother's death always reminded him of the failure of love.

"Love was such a disappointment," she said.

His brain hit overload when he rolled into Bogalusa, Louisiana on the Pearl River. It was the same god-awful smelly, ugly pulp mill smell as Port Royale, but much worse. Port Royale at least had a constant sea breeze to dissipate the putrid pulp mill odor.

Bogalusa was a hell of a place. And it didn't smell any better just because Terri was there. She had locked herself inside room #318 of the Pearl River Motel, afraid to open the door.

He really did not want to know what else Terri had nothing to do with.

CHAPTER THIRTY

The Negro Fort

THE MEMORIAL SERVICE for Cleave Thomas overflowed the wood frame Zion Baptist Church. All day and night, thousands crowded beneath the live oaks surrounding the church, singing and praying, and their prayers were as hot as the sweltering late summer weather.

Beginning from the church in the Section and winding slowly through downtown Belle Rio to the Bridge, and over the Bay Bridge and five miles across the causeway through East Bay, where a throng of crackers, rednecks, and white dragons had gathered, then north past the jail, where they were now holding the only white man they could find who had dared to cause such a travesty, cars upon cars, hundreds, some said thousands of cars, moved in a caravan of final celebration. It was the epiphany of a people, that sudden manifestation of who they were at this place, at this time in history, and what that history meant to them and what it had meant to one of the best of them: outrageous death. This powerful spontaneous emotional outpouring of grief and frustration and rage and love, yes, love too, among the many brothers and sisters, fathers and mothers, would not, could not, be denied.

Overnight, the Sherriff's Department set up a road block to stop the cortege from rolling through East Bay, where a spark could have ignited a conflagration of violence that would have no end.

Sheriff Tatum, after receiving a call from the Governor himself, instructing the Sheriff "to facilitate the memorial service and demonstration in whatever way necessary and possible, within the limits of his manpower, and to be responsive to the human dilemma, the human dimension of anger, and to be a dedicated lawman, an agent for good in the community, and for God's sake, Sheriff, don't let there be any trouble; it's less than three damn months to the November election," ordered his deputies to stand aside and escort and protect with all force necessary, not prohibit, the procession which was increasing with the extended families of cousins, aunts and uncles, from Capital City to Port Royale, and the Talmadge Hannah family from the Chipola swamp, swelling with more cars, people walking, all going to the river, to Jerusalem. The entire extended family of the black community, bound for the preaching and memorial service, was anticipating the long overdue political awakening at the Negro Fort Historical Site, which was located fifteen miles up the highway toward Sumatra, on the eastern bluff of the river. It was at this location, where the curse of history, and the longing of the people for freedom, was to be made manifest.

The choice of the Negro Fort for the memorial service was the inspiration of the Reverend Thomas Hannah Carlton, an uncle, once or twice removed, no one knew for sure, who raised the young boy that came to him upon the death of his mother. He named the boy 'Cleave', for he was torn asunder from the very center of life.

The Reverend Thomas Hannah Carlton, Professor Emeritus of History and Theology at a prestigious Atlanta university, was an imposing figure of outrage: proud and defiant, filled with anger, grief, and sorrow. He silently prayed that his love of God, which he never doubted, and his love of mankind, if that love still existed, and if it did not, that God's love for him would deliver him from the bitter hate that he could taste with this tragic death.

All were family now in this moment of glory, the huge crowd, both black and white, assembled in the open grassy knoll for a solemn celebration under a glaring late afternoon sun, which cast long shadows from the tall hardwoods along the banks of the river.

"When I was a boy," Reverend Carlton's powerful voice filled the afternoon silence, "I treasured the idea of the Negro Fort, the place where we are gathered today. The idea of a Negro Fortress carried great significance in my childhood mind: that the Negro had a Fort of his very own, even if he had to die in it, meant everything to me.. I was moved deep in my soul that our once enslaved African ancestors had fought and died for the dignity that belongs to every man. Our ancestors had a Fort to die in. It was a Mighty Fortress.

"I came with my uncle and my grandfather to this very spot, and we stood on these bluffs, while I listened to my grandfather tell the story of the Negro Fort, and the struggle of the dreams for those who died here.

"My Old Ancestor was carried from Africa in the galley of a Portuguese schooner, and sold at the slave market in Spanish St. Augustine to an English planter from Georgia. My Old Ancestor escaped from the Georgia plantation with five other Africans, and they ran away into the swamps of Spanish Florida, where they lived with the Renegade Indians. And they came with the Indians to this place, where a Fort had been built by English soldiers and merchants who fought against the Americans and Spanish for the wealth of the new world.

"'Renegade Indians and Runaway Free Negroes,' I said to myself, time and again. It had a rhythm, a fascination, a beauty, a dream. It was my personal myth and history.

"In the early spring of long ago, Renegade Indians and Runaway Free Negroes went on a raiding party into South Georgia. They returned to the Fort on the bluff overlooking the river with the white soldiers' rifle, their uniforms, and their scalps. The Negro Fort became the symbol of fear and hatred for every white American frontier settler. They feared and hated Renegade Indians and Runaway Negroes with guns and a place to shoot them from.

"Within a short time, this Fort was impregnable. They brought a halt to all traffic on the river. Earthen bunkers supported an assortment of British artillery. There was an ammunition depot with a supply of pistols and rifles and plenty of powder for the cannons. Cattle grazed on the land just outside the wooden walls and they grew beans and corn and melons. It was a paradise in America for the Renegade Indian and Runaway Free Negros, who would soon fight against Andrew Jackson, the white man's Devil.

"In July of 1816, General Andrew Jackson was working the 'Will of God in History and the Manifest Destiny of America' to capture and return the runaway African slaves to their masters and complete the final extermination or the removal of Indian savages. It was, he said, the unrelenting and unfathomable march of history.

"General Jackson ordered the U.S. Regulars into action against the Renegade Indians and Runaway Free Negroes in Spanish Florida, with instructions to take the Fort, kill the Renegade Indians, and return the Runaway Negroes to slavery.

"As a representative of Andrew Jackson, Choctaw Mad Tiger, with five of his best warriors, came to the Fort to discuss terms of surrender with a runaway slave named General Garcia who commanded the Fort.

"General Garcia said, 'We will never surrender,' and he chastised the Choctaws and ridiculed them for being the stooges of the white American devils. The Renegade Indians and Runaway Free Negroes laughed at the Choctaws and enjoined them to also be free, and kill the white mercenary devils and soldiers of Andrew Jackson.

"Choctaw Mad Tiger called them savages and fools!

"General Garcia negotiated with the Choctaws for two days, while a squadron of American gunboats from New Orleans made their way upriver, and assembled just across the river.

"The following morning, at first light, the American soldiers heated cannonballs in the fire, and quickly loaded them in their fourteen pounders.

"The first two red hots made a direct hit on the ammunition depot inside the Negro Fort, and a tremendous explosion rocked the morning quiet. A fireball rose into the air with the screams and wailing of men, women, and children.

"The Choctaw mercenaries raced into the burning wreckage, and amid the burning timbers, the collapsed buildings, the broken bodies and vomiting soldiers, they killed men, women, and children, and took many Renegade Indians and Runaway Free Negro scalps. It was a scene of awful violence, bloody mayhem, carnage, and the death of a dream.

"The dangerous, runaway Free Negro General Garcia's severed head was placed on a pole along a muddy road in Georgia. It was the promise of what waited for Runaway Negroes when they got to freedom.

"My ancestors escaped from the Negro Fort through the swamps, and after years of wandering, became slaves on a Florida plantation owned by a white man named Thomas Carlton. When Thomas Carlton died, Mrs. Carlton, a free-spirited English woman, took up with the son of my ancestor, a handsome house slave she called Thomas, and their conjugal relationship produced four children.

"Mrs. Carlton returned to England with the two young children who passed for white. She died in England, and her sons, now grown, returned to claim the plantation. They were educated men who assumed they were English gentlemen.

"The oldest son, horrified to discover that his father had been a black man, returned to England with his terrible secret.

"The younger Carlton son also fled the curiosity of his heritage, and for many years lived a vagabond life in New Orleans, where he married an octoroon woman, and his son became a doctor, and his son a doctor, and his youngest son a professor at an Atlanta University.

"All together there were more than twenty children descended from the slave Thomas Carlton, some of them black, others white. That is the family that brought the boy, Cleave Thomas, to me. He was a child of God, an orphan to his mother, a nephew to my uncle, a cousin to my cousin, a brother to his sister, a son without a father, and so he became my son, because we are all one family.

"The time has come to speak the truth. Many of our ancestors in America have the blood of generations of white and black Americans, Africans, Englishmen, Irishmen, Germans, Indian savages, Chinese Coolies, and Spanish conquistadors. Look around you. Look at your family. Look at your friends. Look at the strangers next to you. We are black and white, Spanish, English, African and Indian. Men and women in this holy place. This sacred place—The Negro Fort. Stand up brothers! Stand up sisters! We are free and proud: to live and to die in this Fort, for it is our refuge."

The choir began to sing, and their voices supported the swelling of emotion with a tremolo of supplication. The afternoon air was filled with an overwhelming mantle of peace and salvation.

"WE cannot hate ourselves because we were enslaved against our will and bred like animals for the pleasure and benefit of others. We cannot hate ourselves! We cannot even hate our tormentors! And those who do us harm. For there is not enough hatred to go around! Certainly, There is not enough hate even for those who have unwittingly, not done these iniquities unto us, for they are our father, and our brothers, and our sisters.

"My God is my witness. I speak the Truth. If I do not speak the truth, may God strike me dead."

He looked dramatically to the Heavens; arms upraised.

"We are here today because one of us was loved by one of them. And one of them loved by one of us. So, they killed one of us. They killed Cleave Thomas, my child, the cousin of my cousin, the son of my sister, and the son of my brother. The son of you. And the son of one of them."

The audience was held breathless, waiting for the parting of the Heavens.

"There's a white man out there who has done a grievous injustice on my son, your child. As I pray for his soul, I cannot help but pray, that God strike him dead!"

The throng of mourners voiced loud approval. Reverend Thomas waited for silence.

"We have raised that boy as our own. By his talents he exalted the Glory of God, and made each of us better in our heart. I have loved that boy as my own. Now I carry him in my bosom to the grave. May God forgive the hate I have in my heart. Deliver us from evil. For though we were banished into the land of slavery and suffering, we have been delivered. And we shall be victorious."

A mighty roar escaped from this body of people.

Reverend Thomas Hannah Carlton fell to his knees. The Holy Spirit struggled for his soul, as he cried,

"Save me, Jesus! For I am filled with hate!"

The singing voices grew into a crescendo of celebration, of victory and mourning, for the young man who had no mother, no father, no brothers, no sisters, asking the Lord to make whole and sanctify the horrible wounds inflicted on Cleave Thomas, praying that his soul be accepted among the souls of all the ancestors who had gone long before, who had suffered the agony and insults of this world, before returning home to the bosom of Jesus.

Reverend Thomas Hannah Carlton held aloft the urn with the ashes of the son, Cleave Thomas, the New Deion, *Angus Dei,* the Lamb of God, and scattered them to the wind.

It was the Passion of Belle Rio.

CHAPTER THIRTY-ONE

Terri Cates' Destiny

"YOU WANT ME to start at the beginning?"

"Well, yes. That would be a good place to start." Assistant State's Attorney Ronnie Smith, smiled with an ingratiating attitude.

Her hair sprayed crisp, her taunt face painted glamourous, dressed like she was going to a charity fundraiser at the VFW. She straightened her dress and stared out the large picture window which framed the Bay Bridge against the gulf and the dull gray, foggy morning. A flock of pigeons flew across the sky and settled on the window ledge. The room was enthralled by her presence.

"My name is Teresa Cates."

This formal hearing was Ronnie Smith's big show and he had to make the best of it. Terri Cates was potentially the only known living eyewitness to the death of Cleave Thomas, other than, perhaps, the heavily drugged Katherine Hardaway, whose statement regarding the events of that Friday night after the Riviera Club melee contained no mention of a felony homicide committed against Cleave Thomas at the Hardaway fish camp on the Ochlockonee River. Andrew Percy, who was already under house arrest for the homicide of Cleave Thomas, denied being at the scene of crime. And Cairo Thorne, the other known possible suspect, was still missing.

Billy Ray had stated in his interview that none of them knew anything about Cleave Thomas. Billy Ray's testimony that he discovered his sister on the highway and never went to the fish camp was part of the record. There were a lot of unanswered questions.

"Where do you live, Ms. Cates?"

"I live at the White Sands Motel at Belle Rio with my mother."

"Ms. Cates, is it true that you were with Andrew Percy and Cairo Thorne on the night of July twenty-second and continuing into the morning of Saturday the twenty-third."

"Yes," she answered, barely audible.

"You need to speak up, Ms. Cates, so that the court reporter can hear what you're saying."

"Yes, sir."

"You knew Billy Ray Hardaway, Ms. Cates?"

"Yes."

"Did you consider yourself a friend, his girlfriend? How would you characterize your relationship?"

"You mean was we just friends or lovers or something like that?"

"Yes, how would you characterize your relationship?"

"Well, Billy Ray was my friend. I mean he sometimes wanted to be more than that, you know, but he was a friend. Yes, I would say he was a friend. But we was never lovers."

"And you also knew Mr. Charles Maxwell? Who everyone called Crazy Maxwell?"

"Yes. I seen him around town ever since I can remember."

"Who else was at the Point on the night, the Friday night, after the ruckus at the Riviera Club?"

"Well, Chad was there. He's a boy who sometimes goes with Darlene. Darlene was there and she sometimes was Billy Ray's girlfriend, but she was with Keith Moss at the Point. And there was some other people there off and on. I don't remember everything or everybody who was there."

"Was Mr. Andrew Percy at the Point that night?

"Yes."

"Was Cairo Thorne there?

"Yes, he was there."

"And how do you know Mr. Percy?"

"You mean how did I meet Mr. Percy? Or how long did I know him or what?"

"How did you meet Mr. Percy?"

"Billy Ray took me to Panama City and introduced me to him."

"What does Mr. Percy do in Panama City?"

"He's a businessman."

"What business is he in?"

"He says his business is entertainment."

"How would you further characterize his *entertainment* business? What would you call this type of business?"

"He manages one of them dance clubs."

"Where girls perform naked?"

"Well, almost naked."

"Did you ever perform at Mr. Percy's Club?"

"Yes," she said.

"Did you get up on stage and perform naked, or 'almost naked' as you said?"

"I don't see what this has to do with the murder of Cleave Thomas," Attorney McCutcheon interjected.

"I'll asked the questions I deem appropriate and necessary, Mr. McCutcheon. Your client can answer to the best of her knowledge and ability."

"I said I would answer questions, and so I don't care what you ask me. But I didn't have anything to do with what happened."

"How did you come to dance naked in Panama City? Were you recruited by Mr. Percy? Or someone in his employ?"

"I went to Panama City with Billy Ray. We met Percy at his club on the beach called *Cleopatra's*. It's a sports bar and dance club. Percy asked me did I want to dance. We danced for a while. Talked about his club. I never done anything like that before. He said he thought I could be a regular dancer. Then I went to the club and put on a costume … and I took it off on stage. I was a good dancer, everybody said so. That's all there was to it. I performed there a few more times, and I was good at it."

"I'm sure you were … Did Billy Ray discuss transporting and/or selling marijuana or other controlled substances with Mr. Percy?"

"I don't know nothing about that."

"Did Billy Ray place bets on sporting events with Mr. Percy?"

"I don't know nothing about that. They talked about money, but I don't listen to men talk. Even about money. They just talk."

"Do you know anything about Cairo Thorne's so called 'farming' on Gulf Royale timber land?"

"Like I said, men talk. I hear the same talk everybody hears."

"What is that talk?"

"Cairo grows pot in the woods. Everybody knows that. That don't have nothing to do with what happened that night. What happened that night didn't have nothing to do with any of that other stuff. It was just something that happened when men get crazy."

"That's what we're here to discuss, Ms. Cates, the truth of what happened that night."

"Since what happened that night, I got to tell the truth."

"We appreciate that Ms. Cates ... Did you know the deceased, Mr. Thomas, the football player?

"He was the famous one that played at the Belle Rio High School the year they almost won the state Championship. That was about four years ago. I was just starting in high school. He was cute. Some people didn't like it then, but he went with a lot of white girls when he was in Belle Rio. Others never paid attention to that. I remember the older girls talking about him. It ain't, it's not such a big deal with the young people anymore. He was fun. And a lot of the girls went with him."

"Why don't you tell us in your own words what happened on the Friday night of July twenty-second. Then I'll ask you some more questions."

"Well, Billy Ray picked me up and said there was a really hot band playing at the Riviera Club in Wakulla. So a bunch of us drove over there. The usual bunch: Billy Ray and Darlene and Chad and Keith Moss and Maxwell. There was a big crowd at the Riviera. I mean it was packed and there was all these football players there from the university and their girlfriends and a lot of them was black, and some of them was with white girls, and one of them happened to be Billy Ray's sister, Kate Hardaway. I don't know her personally, but I know who she is. She was with the Thomas boy ... Billy Ray for some reason got really mad, and Maxwell was egging him on, and so was a lot of them hicks from Dixie County. The blacks wasn't helping either. They was all loud and showing out. They started having words. It was some time around then that Percy and Cairo came in.

"I danced with Percy. Billy Ray was being such a jerk, and I wanted to make better acquaintance with Mr. Percy because he said he would let me be a headline dancer, and I could make two thousand dollars a week and live in Panama City. Anyway, Billy started arguing with the blacks, and they all started fighting and throwing things, and we could see the trouble coming.

"Percy and me and Cairo went outside before the Sheriff got there. And Kate and football player got out and drove away in his silver Mazda. Almost all of us got out before the Wakulla Sheriff got there, except for the bad rednecks that wanted to fight and the football players, and they was just wanting to fight too."

"And what happened then?"

"We went out to the Point and we kept on partying. Billy Ray showed up with Maxwell and Keith with Darlene. And anyway, we was all out there with a bonfire and partying, drinking and, ..." she paused.

"I was out on the beach with Billy Ray and he said, 'He's a son of a bitch and I'm gonna kill his ass.' Them was his exact words. And I said, 'Billy Ray you ain't mean enough to kill nobody' and he hit me."

She swung her hand, recreating the backhand slap Billy Ray gave her across her face, and then held her hand up to her painted, wounded face in surprise and regret.

"I said, 'Don't you ever hit me again, Billy Ray.' He's never done nothing like that to me before. It wasn't like him. He was really upset about his sister and that Thomas boy."

"What happened then?"

"I went off with Percy."

"Where did you go off with Mr. Percy?"

"We got in his car. It was parked near the beach."

"What did you do then?"

She didn't answer.

"What happened next, Ms. Cates? Did you have ...

Attorney McCutcheon interrupted, "Not relevant, sir."

Ronnie Smith glared at Matthew. "What happened next, Ms. Cates?"

"Some other cars came and left."

"Tell us, please, what happened next, Ms. Cates, with Mr Percy."

"We was just fooling around in the back of his car. He was drunk and acted fun, making fun of rednecks, ya know."

"I see. What happened then?"

"They was all mad and drunk and hollering. Keith and Chad and Darlene and somebody else with them. And maybe some others. I don't recall everybody that was there ... And the next thing I know we was all driving,"

"Which people, Ms. Cates?"

"Well, there was Cairo driving Percy's car. And Billy Ray and Maxwell in his Corvette. We followed them. And ..."

"What happened then?"

"We turned off the highway onto this dirt road and went down it for a while. Billy Ray was speeding. Percy was in the front seat and Cairo went out of control, and we went every which a way, and slammed into the ditch. Percy got throwed into the windshield. He was all bloody and just lay there like he was hurt."

"Who was driving on this dirt road? How many cars?"

"Just Billy Ray's Corvette and Cairo and me in Percy's car."

"Did Billy Ray pass his sister along the highway? Did Billy Ray stop for his sister, Kate Hardaway?"

"No. He never stopped for nobody. I never seen her again, after she left the Riviera with Thomas."

"Then what happened?"

"Me and Cairo climbed from the car. Percy was still in the car. I heard him making a noise. Cairo got something from under the seat, I think it was a gun, and he grabbed my arm and pulled me and we went down the road where Billy Ray had gone."

"You think Cairo got a gun from Percy's car? Or did he actually get a gun from under the seat? Yes or no. To the best of your recollection."

"Yes, it was a gun he got from the car."

"What road were you traveling on?"

"The sand logging road to the fish cabin."

"The McIntyre Road?"

"I don't know the name of that road we wrecked on."

"How far did you walk down the road?"

"We walked a little ways until we came to a cabin that was at the end of the road, and the silver Mazda that the Thomas boy drives was parked there, and Billy Ray's Corvette was parked with the headlights shining at the cabin, and they was yelling at him and daring him to come out, saying they was gonna kill his ass and stuff like that, calling him bad names an' all that kinda stuff."

She stopped and took a drink of water. She looked at Matthew and took a deep breath. The room exhaled with her.

"Am I telling you what you want to know?"

"You just tell us what you did and what you saw. We just want to know what happened."

"I got scared then. Because I knew something bad was going to happen."

"Ms. Cates, let's go back to Percy for a moment. What condition was he in when you saw him last? You said that you left him in the car, is that correct?"

"After we hit the ditch, I tried to make him talk to me, but he just groaned and mumbled and made no sense. He hit his head on the windshield and got cut real bad. I could see lots of blood. But Cairo grabbed me. I got out of the back seat and went down the road with him in the direction that Billy Ray's car had gone. I don't know what direction it was. We went to the end of the road, but when we got down to the cabin, they was already starting more trouble. I was afraid and walked away because I couldn't stand to see what they had come there to do. I was feeling sick. Felt like I was gonna vomit. I went walking back to the car to help Percy. I didn't want to see what they was gonna do."

"You left the cabin?"

"Yes."

"Did you see any other events that transpired at the cabin? Did you actually witness what went on there?"

"No."

"How do you know what happened?"

"Cairo told me."

"What happened next? What happened that you personally saw or heard? What did you do?"

"There were gun shots."

"You are sure they were gunshots?"

"They wasn't popcorn popping."

"How many gunshots?"

"A lot."

"More than two?"

"There was four or five, maybe more."

"Then what happened?"

"Then Cairo came driving back up the road in the silver car. He stopped and said, 'Get in!' I didn't want to, and he said, 'Get in, you damn bitch!' And I got in. We drove back past the Lincoln. Percy was gone. He wasn't there no more. At the Lincoln. The door was open, and he was gone."

"Did Cairo stop at Percy's Lincoln? Did you look for him?"

"Yes, we looked out for him, but he wasn't there. We drove back on the logging road, and Cairo threw a gun out the window into the ditch.

Then we drove up through the woods to Telogia, then to Dead Lakes, and on back roads from there to Panama City."

The euphoria of being the star witness had vanished. She was getting weary.

"He told me they shot him, and it was not pretty."

"Who told you that?"

"Cairo. We spent two days, maybe three days, in Panama City hiding out in some kind of building that was like a car repair garage. Cairo had clothes there. He and another man took blow torches to the Mazda and cut it all up. Stripped it clean. Some Cuban guy named Degado, or something, came by. He was from Miami, or Palm Springs or Palm Beach, or somewhere, and he was real mad that Percy was not there, and he got real nervous and angry because Cairo and some redneck I'd never seen before got stoned all the time.

"Then the next day Cairo had a bad argument with this Cuban man in the garage office, and I think I heard, I know I saw Cairo hit him with something, and he was quiet, just a lump on the floor, and the other redneck said, 'shit, you killed him.' And Cairo said, 'He was a son of a bitch. I can't have him hangin' on me all the damn time.'

"Cairo left me there for a day locked in the room in the garage, and I was scared, and then we left for New Orleans in Cairo's car. He didn't like being with me, I tell you that. I was with him for a week, day and night in Panama City, except for when he went away the day they dumped the Cuban guy. That was enough for me. He treated me like I was gonna be dead, too, sooner than later."

"That's very good, Ms. Cates. Now on the Friday after the Riviera incident, and the party on the beach, you said that you followed Billy Ray's car, and he did not find his sister on the highway, is that correct?"

"I told you we followed Billy Ray to the cabin, and they killed … Thomas… at the cabin. That's what I told you."

"Did you ever see Kate Hardaway at the cabin?"

"No."

"Did you see them kill Cleave Thomas at the cabin? Did you witness the shooting?"

"I told you I heard gunshots, and Cairo told me, 'We killed him and it weren't pretty.' Why don't you believe what I'm saying, and quit trying to make it sound like I don't know what I'm talking about."

"Were you raped by Mr. Percy?"

"Not relevant, Mr. Smith," Attorney McCutcheon interjected.

"If I was, I'd remember." Terri Cates stated boldly. "Rape's not something you usually forget."

"Billy Ray told the Sheriff, that you told him, that Mr. Percy raped and beat you."

"That ain't something I'd forget. Billy Ray doesn't always tell the truth. Billy Ray just made that stuff up for some reason on his own. Billy Ray wanted to make Percy a bad person. It ain't true. Billy Ray was telling lies to protect himself."

"Are you trying to protect Mr. Percy, Ms. Cates?"

"I ain't got no reason to do that."

"And we are to assume that you're telling the truth, under oath, that Mr. Percy was injured in the wreck on the way to the fish camp? Then he was left unconscious on the road to the fish camp. And yet when you got back to his car he was not there. Gone. Vanished. Disappeared into the woods. Is that what you want me to believe?"

"Believe?" she said. "You believe what you want to believe. That's what happened! When I last saw him he was hurt bad. I would say unconscious even. I know he was never at the fish camp."

Ronnie Smith was frustrated that this event was still a big mess, that the case was slipping away, that his air-tight theory did not stand up. He wanted Percy to be at the fish cabin.

"Then what happened to Mr. Percy after the wreck? Where was he?"

"I told you. He couldn't a gone far. He was bad hurt."

"Could he have gone to the fish camp?"

She exhaled, "I can't make you believe what you don't want to believe. I'm telling the truth. I'm just telling you what happened. I'm telling the truth. Why don't you believe me?" She was getting peeved.

"Ms. Cates. I want to know where Andrew Percy was. I believe he was at the fish camp and for some reason, which I can't fathom, you are lying to protect him."

Suddenly she blew up a storm and stared angrily at Ronnie Smith. Now she was mad at him: for challenging her, for calling her a liar. For dis-respecting her, not taking her seriously. She turned and glared at Matthew. Stuck. Exasperated. Pissed.

Attorney McCutcheon stated calmly, "Mr. Smith, you have to find a credible witness, if there is one alive somewhere, maybe, potentially Cairo Thorne, who will testify what you want to hear: that Mr. Percy was at the cabin."

"That's enough, Mr. McCutcheon."

Attorney McCutcheon cleared his throat. "Mr. Smith, it is clear that she can<u>not</u> make you believe that she is <u>not</u> lying, if you are committed to the position that she is …"

"Counselor!" Prosecutor Smith interrupted bluntly.

"I'm not a liar," Terri Cates stated angrily. "Why don't you believe what I'm telling you?"

"I want to know the truth, Ms. Cates."

"I told you the truth."

"I want to know the truth." Insulting her. That's all. "That you are not a liar. Yes, prove it to me. That you are not a liar. Tell me the truth."

"I am not a liar," she said defiantly. She pointed unquestioningly at Attorney Matthew McCutcheon "I had sex with him. At his house when my mama was staying there. And that's the truth! I am not a liar."

For a brief eternity, the room was tomb quiet.

"Ain't that the truth, Matt? Ain't I telling the truth? Ain't that what you want me to do?"

Then she glared at State's Attorney Ronnie Smith. "I am not a liar!"

She looked at Matthew with a faint, sad smile. Was it regret? Satisfaction? Validation? Or possibly, even, gratitude that she could fulfill her destiny at that moment.

Her testimony was finished. She had done what she said she would do. The room waited in silence.

Matthew McCutcheon was stranded in the awkward, embarrassing moment: between denial and pride, the desire to say that he was innocent and the necessity to say that she was not a liar.

"Yes, that is true," he said, his voice cracking the brittle silence with all the legal dignity he could muster. "She is telling the truth. She is not a liar."

"You people believe what you want to believe," she said. "I just told you what happened. Mr. Percy was not at the cabin. He was knocked unconscious and never came to the cabin. Cairo was there.

"Cairo said, 'We killed him an' it weren't pretty.' It was him and Maxwell and Billy Ray. I can't make up stuff like what happened that night."

Matthew had driven Terri Cates back to Belle Rio and told her, with her frightened, beautiful, painted face, with her proud determined eyes, to tell the truth, because that was all they wanted to know: the truth.

She was not a liar. She was telling the truth. Andrew Percy was innocent. But Matthew was guilty, and strangely, proud of it.

CHAPTER THIRTY-TWO

Redemption

BILLY RAY'S RED CORVETTE was parked under the rambling cedar house that sat fifteen feet off the ground, beneath large pines and shrouded oaks, overlooking St. Cecilia Bay. Without going to the house, Matthew walked down to the dock where Bud was fueling the boat. It was late afternoon.

Soon they were skimming over the water. Thick clouds moved swift and low across the churning water as they sped up the broad Ochlockonee River. They went under the Sopchoppy Bridge, and as the river grew increasingly smooth and placid, the atmosphere became solemn and mysterious, portentous.

The decomposing remnants of the old Belle Rio & Savannah Railroad stretched across the narrows of the Ochlockonee River, which was joined there by the meandering Crooked River. Somewhere on the eastern bank of the river, hidden in the underbrush beyond the cypress stumps and swamp grass the ghost of the old sawmill town of McIntyre, was concealed in the silence of live oak, sweet gum, yaupon and juniper, sycamore, and magnolia, a faint reminder of 'what the land had been before it was ours.'

They floated quietly into a backwater cove where the powerboat slid up to the dock of the Hardaway fish camp. Matthew drank straight hot whiskey and waited for Bud to say whatever he was going to say.

Finally, Bud spoke, "My daughter was a fool getting involved with the Thomas boy, even if he was the biggest hero on campus. She knew what he was. She always was butt-headed. I don't like Ronnie Smith, never have. He's self-serving and too ambitious, but he's done a fair job for what he does. I never trust anybody that ambitious."

He looked at Matthew with a dreary, hopeless expression.

"I was never ambitious, only busy. I just did what I had to do, one day at a time, and sometimes I got lucky. Not always."

That hollow victory hung in the quiet afternoon a long time.

"Well, we all know Thomas didn't kill himself," Bud said after a while. "The blacks are pretty upset over this thing, and they got all them TV people and politicians making hay and getting themselves re-elected by keeping this thing stirred up."

"Did you expect them to do something different?"

"No, I guess not. You know, I've loved my kids, each one in his own way. They were all different. Billy Ray was my failing, when you consider all the things that I gave him to make up for the loss of his sister. And what he didn't get from his mother. I gave him too much. I'd have to say that now. It was a mistake. And it made him useless."

An uneasy feeling had settled on the fish camp, the cabin still partially roped off by yellow stakes that the deputies had placed around the area where Cleave Thomas had died.

"I watched that Thomas boy run back at least six interceptions for touchdowns. And one kick-off the length of the field. He was an natural athlete. He could play baseball, basketball, run track. Not just football.

He was something special at the high school, back when none of us were used to winning. We won big."

Matthew looked at the fish camp bungalow, listened to the wind in the pines for the violence to erupt from the ominous crime scene, but it was quiet like the remains of the McIntyre ghost town.

Bud stood on the dock, looking out across the water that surrounded them in the twilight cathedral silence. High up in the cypress a kingfisher screamed. His whole body was convulsed in agony and his shoulders quivered, then froze.

"Yesterday I mailed a check to your office to retain you as my lawyer." He turned and looked at Matthew. He was exhausted and old.

"There's a letter with it, for you to give Sheriff Tatum."

Matthew was driving in the dark, east on Interstate 90. Bud told him that he first knew the boy had returned when he saw him walking along the street where Jones Hannah lived in the Section. He was about thirteen years old. He knew for certain who the boy was. His heart stopped cold at that moment. He dropped out of the race for re-election to the County Commissioners. He moved his family out of Belle Rio east, to St. Cecilia. Billy Ray was in his last year of high school. He sent Kate to private boarding school in Thomasville when she was nine and then to the school in Chattanooga. She was independent and smart, and everybody said she was going to make something special.

He always knew Billy Ray was useless, even though he'd been a fair baseball player. The year they won the district and went to state, he failed to get a hit, failed to even get on the base, and made two errors at second, one of which cost them the fifth and final game of the championship tournament. But Billy Ray had personal charm and people liked him. He could catch fish.

About the time Cleave Thomas returned to Belle Rio, he had a chance to make some really big money and he took it. Using his shrimp fleet in the deep gulf, before the Marine Patrol had off-shore surveillance, he took delivery of several hundred pounds of Columbian cocaine worth a small fortune in the drug-crazed cities. It was the early eighties. Damn rich suburban kids couldn't spend money fast enough. On numerous occasions, twin engine planes landed at the Belle Rio airstrip, a hundred yards of asphalt on the outskirts of town across the river, and picked up shipments.

Tommy Matson was the contact man with the pilots. He shielded Donny from any illegal activity, for most of his life; his mother saw to that. Donny went to college and studied business. He took in another partner, an ex-marine captain who had been a mercenary in Honduras and had government friends. They shipped guns to Panama and Guatemala and brought back cocaine. They trucked it out of Belle Rio in refrigerated rigs that delivered seafood to the wholesale market in Chicago. Francois set up the connections. Strahorn laundered the money. They started buying land. Lots of land with different corporations. Bought most of East Bay and thousands of acres of woods along the river. Then Tommy got busted. He took the rap. Kept his mouth shut and went to Atlanta. He was going to take care of Tommy, but Liana did that for him. Better than he could have.

Bud lay awake at night in St. Cecilia, where his heart ached and his mind dreaded the day that he would meet his maker. When their little girl died, Nancy, who had never been what he had expected, got worse, more withdrawn, morose, and religious. She had always been the baby of her family. Born late to her mother. A little snob, always. He couldn't say why he married her. Seemed like the thing to do at the time. He wanted to be a snob too. Hell, why do people do anything they do?

A woman came to work for him. A mulatto black woman. Skin like tan suede leather. Not a young girl. A woman. Thirty-five, beautiful to look at. It wasn't the first time he'd had poontang. There was plenty to give it. But this was, this was, this was something different. This was a woman. Her eyes looked straight into his soul, pleading for comprehension, for compassion, for release. She came to the packing house and worked the line, and he discovered she could talk, and she was smart. She had been to school and knew the office business routine. She had worked in Atlanta. Her closest family was in Belle Rio. She'd had trouble in Atlanta. She'd become a woman he could not be without. He could not think, but when he thought about her. He smelled her. Breathed her. He ate her, drank her, slept her. It, she, became an obsession. She never held back. Had no shame. No fear.

"I think she came to love me," he said after a long silence. And I …" He could not say it, probably never said it to anyone about anyone, or thought it, even, about anyone, except maybe his brother who drowned, and since last week, about his daughter Kate, and his mother, the memory of his father, his brother who drowned. He was trying to say it now, but would not, could not. He had felt it about the boy, their son. "I swear, I believe that to this day, she loved me the way I loved her." He finally did say it. "I loved her."

It was five in the morning. The sun came up over the Atlantic, Bud still talking. He had to say it now, for soon it would be over.

"So, I bought the Cypress Ridge Lodge and Fish Camp up the river, and we moved her up there and I let her manage the camp, when I wasn't there bothering her. And I spent a lot of time up there. Pretending. Pretending we were in a world where we could do and be whatever we wanted. We added more docks and built the motel units, one of 'em special for us, and I had architect plans for a restaurant, and I'd go up there and spend weekends in the hot house on the bayou. The rednecks that came to fish at the lodge sorta got wind of what was happening, and the business began to fall off. They were uncomfortable with a white man and a black woman, the way we were so obvious. And Nancy tried to ignore me, but once she said, 'you smell like the nigger woman.' Our marriage was gone. We'd only been together once in many years and it was Kate.

I'd swear the only thing that Kate got from her mother was her contrary nature. Contrary was Nancy's middle name, and self-righteous: Nancy Contrary Self-Righteous Markham Hardaway. Of course, everybody knows how easy I am to get along with."

They almost laughed. But they drove in more silence.

Then Bud spoke from deep within himself, "I would rather have loved that woman with all the hurt it caused than to have had my life without her."

What more could he say? Bud looked tired and subdued by the tremendous emotional sadness which had swollen from deep within him as he realized the horror that was contained by the fact of their love.

"When she got pregnant, she went back up north, and then she got on the drugs and couldn't take it. She sent the boy to Atlanta, then after a few years, when he was about thirteen, he showed up here. Going to high school. He lived with Talmadge Hannah's boy, Jones Hannah. Jones was a always a hardworking, respectable man."

They rode for a long time without talking, then he said, "I need someone to keep this thing quiet, Matthew. Do what you can, or hire somebody you think can do what needs to be done. I know you're gonna ask why I don't get Taghert to do this. Corrupt he is, Taghert always looked down on me. Looked down on her. I don't need no damn 'I told ya so' from that s.o.b. right now."

Bud had lived his life knowing there was no defense for his actions, only reasons, no excuses, only causes, and no cause strong enough to do what he did, only events, and no conclusions to be drawn, but that he did what he did because he did what he did because, because, because that's as far as it got, and there was nothing more he could say, but what he did, what he did because it was what he did. He knew too much now to leave it alone. And what he had done had to be done. He felt that, but could he ever say that in Belle Rio? No, it was just that he did what he did. That's all. Because he did what he did. There was nothing else he could do and even that wasn't what it was. It was just what he did. That's all. What he did. That's how he lived his life: he did. Others watched and talked and waited and wondered. He did.

Now he was dying inside, and all around him was ruin and grief because he had done what he did.

He was in pain: insane with loneliness and a deep sadness. He was marooned, wrecked by fate on the precipice, the mark, the stigma of love and passion, and now neither love nor hate nor even the memory of love could excite him, because all he felt inside was alone. That's the way life is. He did what he did so that he would not be alone.

"He could play ball, my boy."

That was the last thing he had to say.

They drove back toward Capital City, then turned and drove into toward Thomasville. After miles of manicured forest, they arrived at a large traditional Georgian brick mansion, a private sanitarium, the former estate of a Pittsburgh industrialist, who used it for quail hunting. An oriental valet took the car, and they went into the house. Bud talked to a woman who might have been a doctor, while Matthew waited absent-mindedly before one painting after another of dogs and men walking fields and birds in flight across the golden autumn sky.

Kate Hardaway, locked in horror and silence, had been unable to be alone since that night of shame and death. She had cried for days and nights, without end, her face drained, the eyes black, shallow, hollow, depraved with fear, now well beyond her youth, beyond love.

Her innocence was gone.

Matthew sat in the heavy silence of the pleasant room.

Bud said, "This is Matthew McCutcheon. He's a lawyer who will help us."

She said, "Good luck, Jack."

They talked and fought and re-lived the tragic events, as her mind wandered, uncontrolled, for she could see, but could not flee, the vision that he brought with him into the room, and the endless sounds of pitiful death that she still heard, the strange demented sing-song cartoon of voices her brother sang, the weird chant of hate coming from the moon-shadowed darkness, taunting the black son, his brother, her brother: You gonna fuck my sister? You ain't good enough for that white whore. Kate spitting venom. Bud talking back, protesting. Both talking at once, with Billy Ray, her departed brother, interjecting too late his own unhappiness, and the brother, Cleave, crying out in vain from across the void.

From the Riviera Club, they go up the dirt road that ends at the fish cabin, at death, in the night where she spent so many sunlit days and moonlight nights on the river, that were happy.

Don't call me your daughter a whore. I don't care what you I think. You don't care what she does, what I do. Who am I? Don't you care, Daddy? About anyone but you? Don't you know we all know the truth: you loved that dark brown woman. His mother. We all know your lie.

Please don't, Kate, please. Not with him? Your brother. Not with anybody, Daddy. That's what you meant, holding me him naked. Not with anybody.

Bud's boat moves quietly across the placid surface, across the shimmering silence in the dark moonlight. And he watches her white naked, his black brown, flesh in the shadows. Naked their flesh together, as they are one, both of my blood, her legs spread and wrapped around him. Him holding her, giving her so much love, pleasure. Could she hear my cries of love? Why do I have to see my son, and cannot say, my son, with you naked? He goes back to the past, the happy dangerous day, the first hour of lust with his mother, hours and hours of secret lust. Goes back to her childhood before the boy came to Belle Rio.

Cars arrive. The stumbling dead drunk brother and crazy men hiding in the darkness. And there is and was no escape from fear. The road-blocked life. The dead end ghost. The dark dreams of her dead lover surround them. Cartoon voices from Billy Ray's Saturday morning childhood, voices that only Kate and Billy Ray and Daddy could understand. They were all Billy Ray ever had to offer the world, created in solitude and loneliness, far from father's love: Elmer Fudd, the childhood freak show. It was the cartoon Billy Ray making the creature voice, hating me because I loved him who was better than him.

Yes, you can say it, better than your son. In the dark, creatures killed the naked black man, killed Cleave. I loved him, and you and men surrounded me, surrounded us, them dragging me him naked, wet with love, him and me naked with sex in the nightmare violence of love that was all hate and lust and love and blood, and them dragging him dragging me dragging us through the dirt.

Cleave struggling against two, three men, his blood long ago knowing his death, this drying. He loved me, made me a woman like you loved his mother, but he was good as dead as soon as he held me in his arms, sure as death inevitable. Ugly daddy ugly boys caught me her she I screamed and held me, Daddy, fondling me between two world, helpless pleading begging, begging you through suffering eyes, for you to relieve your hurt, his desire. I looked unable to not see the climax yet to be reached, yearned to feel and be and know. Beating, him beaten, dragging him, dragged naked, blood stained with love into the dark night.

The gun blazing sharp, loud, a still-frame burning into my mind, I ran and ran and ran.

But we cannot escape, telling her me to run, but holding me her because he was afraid. And you are the father who takes away all fear. Hold me Daddy, for I am still afraid. Stroke my head, lie here with me. He was so beautiful, Daddy and I loved him, you. He, I was like you, Daddy. Your love, my love, his love, her love was not good enough for you, for me, for him, for us, and he looked at me with such such such such—she cried and the sobbing pain, uncontrolled, the sad, broken love on her face. Is that love? Was that love? I loved you. He loved me. You, I loved you. And then in her mind she is again naked, wanting to be free, running from life, from death, from hate to love to hate to love to death.

Love caught us both, me and you, and I he knew deep down I would get him killed. Be his death. A black man and this white girl. Too hot dancing, Daddy. Remember my ballet, my arms wrapped tight around your neck, felt his love against my loins, and it was a mortal sin. Doomed to hell. And he laughed, you know I love you redneck girl, he said, and I saw your face in his love, Daddy.

A crime is not a sin. Murder is a sin and a crime: loving, killing your son, losing your daughter, your wife, because of your desire, Daddy.

He was good as dead when he loved you, like I loved her, his mother.

You, he held me naked, trembling. He held her there, making her watch, and you, I cried and cried and tried and tried, but cannot forget, never ever, never ever, never forget. Never forget. We, you killed him, your son, my brother, but they killed us both. Too. We died with him.

She woke up in the dawn mist on the floor of her Daddy's boat—curled in fear, knees drawn up tight to her chin—speeding across the ancient river. Then she was carried to the car, then to this quiet place for years of sleep and sorrow. Sleep which now brought dreams of holy terror.

"Have you no memory?" she said. "You killed your son, your blood, my love." Her memory fleeing, racing past the nightmare to another time long ago, a happy time of wind-swept white sand beaches, and waves, rolling waves, peaceful waves, innocent waves, endless, eternal waves, and parties laughing singing melodies, and sea gulls floating on the ocean breeze, then screaming: "No no no! Please don't please don't" until the darkness became a time of terror and horror and the black boy who was her half-brother lover, his better half, and her lover and her other brother that was half man, half cartoon fool, and the man that was her father killed him that was most like himself. For he was the unfortunate man in his own nightmare that would not leave her or him or me alone.

I you don't love you me.

There was finally nothing more to say and she watched but spoke not but watched. He will do it, she thought. I pray you to do it. She watched him and prayed for it. Please do it, she thought.

"Forgive me," he said. "Forgive me."

Do it. Damn you. Was stuck in her mind.

"Forgive me."

"Let God forgive you," she said. "What do we, you, I, say to God for our passion?"

"Can you help you love me," he pleaded. The father, the lover the killer of broken dreams.

"You cannot be helped, father. I am sorry."

"I love you, Kate. Please love me."

"No," she said.

Matthew turned, saw Bud Hardaway, and he knew, suddenly saw, stunned to see, the dark gun barrel against his head, unable to prevent the hand, holding steady in the dreaded silence, before the explosion reached to heaven, reverberating. The shattered heart cried out in bloody silence as the body fell against the TV, arms spread, face missing, across the bed, while the girl, the daughter, the lover, sat numb in the chair, vacant, bleary-eyed, lost in the sudden silence, unable to weep.

His own voice screaming NO! in the peaceful aftermath of the revolver noise, and then from her, the daughter, lover, a piteous wail, crying for her father's redemption, crying until he found peace with her lover, his sons, her brothers, and his brother lost at sea, the dark brown woman, his love, the father and brother, her brother and lover, all dead on a dark moon night when the heavens wept.

CHAPTER THIRTY-THREE

Who is Guilty?

MATTHEW WENT out to the beach at sunset and tried not to think, but the moment kept exploding with a horrible noise in his head.

From the mud flats, exposed by the low tide to the point at the west end of the beach, where the highway ran along the water directly in front of the setting sun, he was alone on the beach. A warm breeze sang with the quiet lapping of the surf. A hawk swept from the pines and caught the current and disappeared back over the marsh behind the pines.

Spindle-legged sandpipers ate their dinner at the water's edge. The sun and full moon hung in equal balance in the sky as the two mated celestial orbs faced each other in perfect harmony, balance and silence. He walked east toward the cove.

The golden setting sun cast his long shadow ahead of him, pursued by the dark horizon line, until it suddenly disappeared and he turned toward the western sky. The black curve of trees along the shoreline, below the layers of dense golden haze, swallowed the sun, but the full moon continued to rise in the eastern sky against the soft, faded background.

The thought of Bud in a white flash of noise and confusion made him feel sick and he tried not to think about Bud anymore and closed the shutter of his mind's eye over the fading spectral images of Kate's tragic sorrow, Cleave Thomas, torn asunder, the cartoon Elmer Fudd, the ghostly descendants of Don the Hard Way, killed by Sugar Walton, the bootlegger ancestor of Talmadge Hannah, the Dominicker Moses wandering through Tate's Hell wilderness.

Belle Rio had consumed him. He heard the crashing waves, the sonorous voice of Bud Hardaway, the daughter who refused his love, the son who was killed on a dark moon night. The secret love which Bud desired more than life without it. The depth of desire and passion that lead to despair and death, the same great love that went beyond all measure of reason, to where there was no reason at all.

A pipe bomb exploded in Tampa at the *Net Ban Amendment* Headquarters. The Capital City newspaper editorial page condemned the "outrageous, unnecessary violence" in the commercial fishing community "and endorsed the statewide *Net Ban Amendment*."

The *Festival Belle Rio* had been cancelled as a precautionary measure to forestall political demonstrations and potential bad publicity. The '94 General Election was just a few weeks away and the Governor's re-election bid generations of was up for grabs. Neither candidate was opposed to the *Net Ban Amendment*, so it was, ninety to one, a done deal.

For Belle Rio, it would be the end of life as they knew it. The good ol' days would be gone with the winds of strange bedfellows. Commercial mullet fishermen would be replaced by sport fishermen and recreational boaters, resort condo developers, and evangelical constitutional amendment environmentalists. Their way of life gone in the name of traditional values, free enterprise, economic growth, and the pursuit of pure profit and a better future. Tourism *dinero* would be the currency of the future. They would all have to change. Nothing would be the same.

The State of Florida promised to build the county a large correctional facility in exchange for the freedom of the open water. The generational fishermen could become prison guards, construction workers and servants to the tourist class. Life in Belle Rio would be grim until it became something new.

While they tried not to forget what it had been.

Through his office window, Matthew watched as the new convertible pulled up outside the Victorian Inn. Terri the Pirate Cates was wearing her glamourous Hollywood shades, ready to travel, ready to meet her destiny.

Andrew Percy stood awkwardly from the new sports car. He walked cautiously with a slight limp; his right arm moved stiffly. He wore a stylish bandana over his half-shaved head, a sport shirt, and a twisted smile. He had grown a salt and pepper beard.

"You probably don't remember me," Percy said, standing in the doorway, waiting for an indication, which didn't come, that he was welcome, so he hobbled into the office and planted himself on the corner of the desk.

"Unfortunately," McCutcheon said, "I remember too well."

"I'm still not exactly myself, as you can see, but I do seem to recall you from your days with the Federal Attorney's gambling probe in Nashville. You were the quiet, youthful, disgusted one."

Twenty some odd years ago, Matthew was a young attorney in the Nashville Federal Prosecutor's office when Andrew Percy laughed in the face of a federal government gambling investigation.

Federal Prosecutors had been investigating high-rolling sports bettors at a fancy private dinner club for several years, when on a frigid December morning, FBI agents, acting without consulting the city boys, raided sixteen homes and businesses. A number of prominent citizens were caught with their pants down, their hands dirty, and illegal betting slips stuffed in their suit coat pockets.

Mr. Percy was talking on one of his six telephones when FBI agents crashed through the doors and windows of his Belle Meade bungalow. The agents carried boxes of gambling material from his house, along with twenty-seven thousand dollars cash hidden in an unlocked wall safe behind a glamourous picture of Dolly Parton.

They took custody of betting forms and football parlay cards, three pistols, and several boxes of ammunition. But they didn't find his book of prominent clients and customers, which he had stashed safely in a heating duct behind an autographed photo of Hank Williams

When questioned by the Crime Task Force, Mr. Percy was genuinely uncommunicative, saying only that he needed large sums of cash for his business, and that he had a federal gambling license. He even paid his taxes.

Percy worked at "Big Al" Catalano's Bordeaux Supper Club, where Las Vegas style gambling took place behind closed doors. The Bordeaux club was frequented by prominent politicians, well-heeled businessmen, their wives, clients, girlfriends, and many country music celebrities after the Saturday night radio broadcast of the *Grand Ole Opry*.

High-stakes gambling fueled the after-hours nightspot until four Sunday morning, when in a concession to Bible Belt sensibilities, illegal activities came to a screeching halt.

A shock wave went through the city: at the Wednesday night church supper, the country club, the pool hall, the corporate board room, the suburban bedroom, and at City Hall. Speculation as to who among the city's elite might be arrested and indicted was front page news.

The most excitement was generated by the revelation of gambling activity at the Downtown National Bank, where large bets were placed by many distinguished, high-minded Episcopalians.

Forty thousand dollars cash had been collected at a desk in a corner of the Downtown National Bank, leased to a stockbroker affiliated with a large national investment company.

A spokesman for the Downtown Bank stated that the desk where the gambling activity transpired was leased as a "professional courtesy" to a retired stockbroker, who, unbeknownst to them, took the illegal bets and paid winners 'at the bank.'

With a wink and a nod, it was the best joke in town.

The federal criminal investigation turned out to be all smoke and mirrors. And soon became low priority. Jimmy Carter replaced Gerald Ford as President. A year went by with no indictments.

Andrew Percy was lost in the shuffle and was already taking bets on the baseball season, and was living the high life, traveling as the personal manager of a famous 'countrypolitan' singer. Some guys have all the luck.

Matthew had naively thought they were going to indict Andrew Percy, along with many of the holier-than-thou respectable citizens and Born-Again sinners who gambled freely in Nashville, the gilded buckle of the Bible Belt. But the real world of social relations was fixed as tight as the sports betting game, where the house always won. There were too many prominent face cards for the house to lose. The case dissolved.

Matthew resigned in disgust from the federal government task force, got married, and moved to Chicago.

"If it had been my decision, we would've put you in jail with the respectable country club Episcopalian types. We listened to you on the wiretap for three months. We had enough information but, as it turned out, nobody was really interested in bringing respectable white-collar crime to justice." Matthew was still disappointed in 'justice'.

"Justice is the gov'ment still owes me twenty-seven thousand dollars."

"I'm sure it's still safe in the Downtown Nashville Bank."

"That gamblin' set-up was one of my biggest grossing cards ever," Percy said with an unusual sentiment. "Big Al was like a second father to me. He died from cancer five years ago. He was selling used appliances on Trinity Lane."

"Sorry to hear it."

"He said I had a 'gift' for making easy money."

Matthew had had enough of Andrew Percy. "What'd you come here for, Mr. Percy?"

"You done a hell of a job for me during this terrible murder nonsense. And I come to thank you. I never was guilty of any of that killing business, but if they could, they were sure gonna hang me."

"I didn't do it for you, Mr. Percy. You can thank somebody else."

"Well, whatever it was you did, you got the situation straightened out, and you put the muzzle on that Prosecutor, one of my least favorite ever. And on a more personal note, Terri, my little travelin' companion, chauffer, said that I should've seen the look on your face when she told them what she told them. She said that you were wide-eyed and speechless, and pale as a sheet. But you did the right thing by her. I know she thanks you for that."

"It was the right thing to do," Matthew said stiffly. "Although, apparently, it was somewhat amusing, at my expense. Yes, Terri has natural dramatic instincts. But no, I didn't do it for you, Mr. Percy."

Matthew didn't have anything else to say on that subject. That subject was closed.

But he did say, "The next time I see your name, Mr. Percy, I hope it's in the obituary section."

It was an unnecessary remark, that was somewhat curious and out of character.

Percy ignored the apparently, intended affront, and said, "Just think, McCutcheon, the gov'ment might've had me in jail twenty-five years ago if they'd let you handle the case."

"Answer me one question, Mr. Percy, just between you and me, off the record of course: Is there anything you're actually *guilty* of?"

Percy thought about that for a moment.

"I don't know guilt, McCutcheon. It's a luxury I can't afford. But I do hate having trouble with the blacks. That's how I got this necklace," Percy said, indicating with his one good arm, the faded scar that ran down from his ear across his throat. "Damn Bantu tried to off me while I was in the Club Fed. When Doctor Ashish's cousin does my cosmetic surgery, it's gonna be a whole new me."

Matthew continued, sarcastically, "You're a real popular guy. I've gotten calls on you from an investigator in Miami regarding a former Jai Alai star, a Cuban Mafioso type named Delgado, who seems to be missing, along with a West Palm Judge, who has completely disappeared, and was evidently on the take from the same Jai Alai crowd that supported Mr. Delgado's sport club interest in Miami. Your dance club too, I understand. Maybe you should stick around, Mr. Percy. I could make a profitable career with one or two clients like you."

"I doubt that," Percy said, "I lead a pretty dull life. Unlike the characters you have around this town. I can tell you this much: Billy Ray wasn't much of a killer. He was a talker. What little I do remember while we were at the beach after the club fracas, is that somebody drove up and said the football guy and the girl were at a place they all knew. And then went looking for them. I'd swear, if I didn't know any better, it was a deputy Sheriff who told where they were. I couldn't identify the officer, even if I was asked. Cause I don't really pay attention to the coming and going of crazy rednecks. You get the picture? The law was in on it, I know that much. Now that's pretty exciting, but I guess, around here, it's best you let sleeping dogs lie.

"If they ever find Cairo, they can hang him for his part. But if I find him first, I'll kill that half-breed son of a bitch."

"Then you would be guilty of something, Mr. Percy."

"Before my luck changes, McCutcheon, I'm going to walk out of here, and never look back."

He turned toward the door, but stopped and looked back at Matthew, "Thanks again, McCutcheon, for what you done for Terri…" He paused and said sardonically, "You must have lived a charmed life. You aint got a scratch on you."

Matthew watched Andrew Percy walk back to the car parked along the square, under the large oaks where Terri Cates sat in the passenger seat, with the sun roof open and the radio playing Oyster Rock.

Terri looked over at Matthew McCutcheon standing at the window. Her look said all that needed to be said: said goodbye, Matthew, said give my love to mother, if you see her, said watch for Venus in the evening sky. Or maybe she didn't even see him, watching her from the window, wanting to forget all that had happened. She saw only her own reflection in the window glass.

As they drove away, Matthew turned from the window and his hand went up to the little scar, which didn't amount to much, on his right cheek beneath the eye.

Driving west, Percy thought how he hated holier'n thou 'Piscopalian types, knowing he was gone for good this time, or until his luck finally ran out and he met the cold, dark, dead hours of night.

What's a relative anyway? Percy thought, somebody that's kin and probably no count, a poor relation. And far as he knew he had no kin, never did, no matter what Momma babbled at him in the hospital. He never had no kin, except for Sister. They had some fun, before he knew how goofy in the head she was. Sister never had nobody to stick up for her but Percy.

"God's will," Momma said. Although he never understood what she meant by that: God's will. There ain't no God, and there's no friend in Jesus to be bothered with, if he lets things happen like what happened to Sister.

Percy thought to himself that the killing at the fish camp must have been one of both great passion and unbelievable stupidity. He thought to himself how the only passion he felt for Judge Traynor was disgust and pity and how hard he had worked to feel even that, surprised he thought of Traynor at all, then he forgot the Judge, and it was something that had never happened. But he had a nagging fear that whatever it was that kept him going, it wasn't there any more, that maybe he'd lost it, or that maybe he'd just used it up, except for the raw survival instinct of his cold-blooded heart, and when that ran out, he would have nothing. He would be dead. Without any glory. That would be God's will. Just like Momma said.

CHAPTER THIRTY-FOUR

Momma Percy & Sister

SARAH PERCY left home about two in the afternoon. She had everything in order. Sister was a nuisance to travel with because there wasn't a car seat big enough for an overgrown forty-year-old with diminished capacity.

She had made the drive not long ago when she went for Billy Ray's burial service. That poor Mrs. Hardaway had never been very nice to her since they were children. She had always resented her being part of the Markham family. It wasn't her fault how she got there. Sarah swore she would never go back after the burying, but then she drove again to Belle Rio to see the lawyer who told her about the kin she didn't know she had, even if it made her illegitimate, and she tried to explain to Percy after his wreck, but he was too drugged to care. When the papers were drawn up, and Percy drove away to the west coast with that young woman, it became important to her to make another trip and see the lawyer: the one who would take care of Sister.

Once Sarah was out of Port Royale, she felt like she had everything under control. She concentrated on the road and drove in the flow of traffic. There was a lot of traffic for a Saturday afternoon, and everyone passed the slow-moving white Impala driven by the shrunken old woman with the big lump in the back seat. Percy was never coming back. Whatever he had done this time he had gone too far. But maybe he was right. She was too old to take care of Sister anymore. Funny, she thought, wrong as the boy was, he was usually right.

When she was getting close to the place where all the statues and collectibles stood in the front yard next to the trailer court, she decided it was probably her last chance to stop and buy one of those concrete painted pelicans for her yard.

She passed Jewel's place many times over the years: *Jewel's Shells & Statues*. The owner had been her friend when they were young girls. Jewel was now short, plump, fake blonde-going-gray, with thick glasses. She painted the animals and figurines and complained that the doctors made her husband a pill-a-holic, and that cost them forty dollars a day, when before the doctor, he had just been an alcoholic for twenty dollars a day.

Jewel's Shells & Statues sat across the highway from the bay, a yard full of concrete mold figurines: pelicans, herons, sea gulls, turtles, frogs, naked nymphs, St. Francis in prayer, squirrels, alligators in all sizes, little black face boys fishing, Hansel and Gretel, large fish, lady frogs in bikinis with sunglasses, male frogs with their privates covered by a lily pad. All cast in concrete.

Jewel painted to order. In her studio was every kind of shell: rare, large conch shells, plastic sacks of polished melampus, bubbles, flamingo tongues, colored periwinkles, moon shells, shark eyes, rare virgin nerites, nutmegs, and greedy dove shells, mounted fish, a shark jaw, a five foot sing ray tail, turtle skulls, stuffed baby alligators, snake skins, decorated sea urchins, and blow fish with cute glued on buttons for eyes hanging from the ceiling, along with her own special design of wind spinners made from large plastic soft drink bottles.

Jewel had all the knicky-knacks and whatnots made from shells and glass that Momma loved. Like a shopping holiday in Mexico, she imagined her visit with Jewel.

If she didn't stop today, she would never stop. After forty-five years, she wanted to talk to Jewel. That would remind her of the days before she knew what she was, and she met A.J. – fine as he was. He never knew how nice her life had been before him. Except for the family Talking to Jewel meant a lot to her.

She had gone to the Hardaway funeral and she didn't belong there. Her sister had all those years to answer her letters. Even the ones she wrote when Aunt Jean died, after the telephone call when Nancy told her not to come for Aunt Jean's funeral because she was no longer welcome. Aunt Jean was the only mother she ever knew. In her life, she said, her life made sense, but other people failed to understand and were, too often, unnecessarily mean and hurtful. Crazy Sister agreed.

There was a parking lot for Jewel's store, across the highway. She had to cross the roadway, so she slowed to a crawl and traffic backed up behind her.

His name was on the driver side cab door of the logging truck: *Last Chance Inc./ Jim Bob Trucking /Dixie County, Florida.* Jim Bob was in a funk.

His Kenworth had cost him more than he was worth. He'd spent the last two days hauling out of the Broad Marsh area, and he had to haul them all the way to the Port Royale mill from Dixie County. That took twice the time to run over there and back. He went out short day before yesterday. He was figuring in his head. The trailer bed of the logging truck was twelve feet across, sixteen feet high, and the trees piled onto the truck were stripped naked and piled higher than the law allowed. He was getting thirty-one dollars a ton for the wood times a hundred and twenty thousand pounds of timber. Divide that by two makes sixty tons. Multiply by thirty-one. Hell, make that thirty. That makes eighteen hundred dollars for the day, if he could make it to Gulf Royale without getting stopped for being ten tons over the weight limit. The damn tourist traffic had cost him nearly an hour, and if he didn't get there before they shut down the line, it would be Monday.

"Gawd Damn" he said out loud. And he picked up speed.

Sister said something, but Momma ignored her. The traffic behind her passed. Some teenager yelled rude insults, and she said, "yea yea you too buddy."

Then, looking back down the highway, she turned to cross the highway and park directly in front of Jewel's shop.

From behind the line of cars that passed, Jim Bob didn't see the Impala turn across the highway, and the logging truck slammed into the back right of Sarah Percy's car, knocked it off the road, and it flipped over into the concrete statues.

Jim Bob jerked the steering wheel and went careening out of control, crossing the center line, headed for the vacant restaurant with the yellow hard-hat roof and red crab claw arms, formerly known as *The Crab Trap*, which sat at the water's edge. Cars swerved to miss the Kenworth and one out-of-control vehicle went charging into the collection of stone frogs, pelicans, toads, alligators, and religious icons.

The Kenworth smashed into the deserted restaurant, and together, the truck and part of the shattered building, went into the water.

Jim Bob climbed slowly from the cab of the over-turned, half submerged Kenworth, surveyed the damaged automobiles and scattered pine logs strewn all over the highway and parking lot.

"It ain't worth the damn trouble."

The telephone rang in his office.

"Mr. McCutcheon. This is Nurse Kelly at Belle Rio Hospital. I hope I am not disturbing you, but we have an elderly woman here named Mrs. A.J. Percy who is asking for you. She was in an automobile accident this afternoon. She keeps asking for you. And she's in critical condition.

It was a short walk across town to the hospital. Outside the Victorian Inn, an impromptu unofficial *Festival! Belle Rio* Celebration was grooving on the verandah to a small jazz combo, mostly young tourists from Capital City: they drank too much, they danced in the streets, they kissed strangers, and they talked to their dogs. A perky photographer's assistant primped a too blonde fashion model perched on the fender of an expensive Excalibur roadster. The fashion model dropped her head, shook out her blonde curls, looked seductively into the camera lens. Her thick hair fell away from her too perfect face and the romantic golden sunlight caught her perfect smile at just the right angle. The strobe light flashed. It looked like the print and it was, the whole damn picturesque new Belle Rio pasted over the remote fishing village he had known since childhood. What have you got when you've lost the real thing? The photo headline read: *For the Memories.*

As he got farther from the downtown square, the late afternoon twilight was peaceful, except for the wailing sirens, with the November sun disappearing through the trees.

He crossed the busy highway to Port Royale and the shadows were cooler as he walked through the old cemetery where the crumbling stones gave mute testimony to the myths and legends of Belle Rio's vainglorious, but mostly insignificant, sometimes turbulent past and its uncertain future.

The Emergency Room at the small Belle Rio Hospital was overloaded with activity because of the multi-car pileup on the highway to Port Royale west of Belle Rio.

"Sorry I kept you waiting," nurse Kelly said. "That wreck on the highway was awful. Two dead already. Six hurt bad enough to keep us really busy.

"Mrs. Percy's in the worst condition of anybody alive, mostly internal injuries, and she apparently suffered a stroke. Another ambulance is on its way to take her to Capital City.

"I don't know what to do with the one that was with her. She's in a room down the hall. Mrs. Percy said you would know what to do to take care of her. She won't say much else, except, 'God's will.' Are you a member of the family?"

"No," he said. "I don't know why she asked for me."

"She was insistent. I mean, she demanded that we call you to come."

He followed Nurse Kelly down the corridor to the room where a frail old woman lay in the garnish light of the under-funded hospital room.

"This is for you. Has your name on it." She indicated a manila folder on the table at the foot of the bed.

Mrs. Percy was the woman he had seen at Billy Ray's funeral. He was sure of that. He thought, strangely, of Donny Hardaway, walking in the rain beside his mother. The strength to endure, to love, and to keep.

"Son," Mrs. Percy whispered, pale as death.

"Yes, ma'am," he answered, still hesitant, confused. He leaned over so that she could see him. She seemed to know who he was.

He reached out and touched her cheek, caressed it with the back of his fingers.

"Son," she repeated in a faint distant voice.

"I'm Matthew McCutcheon," he said. Like who cares, he thought.

"He was good to me," she said faintly. Her eyes were like cloudy glass. "And he loved Sister."

He felt a cold chill, suddenly forgotten and alone.

"She's your sister now," she said. Her cold hand clutched his hand, squeezed it fervently, and would not let go.

Her breathing became heavy and measured, then slower and slower, until she exhaled and was still. She relaxed her grip and breathed imperceptibly, then groaned, as if in pain, and stared intently into his eyes. And she whispered, "Take care of Sister."

He saw her fading into the distance. She opened her eyes and looked at him, but he was not who she remembered. Then she swooned and he felt her soul escape. She smiled faintly from the distant horizon, succumbing to death in the garish fluorescent light.

The monotone piercing scream of the heart monitor machine filled the empty silence. There was a flurry of activity as Nurse Kelly rushed into the room followed by several frantic paramedics, but they could not change what had happened.

He was ushered from the room, clutching the manila folder, where he stood, uncomprehending, in the neon bluish white glare of the hallway. There was a frenzy of activity up and down the hall.

CHAPTER THIRTY-FIVE

The Letter

MATTHEW SAT on a straight back chair in the rag-tag waiting room and read the letter that Sarah Markham Percy, Mrs. Andrew J Percy, had brought for him—from the office of Francois Gellot Taghert, Esq.

Mr. Matthew Patterson McCutcheon
Attorney at Law
Victorian Inn Suite 208
Belle Rio, FL

Dear Mr. McCutcheon:

I am writing to you in my official capacity as attorney for Mrs. Andrew J. Percy to inform you that you have been appointed executor and trustee of the estate of Mrs. Andrew Percy.

You have also been appointed guardian of her daughter, Allison Markham Percy, age forty, a woman of limited mental capacity since birth.

A Trust Fund has been established for Ms. Allison Markham Percy that should be more than adequate for her health and wellbeing. It will be your responsibility, however, to ensure that Ms. Percy receives the maximum benefit of this fund.

I am well acquainted with your character and know you to be of the highest moral standards. It was for this and other reasons that you were chosen for this responsibility. The documents that created the Trust are available for your pursual in my office.

You are aware, of course, that Ms. Allison Percy will need immediate attention, since her mother no longer feels she is capable of providing the assistance necessary to maintain her daughter in favorable circumstances.

I look forward to your immediate attention to this matter, as the health and wellbeing of a very special person is involved.

If for some reason you feel that you cannot assume responsibility, I would mention to you that your grandfather Patterson is the father of Miss Sarah Markham, who upon age, married Mr. A.J. Percy. And therefore, Mr. Patterson was the grandfather of the beneficiary of this Trust, Ms. Allison Markham Percy.

If my understanding of human relations is correct, Sarah Markham Percy would be a half-sister to your mother, Margaret Patterson, and you, therefore, a cousin, both to the beneficiary of this Trust Fund, and her brother, Andrew J. Percy, may God have mercy on his soul.

Should you doubt my knowledge of the facts of this matter, I have in my possession a letter, written just before her death, from Amanda Faircloth, the mother of Sarah Markham, naming your grandfather, Mr. Johnathan Paul Patterson, the Br/T&S railroad man, as the debaucher of her innocent youth.

And on a more personal level, I had a conversation with your grandfather Patterson (I believe ca. 1952) about the woman, Amanda Faircloth, an aunt to the late Bud Hardaway's wife, Nancy Markham Hardaway, and he referred to Amanda Faircloth at that time as "his sweet little passion of Belle Rio" when he was vice-president of the Belle Rio Railroad & Land Company. She was, according to your grandfather, Mr. Patterson, a lovely creature, curious about the ways of love.

Amanda died an ignominious death after the birth of her daughter in 1920. As you may well imagine, in those days, illegitimate births were hardly acceptable to proper families and Amanda Faircloth took her own life to avoid the shame associated with her condition.

The child, Sarah, was protected as well as could be expected from the harsh realities of her situation by her benevolent Aunt Jean, who raised Sarah, along with her other children, until she completed her education at the Beauty College in Capital City.

About that time, Sarah met Mr. Andrew Jackson Percy, a roustabout and bootlegger, married him, and they moved to Port Royale where he worked in the pulp mill.

Of course, we both know the otherwise unsubstantiated accusations of a ruined woman can be malicious and slanderous, but I assure you, as a gentleman, on my word of honor, that the facts are as I have recounted them to you. Our past binds us all together with obligations and responsibilities we cannot deny.

I look forward to your stewardship of this Trust Fund and I know that you will do what is best for your very special family member, Ms. Allison Markham Percy.

I am, respectfully, your colleague at law,
Francois Gellot Taghert, Esq.

CHAPTER THIRTY-SIX

Slow Dancin'

NURSE KELLY returned. There was nothing more that could be done for Mrs. Sarah Percy.

"Would you please look in on the other one. We don't know what to do with her. We're not really prepared for this kind of thing. No one ever is."

Matthew was in a daze, uncomprehending, almost like stone:

"I guess not, there never is. Yes certainly, by all means, why not, sure, whatever you think is best."

"We've got to do something. If it's too much, I understand. I know this must be quite upsetting for you."

"Yes," he said. "No, whatever you think is best. I'll take care of it."

He followed Nurse Kelly down the corridor to a room that was locked. He could hear her inside the room, moaning a sad unhappy sound, like a warped melancholy Gregorian chant, a hymn that droned hypnotically in solitude. Nurse Kelly opened the door, and they went in.

Sister sat in a chair next to the bed, her clothes in disarray, her hair disheveled, with a wild-eyed uncomprehending stare. She was frightened. She had escaped injury in the wreck because she bounced around the back seat like a rag doll. She made a funny noise in her throat and drooled. Nurse Kelly gently wiped her face with a cloth and offered her water. Sister gazed blankly at the gesture but was immobile.

He stepped toward her and she shrank away from him. He reached out slowly and touched her head. Stroked her hair. She grew calm and seemed to relax, then she started to cry, sobbing loud and unformed sounds, and slowly the sounds became words, plaintive and unbearably sad, "Momma…Momma…Momma."

MATTHEW BURST into the chill night air, stunned with overwhelming confusion and disbelief, his head swirling with memories that no longer made sense. The past was the future, now was forever. No matter what it seemed to be, it was what it was. No matter what it had been, it was what it was, and would be what it is, now and forever.

Maybe someday Taghert would rot in Hell with all the secrets of Belle Rio. Taghert's revenge: Grandfather Patterson's sweet little passion of Belle Rio, curious about the ways of love. Andrew Percy his blood kin.

He laughed out loud and shouted, "Damn you!" to the night sky.

Along the residential streets of the Section, which was just north of the hospital, strands of light sparkled through the trees. The crescent moon floated above the lazy, drifting clouds.

A large crowd had gathered for the bar-b-que street party outside the *StarFire Lounge*. Matthew walked absent mindedly along the edge of the crowd, that looked through him, not seeing him, a white ghost from their haunted past.

The interior of the *StarFire Lounge* was a shock to his senses, the music, the laughter, the babble of foreign unintelligible voices. The ceiling fans rotating slowly under the lights created a strobe-light hypnotic trance. There was a crowded bar on one side of the narrow front room and a TV on the far wall with the Gator/Seminole football game seen through a haze of smoke.

At a booth along the back wall, three white cokeheads played the fool taking Polaroid pictures of an ample waitress in a tight, red sequined dress who was sitting on their table.

He made his way past them to the larger room where couples were dancing, and found a spot near the end of the larger bar.

"So, what's with you, Mr. Matt, in here all alone?"

Juanitia was surprised to see him. She knew him from the courthouse where she worked in the Tax Accessor office, and she had recently applied to be one his clerical assistants in his new job as Public Defender for the Circuit Court.

"Didn't you know I also worked here? My husband owns the *StarFire*. That's him down at the end of the bar."

"You'd mentioned it," he managed a smiled. "Everyone's got a private life."

"Well, Ain't that so." She agreed. "I got mine. And this ain't it. You hear what I'm saying?" She had a sassy attitude in her own world.

"I don't want to know," he tried to smile. "It's better that way."

"You look a bit glum. You alright?"

He was slow to respond, searching for courage and understanding, still overwhelmed by Tagert's revelations.

"Lemme get you a drink. What you drinking? ... Hey, lover man!" she called over the din of music and chatter. He came when called.

"This is Mr. McCutcheon from the courthouse. Meet my husband, George. Mr. Matt needs some spirit, honey. Fix 'm something on the house. George lived here forever. He caught a hold a me in Port Royale an' brought me here to work."

Lover man silently confirmed that. "What you drinking?"

"Bourbon. Rocks… Thanks."

Juanitia said, "We glad to have you as Public Defender, Mr. Matt. Many of your future clients will come through the doors here tonight."

"I'm not working tonight," he said, with a faint smile for humor, still numb, trying to comprehend.

"We've had four Public Defenders in as many years," she said. "It's a thankless job."

"Thank me, if I last the year."

"You'll last," she said. "You're a celebrity around here since the Governor gave Possum his pardon… Anyway, what you got to do that's better than Belle Rio? There ain't no better place. Even with all the troubles we've had. Things are gonna get better."

He nodded, "We just got lucky, I guess."

His drink arrived. "Thanks, George," he said. "I've heard many good stories about the *StarFire*." He took a large swallow and felt the jolt as it brushed away a thicket of cobwebs.

"So, tell me Mr. Matt, how'd you come to *StarFire* tonight? You out celebrating *Festiva!*"

He certainly hadn't thought of *Festiva!* He had bolted out the hospital door and ended up where he was, leaning on the bar, without knowing where he was. And he uttered new, strange words that he had yet to figure out:

"My aunt, my mother's sister, was killed in the wreck on the highway from Port Royale. She just died… And… It just happened this afternoon."

Juanitia said with empathy, "I'm sorry to hear that, Mr. Matt. I didn't know you had relatives in Port Royale."

"Port Royale! The loud talker interrupted them as he pushed up to at the bar. "Police got me 'tween here an' Port Royale doin' a hundert ten."

"Me neither," Matthew replied to Juanitia.

"Mad! Y'all talk 'bout mad. I's mad. Damn Cracker police. Ain't nothin' 'tween here an' there 'cept police makin' money off black folks goin' to Port Royale for a Saturday night."

Jaunitia put her hand on Matthew's hand that was holding the glass of bourbon and said, "Bless you, Mr. McCutcheon. I'll bring you another drink. You're gonna need it."

She gave him a sympathetic smile and moved away. The room had suddenly gotten crowded. She went back to work.

A dark-eyed woman leaned in close to him. "Talk to me Sweet Boy. You a Seminole or a Gator?" she asked. "My brother's a Gator an' when the Gators lose, he cries like a baby."

The hip-hop music coming through the sound system segued into smooth Marvin Gaye.

"I's in a jookin mood," she said to Matthew. "I come down here for the *Festival!* an' aint nuthin' happening. I needs to jook! "You wanna jook with me? "I gotta go back to the city later this evenin', but lord, now I got this feeling an' I needs to jook—cause I's the Jookin Queen."

She motioned toward a couple at the far end of the bar, "They jus gonna sit there an' drink. I needs a jook."

She pulled him by the arm to the dance floor where customers were slow dancing in the dark, the disco lights spinning across the walls, and wrapped her arms around him and pressed her full body against him. Her hands moved up and down his back and he was absorbed in the aroma of flesh and bitter sweet perfume.

The first rush of emotion brought a mist of tears to his eyes, then he shuddered. Her hot breath melted him. It was a sublime moment. He suddenly felt, not heard, deep within his chest, the pain of Sister's lonely, sorrowful lament – "Momma… Momma" … She was his sister now. He began to tremble, and she, mother, was holding him, swaying with the soul music, slow dancing in the shattered darkness of memory. Slow dancing on a night that would last forever, although the war had taken him away, and she would have to find another dancer.. Then it was over, released.

"Ain't no good, cryin', boy," the woman said. "Cryin' ain't gonna help."

But he knew it would.

"I can't jook no more," he said. "My Gator's lost."

From behind the bar, Juanitia watched Matthew leave as the Jookin' Queen reclaimed her seat.

"Pour me another Crown an' Seven. White boy was cryin' 'bout his Gator bein' lost. The game ain't even over yet. His Gator jus' need a good Jookin'."

Outside, from a dark street corner, music wafted through the live oak trees. An old man strummed his electric guitar and Sister Salvation vocalized with spiritual fervor from the back of her Cadillac Deville.

***

Acknowledgements

FOR

MARTHA L. LOVE 1916-1986

JACK T MAY 1909-2001

DORNA MCDONALD 1943 - 2009

While writing this novel I spent many days at the 2nd Judicial Circuit Court of Florida in Apalachicola where real life was often more entertaining and poignant than fiction. I read extensively at the Florida State Archives and at the municipal libraries of Carrabelle, Port St Joe and Nashville. For oral history and folklore, I am indebted to *Florida, a Guide to the Southern Most State*, Compiled and written by the Federal Writer's Project of Work's Progress Administration of the State of Florida, 1936-1939.

I wish to thank Christine Bell for her support and good example; also my appreciation to Phil Treon and Coke Sams for their contribution at different times in the process, my son & daughter, Duncan and Tallahassee, for their continuous support and enthusiasm, Catherine Fleming for editing and Peter Honsberger for publishing the first addition, Patsy Arant for her encouragement & endurance, and Tracy Atkins for his stewardship during the difficult times of the 2nd edition; and ultimately, the people of Franklin County, Florida for being who they are.

www.ingramcontent.com/pod-product-compliance
Lightning Source LLC
Chambersburg PA
CBHW020454100426

42813CB00031B/3357/J